India's Military Strategy

India's Military Strategy

Countering Pakistan's Challenge

S. Kalyanaraman

B L O O M S B U R Y
NEW DELHI • LONDON • OXFORD • NEW YORK • SYDNEY

BLOOMSBURY INDIA
Bloomsbury Publishing India Pvt. Ltd
Second Floor, LSC Building No. 4, DDA Complex, Pocket C – 6 & 7,
Vasant Kunj, New Delhi, 110070

First published in India 2023
This edition published 2023

Bloomsbury Academic India
An imprint of Bloomsbury Publishing Plc

ISBN: HB: 978-93-56400-02-3; eBook: 978-93-56400-04-7
2 4 6 8 10 9 7 5 3 1

For sale in the Indian subcontinent only

Typeset in Manipal Technologies Limited
Printed and bound in India by Replika Press Pvt. Ltd.

Contents

Tables

Preface and Acknowledgements

In this book, Dr S. Kalyanaraman, my late husband, assessed the evolution of India's conventional military strategies towards Pakistan in the last seven decades. These military strategies were in response to the persistent challenges posed by Pakistan to India's territorial sovereignty, national security, and regional leadership in the Indian subcontinent. In the process, Dr Kalyanaraman traced the transformation of the notion of strategy from its original military moorings to a more policy-oriented and -influenced conception. He elaborated upon a tripartite framework of policy, strategy, and doctrine to think about, understand, and analyse the use of force. This work is the first study to assess India's wars with Pakistan at the politico-strategic as well as the doctrinal levels.

My late husband had been working on the manuscript for quite a while. He had drafted and redrafted the chapters multiple times, but the perfectionist in him was never satisfied. I would often prod him to finish the manuscript quickly and send it for publication, but he remained steadfast on his principle that quality cannot be compromised. As fate would have it, he contracted the deadly coronavirus in April 2021. Within days of his test results returning positive, the virus spread to his lungs, and he had to be hospitalised. Even while he was in the critical care unit, my husband was anxious about the book. He told me, 'I have so many things to do; the most important is to publish my book.' He passed away a few days later.

I remembered his last words and decided to publish his book as my tribute to him. I, however, was apprehensive if I would be able to do so, given that the subject he was dealing with was a specialised one and outside my comfort zone. I also had no idea how much of the manuscript was complete. But my family and friends encouraged me. Gradually, I began to peruse the manuscript, and, to my delight, almost all the chapters were complete. I showed the manuscript to my sister, who opined that it is good to be published. He, of course, would have thought otherwise and would have worked some more on the manuscript, adding and subtracting paragraphs, reinforcing arguments, adding footnotes, etc. Anyway, once she and I completed the manuscript, I approached Bloomsbury India, which graciously accepted the manuscript for publication. I express my sincere thanks to Ambassador Sujan R. Chinoy, DG MP-IDSA, Mr Chandra Sekhar of Bloomsbury and Professor P. Kumaraswamy for facilitating the publication of the book.

On behalf of my late husband, I express my heartfelt thanks to friends, colleagues, and people concerned who have assisted him in writing this book. I sincerely thank the referees for reading the manuscript and offering their valuable comments and suggestions.

I hope the readers will find this book to be insightful and informative. I also hope that it will open new lines of inquiry on this subject as envisioned by Dr Kalyanaraman.

Dr Pushpita Das

Introduction

Pakistan has posed a persistent challenge to India's territorial integrity and national security since Partition and Independence. This has resulted in four wars and multiple militarised crises during the last 74 years. Perceiving Pakistan as the primary adversary, India has devoted the bulk of its military energies to the task of tackling the challenges that have been emanating from across India's western borders. How India has militarily responded to the security challenges from Pakistan is the subject of this book. Specifically, it details how India has employed the threat or use of military force against Pakistan by answering three questions:

1. What political aims did India pursue in past wars and crises?
2. What strategy did India adopt to translate political aims into appropriate military objectives, and what was the level and type of effort employed by the armed forces to attain them?
3. What doctrines did the armed services employ to attain the assigned military goals?

Answers to these questions help clarify the politico-military framework hitherto employed by decision makers to think about and decide upon the circumstances under which to use force, the political aim pursued through war, the strategy employed for translating the political aim into the overall military objective and directing the war, and the doctrines that the armed services employed to attain the military objectives assigned to them. In short, this book traces the evolution of Indian military strategy for dealing with the Pakistan challenge.

Given this focus, the book does not delve into India's counter-insurgency and counter-terrorism strategies. While there is no denying Pakistan's support for and sponsorship of anti-India insurgencies and cross-border terrorism, counter-insurgency and counter-terrorism efforts are ultimately embedded in the domestic political context

(Kalyanaraman 2003, 85–100; Kalyanaraman 2012, 107–115). The book's focus is limited to the threat posed by Pakistan and India's use of military force against it, irrespective of whether force has been employed in response to conventional or sub-conventional challenges.

The Challenge of Strategy Formulation

Gaining a clearer sense of the road travelled thus far is not only useful but a necessity for decision makers. Knowledge of the past provides a sound basis for devising a politico-military framework through which to approach war and the critical decisions associated with it. Further, as Michael Howard has noted, by casting a backward glance at the origins and development of an issue or phenomenon, history helps in diagnosing the problem or, even better, in exposing false diagnoses. By informing us about where we started and 'how we have got to where we are now', history also helps in determining 'where we should be going' (Howard 1982/83).

This is all the more important because of the calamity that might befall if the two nuclear-weapon states were to take a false step. Given the real possibility of an India–Pakistan war, and because of the danger of it escalating to the nuclear level, decision makers need to evolve a clear politico-military framework for the effective application of military force. Such a framework is essential to translate the political aim into an appropriate set of military objectives, determine the quantum and type of military effort to be expended, and devise a military plan to attain them. In effect, decision makers need to craft a strategy that integrates political ends with military means and charts the way to attain them.

Normally, the crafting of such a politico-military framework is a task that is undertaken in the run-up to war. As General Carl von Clausewitz pointed out, it is devised after evaluating three sets of factors. The first set of factors involves the political aim sought by decision makers, the state of the economy, and the capabilities and readiness of the military apparatus. A similar appraisal needs to be made about the adversary against which war plans to be waged. Thus, the likely political aim(s) of the adversary state, its economic and financial capacity, and its military capabilities constitute the second set of factors. The third set of factors to be considered before embarking on war is the international context. In particular, it would be important to take into account the positions likely to be adopted by allies, major powers, and neutral countries in the event of war, towards which side their sympathies are likely to lean, and the probability of their participation or intervention in the war. Although an evaluation of these factors may appear quite simple, Clausewitz cautioned that a methodical approach to assessing them is likely to prove impossible in the limited time available to decision makers. He recalled Napoleon's observation that even a genius like Sir Isaac Newton 'would quail before the algebraic problems' posed by such a task (Clausewitz 1976, 586).[1]

Even though modern governments with their institutionalised bureaucracies may be in a better position to carry out such methodical evaluations, the fact remains that the ultimate decisions are invariably made by a small group of influential decision makers. This led the political philosopher Isaiah Berlin to emphasise the importance of what he termed 'political judgement'. In a memorable analogy, Berlin compared the situation facing a statesman with that of the driver of a car who is in 'desperate haste' and comes across 'a rickety-looking bridge' (Berlin 1996). Even if the driver were to have 'some knowledge of the principles of engineering', he does not have the luxury of time 'to stop to survey and calculate' whether the bridge would be able to bear the weight of the car. The only way such knowledge would prove useful to the driver in that time of crisis is if the situation had 'given rise to a semi-instinctive skill—like the ability to read without simultaneous awareness of the rules of the language'. Berlin termed this instinctive, intuitive, knowledge as political judgement, which involves having a sense of what will work and what will not under a set of circumstances. It requires 'a capacity … for synthesis rather than analysis' (Berlin 1996). What successful statesmen need is the instinct to grasp the fundamentals of a situation in the mind's eye and espy a way forward.

The complexities involved in crafting a strategy are something that the Indian political leadership is aware of. An indication was provided in late December 2001 by then Prime Minister Atal Bihari Vajpayee in the wake of the military mobilisation he ordered in response to the terrorist attack on the Indian Parliament by Pakistani jihadi groups. During a conversation with a senior journalist, Vajpayee observed,

> [E]verybody wants to go to war, particularly the armed forces, they really want to thrash Pakistan. But I am asking the chiefs, when the history of this war is written, what name will be given to it? The war of destruction of Pakistan, liberation of Kashmir, annihilation of the Pakistani army, what? We must have a clear objective before we go to war. We can't launch what history would merely call a war of anger. The problem with a war is, how you start it, when and where you start it, is in your hands. But how it will end, and when, is never in your control. That is why the decision to go to war is never taken lightly or in anger. (Gupta 2014)

The military objectives referred to by Vajpayee appear to have been advocated by the then Chief of the Army Staff, General S. Padmanabhan, who subsequently confirmed that 'degradation of the other force, and perhaps the capture of disputed territory in Jammu and Kashmir' could have been achieved in January 2002 if the Cabinet had given the go-ahead for war (Swami 2004). However, all that the political leadership was willing to envisage at that point in time was hot pursuit and calibrated surgical strikes across the Line of Control in response to the terrorist attack on Parliament (*The Telegraph* 2000; *The Times of India* 2001). As is clear from Vajpayee's thought process, neither the destruction of Pakistan nor the annihilation of the Pakistan Army was conceivable without a decisive military victory in a full-scale war. The pursuit of victory in a full-scale war was simply unthinkable, given Pakistan's possession of nuclear weapons. Even the more limited military objectives of liberating all or portions of Pakistan-occupied Kashmir and degrading the Pakistani army's capabilities were not something that the Indian leadership could nonchalantly envisage under prevalent circumstances. Only a year and a half earlier, in the summer of 1999, the same government had directed a war in the heights of Kargil to restore the sanctity of the Line of Control. All in all, the military objectives identified by the leadership of the armed forces were not considered by the Vajpayee government as appropriate under extant diplomatic and military circumstances.

That, however, does not mean that there was a failure on the part of the military leadership. The Indian Army, indeed, any army and, for that matter, any armed service, is only capable of achieving a limited set of objectives through the application of force. In conventional war, land forces capture territory and degrade or destroy adversary forces ranged against them—exactly the objectives that General Padmanabhan had proposed. Naval forces secure local or general command of the sea by either bottling up the adversary fleets in ports or defeating them decisively. They accomplish such objectives by projecting firepower on shore to degrade civilian and military infrastructure, facilitating amphibious operations, and disrupting or destroying adversary commerce. For their part, air forces gain local air superiority or command of the air through aerial pursuit and offensive counter-air operations, attrite the adversary's land forces through close air support and battlefield interdiction, degrade adversary forces at sea, and disrupt or destroy the adversary's home front through strategic bombing. There is no readymade formula to translate these military objectives, which the services could achieve singly or together, into the specific political aim for which a particular war is waged. The only political aim that can be translated into a precise military objective is the conquest of a particular piece of territory because the political aim and the military objective are one and the same in such a case. All other political aims can only be approximately translated into military objectives. The only way in which this gap between the political aim and the military objectives could be narrowed is through continuous dialogue among political and military leaders.

Yet, no concerted effort appears to have been made since 2001 to bridge the gap between the thought processes of the political leadership and the military brass. Seemingly of its own accord, the Indian Army articulated the Cold Start doctrine in 2003 based on the lessons learnt during Operation Parakram, especially the importance of vesting the holding corps with some offensive capabilities, so that it has the capacity to initiate quick action from a standing start and reducing the time taken to move the strike corps to the front. Another important factor that drove the army to devise the Cold Start doctrine was to ensure that the political leadership did not get an opportunity to wilt under international pressure during the weeks it takes to move offensive formations to the border (Kapila 2004).

The Cold Start doctrine indicated how the army would apply force in an envisaged limited war against Pakistan and for what military objectives. But it appears to have evolved in a political vacuum without consulting the civilian leadership and, by extension, without considering or merely guessing what political aim the latter might seek to pursue. The result was the doctrine's disavowal by the political leadership and subsequently even by the army's own leadership in the aftermath of the November 2008 Mumbai terrorist attacks (Unnithan 2010). Recently, however, the doctrine appears to have received a new lease of life. During his tenure as the Chief of the Army Staff, General Bipin Rawat acknowledged that the Cold Start option does exist, but he added that its employment in war would depend upon political authorisation (Unnithan 2017). The political leadership has not given any indication about its views on the Cold Start doctrine and the military objectives identified therein.

Lack of synchronisation between what political leaders may aim to achieve and what the armed forces have the capacity to deliver is not conducive to the effective application of military force. To be reasonably effective, the quantum, intensity, and manner of force employment need to be in tune with the political aim of the war. In other words, the political end sought and the military means employed have to be brought into alignment in a suitable way. That 'way' is strategy. Given that strategy is the bridge that connects the political end with the military means, it can only be devised through close and sustained dialogue between political and military leaders. Strategy, as Hew Strachan has observed, is 'the product of the dialogue between politicians and soldiers' and its 'essence is the harmonisation' of the political aim and the application of military force (Strachan 2013, 77–78). In other words, strategy is the politico-military framework that enables the political leadership and the military brass to think clearly about war in terms of the following: the political aim that is attainable given one's own strengths and weaknesses and those of the adversary's as well as international diplomatic factors; the military objectives to be derived from the political aim; and, finally, the quantum of force to be used, the sequencing of the operations of the armed services, and the manner in which the services would employ force to attain the assigned goals. In the absence of such a politico-military framework that ties these critical aspects of war together, 'a coherent plan of war' can neither be evolved nor implemented (Corbett 1911, 5; Clausewitz 1976, 71, 141). The use of force without a coherent plan is likely to prove ineffective or might cause catastrophe. The alternative is inaction, resulting in loss of domestic credibility and further emboldening of the adversary.

The Literature on India's Use of Force

Issues relating to India's use of force have been addressed in published works over the last several decades, albeit largely in the contexts of individual wars, operations of an individual service, and specific time periods. At the top of the list are the official histories of India's wars prepared by the History Division of the Ministry of Defence and the authorised histories of the Indian Air Force and the Indian Navy. While the former offer detailed narratives of India's war plans and objectives as well as the course of the campaigns during the 1947–1948 War, the 1965 War, and the 1971 War (Prasad and Pal 2005; Chakravorty 1992; Prasad 1992), the latter embed the roles of the air force and navy in these wars within a broader narrative of their growth and development (Singh 2007; Hiranandani 2000; Hiranandani 2005; Hiranandani 2009). These official histories have been supplemented by the personal recollections and reflections of military leaders who participated in these wars (Sen 1969; Sinha 1977; Singh 1991; Kohli 1989; Jacob 2001; Lal 2008; Malik 2006). In addition, there are historical accounts of the origins of these wars, the regional and international contexts in which they unfolded, the diplomatic campaign that accompanied military operations, the course of the military campaigns, and the roles of individual services (Brines 1968; Lehl 2005; Palit 1972; Ayoob and Subrahmanyam 1972; Mankekar 1972; Jackson 1975; Singh 1980, 1981; Ganguly 1986; Krishna Rao 1991; Dasgupta 2002; Bammi 2002; Lavoy 2009; Raghavan 2010; Raghavan 2013; Singh 2013; Subramaniam 2016; Subramaniam 2020). These studies constitute a rich vein of information on and insights into particular wars and on the roles played by individual services. This corpus also constitutes an excellent archive for beginning the process of comprehending India's strategic praxis and its evolution over the last seven decades.

A second category of publications consists of analyses of India's defence and security policies, including issues relating to force posture, defence modernisation, military expenditure, and service doctrines (Kavic 1967; Thomas 1978; Thomas 1986). Overall, these are excellent secondary sources on the trends in the evolution of defence and security policy in general. There are, however, varied interpretations and emphases in these publications. Jasjit Singh, for instance, argued that India's force posture is essentially characterised by a '*defensive defence doctrine* and strategy against external threats' [emphasis in original] (Singh 1989, 230). In a similar vein, Stephen Cohen and Sunil Dasgupta have highlighted India's 'longstanding restraint in military strategy' since Independence and the likelihood of its persistence (Cohen and Dasgupta 2010, 1–28).[2] Ali Ahmed has, however, pointed to multiple shifts in India's 'strategic doctrine' between the defensive and offensive since the 1970s. In addition, Ahmed has also argued that the shift in strategic doctrine from the defensive to the offensive in the early 2000s led to the army changing the orientation of its doctrine from 'defensive deterrence' to 'offensive deterrence' (Ahmed 2014, 38–41). More recently, Arzan Tarapore has argued that although India is wont to pursue defensive war aims, the Indian Army, in particular, and Indian defence policy, more generally, are driven by an 'orthodox offensive doctrine' centred on 'large army formations, operating relatively autonomously from a political direction, seeking to impose a punitive cost on the enemy' (Tarapore 2020, 1).

For their part, studies on defence modernisation have variously characterised India's efforts as militarisation run amok (Rikhye 1990), a puerile yearning for imported toys ('I want my MiG') (Gupta 1995, 441–458), and 'arming without aiming' in the absence of 'strategic purpose' (Cohen and Dasgupta 2010, xii)—with the end result of these impulses being an 'ad hoc arsenal' (Smith 1994). An extraordinary conclusion in this regard is George Tanham's contention that India has not devised an 'overall strategy to deal with Pakistan', suffers from 'lacunae in strategy and planning', and exhibits an absence of 'strategic thinking' (Tanham 1992, 35, 50). Tanham arrived at these conclusions not after conducting an in-depth study of India's strategic praxis but after having conversed with a range of Indian officials, serving and retired as well as civilian and military. Indeed, the statement that '[t]here is no strategic thinking in India' was made by one of his interlocutors (Tanham 1992, 141).[3] According to Inder Malhotra, that interlocutor was K. Subrahmanyam (Malhotra 2011). What Subrahmanyam appears to have actually meant thereby was the 'absence' in the minds of senior civilian and military officials he had interacted with 'of an integrated view of international developments at various levels of the government in spite of Prime Minister Nehru's own uncluttered perception of them' (Subrahmanyam 1976 [1990 reprint], 103). Such an interpretation is substantiated by the fact that Subrahmanyam subsequently delineated Nehru's three-pronged grand strategy comprising 'non-alignment to deal with external security problems, the ... Constitution to address governance challenges, and a partly centrally planned development strategy to accelerate growth' (Subrahmanyam 2012, 2). Yet, Tanham's contention about the absence of strategic thinking continues to be invoked to castigate the Indian state's inability to engage in purposive action and its penchant for reacting in an ad hoc manner to the actions and initiatives of other countries (Karnad 2015, 6, 63; Malik and Kanwal 2005, 6–7).

Since the 1990s, a third set of publications has offered appraisals of the India–Pakistan conventional balance and its interface with the nuclear dimension (Tellis 1997; Jones n.d.), the militarised crises that have occurred between the two countries under the nuclear shadow (Bajpai et al. 1997; Chari et al. 2008; Ganguly and Kraig 2004, 290–324), and their military interaction along the sub-conventional–conventional-nuclear conflict spectrum (Raghavan 2001, 1–18; Ladwig 2007/08, 158–190; Narang 2009/10, 38–78; Ganguly and Kapur 2010; Joshi 2013, 512–40). These analyses explore the destabilising consequences of India's and Pakistan's evolving conventional and nuclear postures and doctrines as well as the very real nuclear dangers involved in the use of force (Kapur 2008; Kapur 2009). Some studies in this category focus on India's limited war option, the strategic and doctrinal issues associated with it, and prescriptions thereof (Singh

2000, 2179–2183; Singh 2000, 1205–1220; Sethi 2009, 415–425; Bakshi 2010).

In sum, each of these three categories of publications highlights different aspects and periods of the India–Pakistan military interaction. Based on these sources and the insights they offer, the present study seeks to tease out the story of the evolution of India's conventional military strategies towards Pakistan during the last seven decades.

Overview of the Study

Following this introduction, which has laid out the aim, scope, and rationale of the study, chapter 1 explores what military strategy is and how it is interconnected with policy on the one hand and military operations on the other. In the process, the chapter traces the transformation of the notion of strategy from its original military moorings to a more policy-oriented and -influenced conception. Thereafter, the chapter elaborates upon a tripartite framework of policy, strategy, and doctrine to think about, understand, and analyse the use of force.

Chapter 2 explores the politics of India–Pakistan conflict in order to root the study of Indian military strategy in the political sphere. The chapter discusses three main issues that have ensured the persistence of conflict: incompatible national identities, Pakistan's congenital quest for parity with and compulsion to challenge India, and irreconcilable positions on the Kashmir issue. In the process, the chapter carries out a quantitative comparison of the differential between the economic and military capabilities of India and Pakistan from the 1960s until now. In addition, it details the various unsuccessful bilateral efforts to forge a compromise solution based on the territorial status quo in Kashmir and highlights the recent change in Indian policy in this regard as well as the roots of that change in the long-held position of the Bharatiya Janata Party, its predecessor the Bharatiya Jana Sangh, and their parent body the Rashtriya Swayamsevak Sangh.

Chapter 3 elaborates upon the origins of the Kashmir conflict in the immediate aftermath of Partition, the issues which contributed to that conflict remaining a half-war between Indian forces and Pakistani raiders led by Pakistani military personnel and later backstopped by units of the Pakistan Army. The chapter deals with the framework that India developed—the strategy of exhaustion in the context of a full-scale war—to counter a Pakistani military challenge to its territorial integrity as well as the doctrines that governed the operations of the army (attrition) and air force (primarily aerial combat but with a significant component of air interdiction). It discusses the factors that drove India's military modernisation during the 1950s.

Chapter 4 analyses the factors which shaped India's strategy and force structure in the 1950s. The threat posed by Pakistan, defence expenditure, retarding economic growth, P.M.S. Blackett's report, and India's anxiety over the US military aid to Pakistan are factors identified in the chapter. The chapter also discusses how, after the shocking defeat of 1962, India's political aims were brought into alignment with the application of force by initiating a major rearmament programme in 1964.

Chapter 5 discusses the events and war plan which precluded the 1965 War. After presenting a detailed discussion on the military plans, the chapter discusses the factors that led to changes in the Indian Army's strategy and war plan and the restricted military objectives that were eventually pursued during the course of the 1965 War with Pakistan. This chapter argues how the strategy of exhaustion was adopted to attain strategic success and how the doctrine of attrition was adopted to secure positions and undertake a methodical advance. It also critically evaluates the reasons for the middling success achieved in that war.

Chapter 6 discusses the changes effected in strategy and service doctrines beginning with the 1971 War and the reasons for that change. During this war and in the following two decades, India pursued the strategy of annihilation through the doctrines of manoeuvre on land, aerial combat and air interdiction, and naval blockade. The chapter also discusses how the victory encouraged India to establish a force structure and military doctrines that would deter neighbours to achieve their objectives through war.

Chapter 7 discusses the change in India's strategy to one of exhaustion in the context of limited war as well as the ongoing adaptation of the doctrines of the three armed services since Pakistan's acquisition of nuclear weapons and the consequent impossibility of seeking a decisive victory.

The concluding chapter presents the strategies and doctrines implemented during India's war with Pakistan. It highlights the importance of designing an overall military strategy for waging limited war and pursuing carefully calibrated political and military objectives by creatively combining the individual doctrines of the three services. The chapter then goes on to discuss the features of civil–military relations in India and analyses the new pattern of this relation in the light of formation of the office of the chief of defence staff.

Notes

1 On the importance of these factors in determining strategy, see Clausewitz (1976, 585–586). The quoted phrases are on p. 586.

2 The quoted phrase can be found on p. 1 (Cohen and Dasgupta 2010).

3 See Footnote 4 in George Tanham (1992, 141).

References

Ahmed, Ali. 2014. *India's Doctrine Puzzle: Limiting War in South Asia*. New Delhi: Routledge.

Ayoob, Mohammed and K. Subrahmanyam. 1972. *The Liberation War*. New Delhi: S. Chand and Co.

Bajpai, Kanti, P.R. Chari, Pervaiz Iqbal Cheema, Stephen P. Cohen, and Sumit Ganguly. 1997. *Brasstacks and Beyond: Perception and Management of Crisis in South Asia*. New Delhi: Manohar.

Bakshi, G.D. 2010. *Limited Wars in South Asia: Need for an Indian Doctrine*. New Delhi: Knowledge World Publishers.

Bammi, Y.M. 2002. *Kargil: The Impregnable Conquered*. Noida: Gorkha Publishers.

Berlin, Isaiah. 1996. 'On Political Judgment'. *New York Review of Books*, 43(15). Available at: http://www.nybooks.com/articles/archives/1996/oct/03/on-political-judgment/ (accessed on 22 April 2015).

Brines, Russell. 1968. *The Indo-Pakistani Conflict*. London: Pall Mall Press.

Chakravorty, B.C. 1992. *History of the Indo-Pak War, 1965*. New Delhi: History Division, Ministry of Defence, Government of India.

Chari, P.R., Pervaiz Iqbal Cheema, and Stephen P. Cohen. 2008. *Four Crises and a Peace Process: American Engagement in South Asia*. New Delhi: HarperCollins Publishers India.

Clausewitz, Carl von. 1976. *On War*, translated and edited by Michael Howard and Peter Paret. Princeton, NJ: Princeton University Press.

Cohen, Stephen P. and Sunil Dasgupta. 2010. *Arming Without Aiming: India's Military Modernization*. New Delhi: Penguin/Viking.

Corbett, Julian Stafford. 1911. *Some Principles of Maritime Strategy*. London. Available at: http://www.gutenberg.org/ebooks/15076 (accessed 12 on April 2012).

Dasgupta, C. 2002. *War and Diplomacy in Kashmir 1947–48*. New Delhi: Sage.

Ganguly, Sumit and S. Paul Kapur. 2010. *India, Pakistan and the Bomb: Debating Nuclear Stability in South Asia*. New Delhi: Penguin.

Ganguly, Sumit and Michael Kraig. 2004. 'The 2001–2002 Indo-Pakistani Crisis: Exposing the Limits of Coercive Diplomacy'. *Security Studies*, 14(2): 290–324.

Ganguly, Sumit. 1986. *The Origins of War in South Asia: Indo-Pakistani Conflicts Since 1947*. Boulder: Westview Press.

Gupta, Amit. 1995. 'Determining India's Force Structure and Military Doctrine: I Want My MiG'. *Asian Survey*, 35(5): 441–458.

Gupta, Shekhar. 2014. 'Narendra Modi: Getting his foreign policy right'. *India Today*, New Delhi, 4 September.

Hiranandani, G.M. 2000. *Transition to Triumph: History of the Indian Navy 1965–1975*. New Delhi: Naval Headquarters/Lancer Publishers.

Hiranandani, G.M. 2005. *Transition to Eminence: The Indian Navy 1976–1990*. New Delhi: Naval Headquarters/Lancer Publishers.

Hiranandani, G.M. 2009. *Transition to Guardianship: The Indian Navy 1991–2000*. New Delhi: Naval Headquarters/Lancer Publishers.

Howard, Michael. 1982/83. 'Reassurance and Deterrence: Western Defense in the 1980s'. *Foreign Affairs*, Winter. Available at: https://www.foreignaffairs.com/articles/1982-12-01/reassurance-and-deterrence-western-defense-1980s (accessed on 9 December 2018).

Jackson, Robert. 1975. *South Asian Crisis: India-Pakistan-Bangla Desh*. London: Chatto and Windus.

Jacob, J.F.R. 2001. *Surrender at Dacca: Birth of a Nation*. New Delhi: Manohar.

Jones, Rodney. n.d. *Strategic Stability and Conventional Force Imbalance: Case of South Asia*. South Asian Strategic Stability Institute. Available at: http://www.sassi.org/pdfs/conventional_imbalance_rjones.pdf (accessed on 7 May 2011).

Joshi, Shashank. 2013. 'India's Military Instrument: A Doctrine Stillborn'. *The Journal of Strategic Studies*, 36(4): 512–40.

Kalyanaraman, S. 2003. 'The Indian Way in Counterinsurgency'. In *Democracies and Small Wars*, edited by Efraim Inbar, 85–100. London: Frank Cass.

Kalyanaraman, S. 2012. 'Thinking about Counter Terrorism in India's National Strategy'. In *Grand Strategy for India: 2020 and Beyond*, edited by Krishnappa Venkatshamy and Princy George, 107–115. New Delhi: Institute for Defence Studies and Analyses/Pentagon Security International.

Kapila, Subhash. 2004. 'India's New "Cold Start" War Doctrine Strategically Reviewed'. South Asia Analysis Group Paper, No. 991, South Asia Analysis Group, India.

Kapur, S. Paul. 2008 *Dangerous Deterrent: Nuclear Weapons Proliferation and Conflict in South Asia*. New Delhi: Oxford University Press.

Kapoor, S. Paul. 2009. 'Deterrence and Asymmetric Warfare'. *Seminar*, No. 599. Available at: http://www.india-seminar.com/2009/599/599_s_paul_kapur.htm (accessed on 4 April 2014).

Karnad, Bharat. 2015. *Why India is Not a Great Power (Yet)*. New Delhi: Oxford University Press.

Kavic, Lorne J. 1967. *India's Quest for Security: Defence Policies, 1947–1965*. Berkeley: University of California Press.

Kohli, S.N. 1989. *We Dared: Maritime Operations in the 1971 Indo-Pak War*. New Delhi: Lancer International.

Krishna Rao, K.V. 1991. *Prepare or Perish: A Study of National Security*. New Delhi: Lancer Publishers.

Ladwig, Walter C. 2007/08. 'A Cold Start for Hot Wars? The Indian Army's New Limited War Doctrine'. *International Security*, 32(3): 158–190.

Lal, P.C. 2008 edn. *My Years with the IAF*, edited by Ila Lal. New Delhi: Lancer.

Lavoy Peter R. ed. 2009. *Asymmetric Warfare in South Asia: The Causes and Consequences of the Kargil Conflict*. Cambridge: Cambridge University Press.

Lehl, Lachhman Singh. 2005 edn. *Missed Opportunities: Indo-Pak War 1965*. Dehradun: Natraj Publishers.

Malhotra, Inder. 2011. 'Our strategic asset'. *The Indian Express*, New Delhi, 3 February.

Malik, V.P. 2006. *Kargil: From Surprise to Reckoning*. New Delhi: HarperCollins Publishers India.

Malik, V.P. and Gurmeet Kanwal. 2005. *Defence Planning in India*. New Delhi: Observer Research Foundation.

Mankekar, D.R. 1972. *Pakistan Cut to Size*. New Delhi: Indian Book Company.

Narang, Vipin. 2009/10. 'Posturing for Peace? Pakistan's Nuclear Postures and South Asian Stability'. *International Security*, 34(3): 38–78.

Palit, D.K. 1972. *The Lightning Campaign: The Indo-Pakistan War 1971*. New Delhi: Thomson Press.

Prasad, S.N. and Dharam Pal. 2005. *History of Operations in Jammu and Kashmir (1947–48)*. New Delhi: History Division, Ministry of Defence, Government of India and Natraj Publishers.

Prasad, S.N. 1992. *The India–Pakistan War of 1971*. New Delhi: History Division, Ministry of Defence, Government of India.

Raghavan, Srinath. 2010. *War and Peace in Modern India: A Strategic History of the Nehru Years*. Ranikhet: Permanent Black.

Raghavan, Srinath. 2013. *1971: A Global History of the Creation of Bangladesh*. Ranikhet: Permanent Black.

Raghavan, V.R. 2001. 'Limited War and Nuclear Escalation in South Asia'. *The Nonproliferation Review*, Fall/Winter: 1–18.

Rikhye, Ravi. 1990. *The Militarisation of Mother India*. Delhi: Chanakya Publications.

Sen, L.P. 1969. *Slender was the Thread: Kashmir Confrontation 1947–48*. New Delhi: Orient Longman.

Sethi, Manpreet. 2009. 'Conventional War in the Presence of Nuclear Weapons'. *Strategic Analysis*, 33(3): 415–425.

Singh, Harbakhsh. 1991. *War Despatches: Indo-Pakistan Conflict 1965*. New Delhi: Lancer International.

Singh, Jasjit. 1989. 'The Indian Experience'. In *Non-Provocative Defence: The Search for Equal Security*, edited by Jasjit Singh and Vatroslav Vekaric, 215–233. New Delhi: Lancer International and IDSA.

Singh, Jasjit. 2000. 'Dynamics of Limited War'. *Strategic Analysis*, 24(7): 1205–1220.

Singh, Jasjit. 2013. *Defence from the Skies: 80 Years of the Indian Air Force*, 2nd edn. New Delhi: Knowledge World and Centre for Air Power Studies.

Singh, Pushpinder. 2007. *Himalayan Eagles: History of the Indian Air Force*, 3 vols. New Delhi: The Society for Aerospace Studies.

Singh, Sukhwant. 1980. *India's Wars Since Independence: The Liberation of Bangladesh, Vol. 1*. New Delhi: Vikas Publishing House.

Singh, Sukhwant. 1981. *Defence of the Western Border, Vol. 2*. New Delhi: Vikas Publishing House.

Singh, Swaran. 2000. 'Indian Debate on Limited War Doctrine'. *Strategic Analysis*, 23(12): 2179–2183.

Sinha, S.K. 1977. *Operation Rescue: Military Operations in Jammu and Kashmir 1947–49*. New Delhi: Vision Books.

Smith, Chris 1994. *India's Ad Hoc Arsenal: Direction or Drift in Defence Policy?* Oxford: Oxford University Press.

Strachan, Hew. 2013. *The Direction of War: Contemporary Strategy in Historical Perspective*. Cambridge, UK: Cambridge University Press.

Subrahmanyam, K. 1976, 1990 reprint. 'Nehru and the India–China Conflict of 1962'. In *Indian Foreign Policy: The Nehru Years*, edited by B.R. Nanda, 102–130. New Delhi: Radiant/Nehru Memorial Museum and Library.

Subrahmanyam, K. 2012. 'India's Grand Strategy'. *Scholar Warrior*, Spring: 2–8.

Subramaniam, Arjun. 2016. *India's Wars: A Military History 1947–1971*. Noida: HarperCollins.

Subramaniam, Arjun. 2020. *Full Spectrum: India's Wars 1972–2020*. Noida: HarperCollins.

Swami, Praveen. 2004. 'Gen. Padmanabhan mulls over lessons of Operation Parakram'. *The Hindu*, New Delhi, 6 February.

Tanham, George K. 1992. *Indian Strategic Thought: An Interpretive Essay*. Santa Monica, CA: RAND.

Tanham, George K. 1992. 'Indian Strategic Culture'. *The Washington Quarterly*, 15(1): 129–142.

Tarapore, Arzan. 2020. *The Army in Indian Military Strategy: Rethink Doctrine or Risk Irrelevance*. Carnegie Endowment. Available at: https://carnegieendowment.org/files/Tarapore_Ground_Forces_in_Indian_Military.pdf (accessed on 11 August 2020).

Tellis, Ashley J. 1997. *Stability in South Asia*. Santa Monica, CA: RAND.

Telegraph. 2000. 'Hot Pursuit Back on BJP Agenda'. *The Telegraph*, New Delhi, 12 August.

Thomas, Raju G.C. 1978. *The Defence of India: A Budgetary Perspective of Strategy and Politics*. Delhi: Macmillan.

Thomas, Raju G.C. 1986. *Indian Security Policy*. Princeton, NJ: Princeton University Press.

Times of India. 2001. 'Hot Pursuit Legitimate: Advani'. *The Times of India*, New Delhi, 19 October.

Unnithan, Sandeep. 2010. 'War Strategy: The Collapse of Cold Start'. *India Today*, New Delhi, 4 December.

Unnithan, Sandeep. 2017. '"We will cross again"—Interview with General Bipin Rawat'. *India Today*, New Delhi, 4 January.

1

Policy, Strategy, and Doctrine: A Framework of Analysis

While war is the continuation of policy and political intercourse by military means rather than through the despatch of diplomatic notes (Clausewitz 1976, 87, 607), it is strategy that translates political aims into military objectives and directs the armed services to achieve them. Strategy, thus, acts as a transmission link between policy and the application of military force. Its purpose is to align political aims with the magnitude of force as well as the manner in which it is to be employed. But what exactly is strategy? Does it belong in the political or military domain, or does it straddle them? How to distinguish strategy from policy on the one hand and military operations on the other? What is the relationship of strategy in land, naval, and aerial warfare? How is strategy in war different from grand strategy and national strategy? Finally, what is the contemporary understanding of strategy? These are the questions explored in this chapter. The chapter is divided into two parts. Part one examines how strategy, which originated as a concept to describe the art of the general, expanded in scope and meaning during the course of the 19th and 20th centuries to encompass the naval, aerial, and nuclear dimensions as well as the non-military elements of national power to emerge as grand strategy. Isolating the military dimension of strategy, the second part of the chapter postulates the framework of political aims, military-strategic objectives, and military doctrinal goals to think about and evaluate the use of force.

Military Origins of Strategy

Until the 18th century, war was seen to consist of two main elements: policy, which sought to attain an objective through the use of force; and, grand tactics, which determined how military force was arrayed and applied in battle. It was only in the wake of the French Revolution, when the size of armies greatly increased with the coming into being of the nation-in-arms, that strategy emerged as a recognisable third element of war. The dramatic increase in the size of armies necessitated planning and coordination for their movement and employment in multiple engagements, and later in multiple theatres, as well as for keeping them sufficiently provisioned. These tasks were different from, and had to be performed prior to, those involved in the actual conduct of battle—a responsibility of higher magnitude that automatically fell on generals. Strategy, in essence, thus, originated as a concept to describe the art of the general in a theatre of war or that of the commander-in-chief. The broad initial understanding of strategy and its relationship to tactics was as follows: tactics pertained to 'what happened on the battlefield', and strategy was about 'what happened off it' (Strachan 2013, 28).[1]

This was a very Jominian understanding of the art of war. Baron Henri de Jomini had served with Napoleon Bonaparte and later emerged as the chief interpreter of the God of War's method. He defined strategy as 'the art of making war upon the map' and comprehending the 'whole theatre of operations'. In contrast, grand tactics involved 'the art of posting troops upon the battle-field according to the accidents of the ground, of bringing them into action, and the art of fighting'. In other words, '[s]trategy decides where to act; logistics brings the troops to this point; grand tactics decides the manner of execution and the employment of the troops' (Jomini 1862, 69; Project Gutenberg 2004). During his exile, Napoleon concurred with Jomini, defining strategy as 'the art of plans of campaign' and tactics as 'the art of battles' (Freedman 2017). Jomini's basic ideas about strategy proceeded in three steps. First, strategy is 'the key to warfare'. Second, strategy is governed by 'invariable scientific principles'. Third, these principles prescribe offensive action that involves massing own force against weaker adversary forces 'at some *decisive point*' to attain victory [emphasis in original] (Shy 1986, 146).

General Carl von Clausewitz, the other great theorist of war to emerge in the wake of the revolution in warfare that Napoleon ushered in, agreed with Jomini that strategy is 'the central point on which all other threads converge'. He, however, criticised Jomini for excluding 'all moral qualities from strategic theory' and reducing 'everything to a few mathematical formulas of equilibrium and superiority, of time and space, limited by a few angles and lines'. Instead, Clausewitz viewed war as 'a paradoxical trinity' driven by the three 'dominant tendencies' of passion, reason, and chance. Passion, that is, the hatred and enmity that one people or nation harbours against another, drives war towards 'primordial violence'. Reason subordinates war to the purpose and objectives of the policy pursued. And 'chance and probability' afford an opportunity for a 'commander and his army' to creatively devise and practice strategy. Coming from such an understanding of war, Clausewitz defined strategy as 'the use of engagements for the object of the war', while tactics involved '*the use of armed forces in the engagement*' [emphases in original] (Clausewitz 1976, 89, 128, 178, 577). Given their association with chance and probability as well as emotion and violence, war and strategy were not unchanging but malleable phenomena.

Civil–Military Tussle over Strategy

For most of the 19th century, strategy was regarded as 'a purely military concept, interacting with tactics but not with policy' (Freedman 2017). As a result, military leaders insisted on strict distinctions between policy and strategy. For example, during the Franco-Prussian War of 1870–1871, Field Marshal Helmuth Karl Bernhard Graf von Moltke argued that 'strategy works uniquely in the direction indicated by policy, but at the same time it protects its complete independence to choose its means of action' (Strachan 2013, 30). The politician should, therefore, 'fall silent' after ordering mobilisation and 'not resume his precedence' until the strategist has completed his task by totally defeating the adversary (Howard 1957, 19–20). As per this view, strategy was not only independent of policy, but it also took the place of policy during the course of war.

Statesmen were, however, loath to accept this Jominian mode of thought and the contention flowing therefrom that the commander-in-chief needs only to 'agree' at the outset 'with the head of the state upon the character of the war' and thereafter independently devise strategy for its conduct (Jomini 1862, 66). Prussian Chancellor Otto von Bismarck disagreed with von Moltke's argument and asserted a role for politics during the course of war. Bismarck contended that

> [t]o fix and limit the objects to be attained by the war, and to advise the monarch in respect of them, is and remains during the war just as before it a political function, and the manner in which these questions are solved cannot be without influence on the conduct of the war. (Freedman 2013, 106)

Although Bismarck had never read Clausewitz, his argument was in line with the latter's reasoning. Clausewitz had noted that policy cannot 'wholly cease to count on the outbreak of war … unless pure hatred made all wars a struggle for life and death'. War, in Clausewitz's view, 'is simply a continuation of political intercourse, with the addition of other means'. That is, political intercourse does not cease at the outbreak of war but continues in the form of 'fighting battles rather than by sending diplomatic notes'. Consequently, '[t]he main lines along which military events progress, and to which they are restricted, are political lines that continue throughout the war into the subsequent peace.' War, thus, cannot be divorced from policy. In fact, war is created by policy and is an instrument of policy. The form and character that each war assumes are, therefore, bound to change in accordance with the aim of policy. While policy 'will not extend its influence to operational details', such as 'the posting of guards or the employment of patrols', political considerations 'are the most influential in the planning of war, of the campaign, and often even of the battle' (Clausewitz 1976, 605–607).

In Bismarck's and Clausewitz's conception, strategy, thus, fell partially in the realm of policy, and the policymaker did have a role in its crafting. Despite prolonged resistance from military leaders, the logic of the Bismarck–Clausewitz conception of the relationship between policy and strategy came to be increasingly acknowledged and accepted as the century progressed. During the American Civil War, for instance, Abraham Lincoln 'exercised a constant oversight of the war effort from beginning to end'. He controlled and directed his generals and even replaced them when he felt it was necessary. He was determined to mould the war and 'dominate the making of peace at its end'. Recording how Lincoln had directed the war, his secretaries-turned-biographers later asserted that

> [e]very war is begun, dominated, and ended by political considerations.... War and politics, campaign and statecraft, are Siamese twins, inseparable and interdependent; and to talk of military operations without the direction and interference of an Administration is as absurd as to plan a campaign without recruits, pay, or rations. (Nicolay and Hay 1890, 359–360)[2]

These views were re-emphasised by G.F.R. Henderson, a British commentator on the American Civil War, who noted that just like war is an instrument of diplomacy, so is the soldier 'the servant of the statesman'. Observing that effective strategy depended on able statesmanship, he concluded that '[i]t is difficult, if not impossible, to divorce soldiering and statesmanship' (Freedman 2018). How far the political and military spheres are intermeshed becomes clear when we consider what strategy actually entails. In his biography of Field Marshal Alan Brooke, David Fraser broke down the 'art of strategy' into five essential steps:

1. Determination of the political aim.
2. Derivation of military objectives from the political aim.
3. Assessment of the military requirements as well as preconditions necessary for attaining the selected objectives.
4. Measurement of 'available and potential resources against the requirements'.
5. Drawing up of 'a coherent pattern of priorities and a rational course of action' (Craig 1986, 481).

Further, if we take Clausewitz's reasoning to its logical conclusion that political considerations influence war plans, campaigns, and battles, a statesman will also need to consider how to translate strategy into operations. That, in turn, throws up another set of technical issues that statesmen need to grapple with. As elaborated by Edward Spears, these include

> examining plans and maps and working out the meaning of the vast number of orders based on these, issued by Army Groups and Armies to artillery of every description, to the air force, the cavalry, infantry, tanks, etc [as well as] estimating such things as the firepower on ... own side and the power of resistance of the enemy, the weight of the shock of the attacking infantry and its tactical dispositions... (Spears 1939, 377)

Notwithstanding the fact that political leaders may not have even basic knowledge of these technicalities, they cannot afford to adopt a hands-off approach because military operations have political consequences in terms of attaining war aims, expanding its scope, and influencing allies on both sides. Consequently, civilian leaders have a natural incentive to monitor the progress of war. They, however, need to guard against too intrusive an approach to avoid interfering with the conduct of military operations. In short, political leaders need to evolve a balanced approach to the conduct of war. As Craig explained,

> If excessive meddling in operational planning and decision making by political leaders can have disruptive consequences, inability or unwillingness on their part to exercise critical control over such plans and decisions runs the risk of placing in military hands powers that can jeopardize the national security for which the political leadership has ultimate responsibility. (Craig 1986, 482)

What crafting of strategy and its translation into military operations require, therefore, is the adoption of an approach that maintains a fine balance between excessive political meddling and granting a blank cheque to the military brass. The relationship of strategy with, and subordination to, policy deepened during the course of the 20th century as the term was expanded to successively include the naval, aerial, nuclear, and non-military elements of national power.

Naval Strategy: Mahan and Corbett

In their original conceptions, strategy and grand tactics had been discussed exclusively in the context of land warfare. Given his continental outlook, Clausewitz completely ignored naval warfare. Jomini devoted a few pages to the naval dimension because Napoleon had considered a seaborne invasion of England. Consequently, although Jomini acknowledged the criticality of establishing and maintaining command of the sea, his discussion was limited to pointing out the difficulties involved in transporting and landing even a small expeditionary force and the importance of securing a harbour to maintain communications (Jomini 1862, 249–252). Naval strategy, thus, remained unaddressed until Alfred Thayer Mahan and Julian Stafford Corbett did so: They aligned naval strategy with land-war strategy, and, in the process, they expanded the meaning and scope of strategy.

Mahan, influenced as he was by Jomini, identified the word 'contact' to be a good indicator of the dividing line between tactics and strategy. He not only cited Jomini's definition of grand tactics but also laid stress upon the strategic principle of bringing to bear superior strength on a weaker portion of the adversary's force in a decisive battle (Mahan 1890, 12th edn. Kindle Version, 898, 932–941). For Mahan, the destruction of the 'organised forces' of the adversary was the 'chief objective' in war, both on land and at sea. Accordingly, the 'role of navies in war was to compete with other navies for the command of the sea' (Freedman 2013, 116–117). A second principle of naval strategy that Mahan emphasised upon, using the example of the Battle of Trafalgar that sealed the fate of Napoleon's expeditionary force in Egypt, was the importance of maintaining one's own, and disrupting the adversary's lines of communication during overseas expeditions. In addition, Mahan identified several other strategic questions, 'covering the whole plan of operations throughout the theatre of war', which had to be decided before the fleet made contact with the adversary's naval force. These included the navy's role and objective in war and the 'points upon which it should be concentrated', establishing fuel and supply depots and maintaining communications with them, and determining whether commerce destruction should be undertaken as 'a decisive or secondary operation' as well as the most efficient way of carrying it out—by scattering cruisers at various places or by establishing control over critical choke points 'through which commercial shipping must pass' (Mahan 1890, 12th edn. Kindle Version, 902).

Mahan's more enduring contribution lay in his identification of the close relationship between naval power and economic strength. 'The necessity of a navy', he wrote, essentially 'springs … from the existence of … peaceful shipping, and disappears with it' (Mahan 1890, 12th edn. Kindle Version, 1202). So did the necessity for securing access to foreign ports as well as establishing naval stations and colonies. In other words, naval superiority is essential for protecting maritime trade and promoting the interests associated with it so that national well-being and prosperity may be safeguarded and enhanced (Strachan 2013, 32). That, in turn, led Mahan to prefer a definition of naval strategy that extended its ambit to peacetime as well. In this regard, he cited an unnamed French author who argued that naval strategy, unlike land warfare strategy, is 'as necessary in peace as in war' because the most favourable and excellent positions on the map are obtained through 'purchase or treaty' during the years of peace. The objective of naval strategy should, therefore, be 'to found, support, and increase, as well in peace as in war, the sea power of a country' (Mahan 1890, 12th edn. Kindle Version, 1112–1116).[3]

If Mahan was influenced by Jomini, Corbett was inspired by Clausewitz. But unlike Mahan, who 'integrate[d] and synthesize[d] Jomini's work with his own', Corbett used Clausewitz's ideas as 'a heuristic point of departure' (Handel 2001, 277). Corbett, however, did not consider the ideas of Jomini as incompatible with those of Clausewitz. On the contrary, he highlighted the similarity in the views of these 'two apostles of the Napoleonic method' on the critical question of the influence of policy, and the limitations it imposed, on war. Though he conceded the difference between Jomini and Clausewitz on the 'details of means' to be employed, Corbett pointed out that they agreed that 'the fundamental conception of war is political' as evident from Jomini's classification of the nine types of war according to the political objective pursued and Clausewitz's definition of war (Corbett 1911, 30, 47).

In Corbett's view, Clausewitz's definition of war as 'a continuation of policy' and 'a form of political intercourse' had wrought a revolution in 'the study of strategy' (Corbett 1911, 18).[4] It indicated that the character of war is bound to change in tune with the aim and scope of policy. War could, thus, be waged for offensive or defensive purposes and to attain limited or expansive objectives. Strategy consequently involves crafting a military plan that matches the quantum, intensity, and manner of force employment with the war's political aim. While there were bound to be compromises between political compulsions and military necessities, 'policy must always be the master [and] the means adopted must conflict as little as possible with the political conditions from which the war springs' (Corbett 1911, 27).

As to the military means employed, since states are territorial entities and the outcome of war is ultimately dependent on what happened on land, the navy has to necessarily adopt a role that is complementary to that of the army. How the mutual relationship between the two services is defined, and what role the navy is assigned, in a plan of war is the function of maritime strategy. Once maritime strategy determines the part to be played by the fleet in relation to the army's actions on land, naval strategy translates the role and function assigned to the fleet into a pattern of deployment and a set of objectives (Corbett 1911, 15–16). Corbett hewed to the common understanding that securing command of the sea was the object of naval strategy. But his explorations with respect to what command of the sea meant, its different types, the means through which it can be secured, and the ultimate purpose it serves represented a significant departure from contemporary articulations.

For Corbett, what command of the sea really meant was the establishment of control over maritime communications for both naval and commercial purposes because, unlike land, the sea can neither be owned (except for territorial waters) nor can an armed force subsist upon it. Further, while the lines of communication on land run more or less in opposite directions towards the theatre of war, the maritime lines of communications of adversaries either 'run approximately parallel' to each other or may even be 'identical'. Control over maritime communications is, therefore, essential for own naval and commercial use of the sea as well as for preventing the adversary from using it. The degree of control established over maritime communications could vary in accordance with the aim and scope of war. It could be general or local, that is, it could exist in all theatres of war or be restricted to a single theatre. Control over maritime communications could also be permanent or temporary, that is, endure throughout the war or exist only for a limited period. Local command, invariably temporary in nature and sufficient for the purposes of limited war, may be secured by establishing a close blockade of the relevant adversary naval base in order to prevent that portion of its fleet from being put to sea (Corbett 1911, 184, 340).[5] However, only a victory in a decisive naval battle can secure general command of the sea.

While general command of the sea enables own amphibious operations and prevents those of the adversary, what it ultimately provides is the power to strangle the latter's seaborne commerce and, over time, its 'whole national life'. Corbett conceded that, on its own, such naval pressure can work only slowly and through 'a process of exhaustion'. Nevertheless, it is the exertion of such 'pressure on the citizens and their collective life' that ultimately compels the adversary to 'make peace' and agree to the demands placed upon it (Corbett 1911, 15–16, 93–94, 97, 103–104, 201, 322). In effect, Corbett envisaged an expansion in the scope and application of strategy beyond the battlefield to the civilian sphere—a thought process that was carried forward in the 1920s by air-power theorists.

Corbett's location of naval strategy as a distinct element, within the broader strategy employed in war, led him to draw a distinction between the two levels of strategy. In order to clearly delineate the boundaries between the larger conception of strategy, on the one hand, and naval strategy and land-warfare strategy, on the other, Corbett termed the former as 'major strategy' and the latter as 'minor strategy'. In his conception, major strategy

> regards the fleet and army as one weapon … co-ordinates their action … indicates the lines on which each must move to realise the full power of both … will direct us to assign to each its proper function in a plan of war … will enable each service to realise the better the limitations and the possibilities of the function with which it is charged, and how and when its own necessities must give way to a higher or more pressing need of the other. (Corbett 1911, 10–11)

In essence, major strategy crafts the war plan, selects the overall military objective in tune with the political aim, and chooses the appropriate mix of land and naval forces to be employed for attaining the aim. For its part, minor strategy—naval, military or combined—derives its specific objectives from the overall military objective in the form of 'the particular forces of the enemy or the strategical points to be dealt with in order to secure the object of the particular operation' and directs the force 'assigned for the operation' (Corbett 1911, 308).

Even as he thus delimited the scope and ambit of major and minor strategies, Corbett was conscious of the fuzzy boundaries between major strategy and policy. Alternatively referring to major strategy as grand strategy, he defined major strategy as 'a branch of statesmanship', which 'in its broadest sense has also to deal with the whole resources of the nation for war'. Therefore, in addition to regarding the army and navy as a single military instrument, major or grand strategy also needs to consider the country's 'politico-diplomatic position' as well as its 'commercial and financial position'. For, without a favourable diplomatic position, force cannot be applied effectively; and without a sound economy, 'the energy for working the [military] instrument' cannot be 'maintained'. Consequently, major or grand strategy and the minor strategies flowing therefrom have to necessarily take into consideration the diplomatic and economic factors and treat them 'as part of the inevitable "friction of war"' (Corbett 1911, 308). Thus, Corbett too, like Mahan, acknowledged the intricate links between strategy and policy as well as the fuzzy boundaries between them.

Air Power Strategy

The aerial dimension emerged during the First World War, with airplanes being at first used for reconnaissance and later for attaining control of the air by shooting down enemy aircraft as well as for attacking targets on the ground—both on the battlefield and in urban areas such as London and Antwerp. Three main ideas about the offensive employment of air power emerged during the war: destroying targets on the battlefield (close air support), disrupting the movement of supplies and reinforcements to the battlefield (interdiction), and bombing civilian and industrial targets to cause the collapse of popular and political resistance (strategic bombardment) (Ledwidge 2018, 38–59).

From the perspective of strategy and its expanding conception, strategic bombardment was the most consequential of these ideas because it expanded the application of military force beyond the battlefield to not just include but actually concentrate upon civilian targets. Giulio Douhet, the foremost advocate of this approach, contended that strategic bombardment was the most efficient means of attaining swift victory in an era of total wars, marked by mass armies with extended battle lines that did not permit an easy breakthrough. As a result, the First World War had ended not because the German military lay defeated but because political and popular will in Germany had collapsed. Instead of such a result occurring under the cumulative impact of several years of attrition wars on land and naval blockades, Douhet advocated the speeding up of the process through the massive bombardment of the adversary's centres of population, government, and industry. If carried out with a mix of bombs containing explosives, incendiaries, and poison gas, strategic bombing, he argued, would destroy entire cities, cause the collapse of 'the physical and moral resistance of the people', and compel them to demand an end to the war, even through a revolutionary change of government (Douhet 1998, 5, 8–9, 19–20, 58, 126).

A prerequisite for wreaking such destruction was attaining the command of the air—a concept that was first proposed in 1893 by Major J.D. Fullerton of the British Royal Engineers (MacIsaac 1986, 627). Douhet, for his part, gave the concept full expression by defining it in Mahanian terms: 'To have command of the air means to be in a position to prevent the adversary from flying while retaining the ability to fly oneself.' Only the retention of such a capacity to wreak destruction upon the adversary's armed forces, government establishments, industrial infrastructure, and population centres, while at the same time denying it to the adversary, would ensure victory. What it involved was the destruction, through both aerial combat and offensive counter-air operations, of all the adversary's 'means of flying', including airplanes, operational and supply bases, and production centres (Douhet 1998, 23–28, 34, 96–97, 105).

While Douhet advocated the indiscriminate bombing of civilian areas, Billy Mitchell and the Air Corps Tactical School in the United States favoured a modified version of strategic bombardment that emphasised on the precision bombing of key nodes, such as military and industrial hubs, rather than population centres. Mitchell and the Tactical School contended that the destruction of these targets would result in the collapse of the adversary's ability to continue the war. Known as the industrial web theory, the origins of this approach lay in the attempts of the Royal Flying Corps and its commander, General Hugh Trenchard, to disrupt the German Army's lines of supply during the First World War through 'concentrated attacks against chosen targets in sufficient numbers and with sufficient continuity to make a decisive impact' (Ledwidge 2018, 47; Freedman 2013, 124–125). Notwithstanding this focus on destroying military and industrial hubs, as opposed to Douhet's call for indiscriminate bombing of population centres, the fact remains that both versions of strategic bombardment expanded the ambit of strategy beyond the battlefield to the civilian sphere.

Grand Strategy

The First World War reinforced the tendency for strategy to be conceived of in grand strategic terms. This was inevitable given that it was a total war in terms of the political aims pursued, the military objectives sought, and the national resources mobilised. Writing in its aftermath, Basil Liddell Hart followed Corbett in drawing a distinction between 'grand strategy' and 'pure strategy'. Grand strategy involved the coordination and direction of 'all the resources of a nation, or band of nations, towards the attainment of the political object of the war'. In that sense, grand strategy was 'practically synonymous with the policy which guides the conduct of war' and also 'serves to bring out the sense of "policy in execution"' (Liddell Hart 1967, 335–336). Pure strategy, for its part, was related to the application of force by the individual armed services.

Thus far, with the exception of Mahan, theorists had invariably discussed strategy, including grand strategy, only in the context of war. But the links between both 'peacetime preparation and the conduct of war' and 'economic capability and military applications' demonstrated by the First World War prompted J.F.C. Fuller to expand the ambit of grand strategy to peacetime as well (Strachan 2013, 33). Fuller contended that it was a waste of material, moral and physical resources to have 'two forms of strategy, one for peace and one for war'. Instead, 'our peace strategy must formulate our war strategy'. Consequently, the grand strategist must first evaluate the country's economic position and, second, its 'moral characteristics' that underpin military power. Applying the same logic to the lesser form of strategy, Fuller pointed out that its division into military, naval, and aerial components is 'a direct violation of the principle of economy of forces as applied to a united army, navy and air force, and hence a weakening of the principle of the objective' (Strachan 2013, 33).

The view that strategy is equally applicable during both peace and war reached its apogee with the introduction of nuclear weapons. By severing 'the link between victory and self-preservation' (Creveld 2000, 28), nuclear weapons robbed war of its very logic—the political purpose, which tames war's 'destructive element' and transforms it into a 'mere instrument' (Clausewitz 1976, 605–606). In the process, nuclear weapons rendered the avoidance of war itself as the purpose of both policy and strategy. As Bernard Brodie presciently noted at the dawn of the nuclear age: 'Thus far the chief purpose of our military establishment has been to win wars. From now on its chief purpose must be to avert them. It can have almost no other useful purpose' (Brodie 1978, 65). The purpose of nuclear strategy was not to win wars. It was to either prevent war by threatening absolute destruction or manipulate the threat of such a cataclysm for pursuing limited objectives. As Thomas Schelling observed, '[t]he power to hurt is bargaining power. To exploit it is diplomacy—vicious diplomacy, but diplomacy' (Schelling 1966, 2). In effect, the new concern of strategy with 'the exploitation of potential force' instead of with its 'efficient application' eroded the distinction between war and peace during the Cold War—a distinction that was reinforced by the nuclear arms race as well as by proxy and guerrilla wars becoming substitutes for war between the superpowers (Strachan 2013, 36).

Erosion of the distinction between war and peace, constraints imposed by nuclear weapons on the use of force, and recognition of the importance of non-military instruments of national power led to the conception of military strategy as just another arm of grand strategy alongside political strategy, economic strategy, and diplomatic strategy

(Strachan 2013, 36). Indeed, grand strategy came to be envisaged as a plan for the application of the military, economic, diplomatic, and psychological instruments of national power in a conjoint manner to attain foreign policy goals (Baylis 2001, 2). A grand plan to achieve long-term foreign policy objectives by employing various instruments of national power is, however, only one of three prevalent conceptions of grand strategy. A second conception is that it is a grand organising principle or set of principles that provides a framework for decision-making. In its third conception, grand strategy is a grand pattern of state behaviour over time (Silove 2018, 27–57).

With 'grand' strategy emerging as the framework for interrelating policy with the various instruments of national power, the ways in which the armed services applied force acquired the new appellation of military doctrine. It was also assigned a new medium of operation—the operational level of war located between grand strategy and tactics (Strachan 2013, 37–38). Yet, confusion persists as to the difference between strategy and doctrine, with both terms being used interchangeably. For instance, Barry Posen calls blitzkrieg a doctrine, whereas John Mearsheimer refers to it as a strategy (Posen 1984, 14; Mearsheimer 1983, 29). The reason for this difference in appellation lies in their respective conceptions of strategy. Posen conceives of strategy in grand strategic terms, with military doctrine being one of the sub-components of grand strategy. Mearsheimer, however, understands strategy in the original Clausewitzian sense of using the battle to attain the object of the war and, hence, classifies blitzkrieg as a strategy along with attrition and fait accompli (Mearsheimer 1983, 29–30).

Political Aims, Strategies, and Doctrines

During the course of its evolution during the 20th century, strategy, thus, shed its original military connotation as the art of the general and became a concept that was political in orientation. In the contemporary understanding, strategy no longer means 'the use of the battle for the purposes of war'; instead, it has come to mean 'the use of war for the purposes of policy' (Strachan 2019, 173). This reformulation of the meaning of strategy during the course of the 20th century helps distinguish it from both policy and military operations, while at the same time providing an overarching framework for directing military operations on land, at sea, and in the air towards the attainment of political objectives. In effect, strategy has become the politico-military framework that brings into alignment policy aims and the application of military force. This definition of strategy is more restricted than the notion of grand strategy, which includes within its ambit the application of non-military elements of national power during both war and peace.

Accordingly, each war may be conceived of as consisting of three interrelated components: policy, strategy, and doctrine. Policy determines the political aims to be attained. Strategy translates political aims into military objectives, determines the form of war (defensive or offensive) to be waged, and evolves an overall plan for the application of military force. Doctrine governs how the armed services apply force to attain the military goals flowing from the overall military objectives.

Political Aims

Throughout history, political entities have used military force to pursue a variety of aims. For instance, Kalevi Holsti identified 35 distinct issues that led to war among modern states between the years 1648 and 1989 (Holsti 1991, passim). Holsti's list included wars to safeguard autonomy, uphold national honour, ensure national security, protect nationals and commercial interests abroad, obtain compensation, enforce or revise treaty terms, gain or preserve territory, unify ethnic or religious populations, change the composition of government, practice ideological liberation, support ethnic/religious/ideological compatriots abroad, acquire colonies, access or control resources, defend or support allies, preserve alliance unity, maintain free trade and freedom of navigation, sustain the balance of power, establish regional dominance, and seek hegemony.

These and other issues that generated inter-state wars before 1648 and after 1989 broadly fall under the two general categories of what Christopher Bassford has termed high-end and limited political aims. What differentiates the two categories is the survival of the state against which war is being waged. While high-end aims threaten the adversary's survival, limited aims stop short of eliminating it as a political entity. High-end political aims threaten state survival because they variously seek to change the adversary's governance system or structure, eradicate it as a political entity, and, in the extreme, eliminate its population. In other words, high-end political aims involve replacing a ruler or regime, changing the form of government, enforcing a confederation or engaging in outright conquest, and committing genocide. In contrast, limited political aims strive to change only the adversary's policy or erode its national capacity. Specifically, limited political aims include intimidating the adversary, compelling it to change policy, partially destroying its military capacity, capturing a portion of its territory, damaging its economy, and causing suffering to its population (Bassford 1997, Chapter 3).

Strategic Objectives

Once political aims are determined, the task of strategy is to translate them into appropriate military objectives. To be successful, the military objectives identified should be such that their achievement compels the adversary to concede, and not continue to resist, the state's political aims. War, as Clausewitz made us realise, is '*the continuation of policy with other means*' as well as the ultimate instrument for compelling the adversary '*to do our will*' [emphases in original] (Clausewitz 1976, 69, 75). It follows therefrom that an adversary would feel compelled to stop resisting and abide by the state's will only when it is no longer capable of putting up either physical or moral resistance or both.

To render an adversary incapable of physical resistance, it needs to be made defenceless. That, in turn, requires the destruction of its armed forces. The German historian Hans Delbrück termed this method of one state imposing its will on another and thereby achieving its political aims as the strategy of annihilation. The word 'annihilation' does not mean the extermination of the adversary's armed forces, only their destruction as coherent fighting forces (Delbrück 1985, 293).

Success in the strategy of annihilation is contingent on sufficient military superiority over the adversary. If a state does not enjoy sufficient military superiority or does not wish to destroy the adversary's armed forces due to balance of power or geopolitical considerations, it could adopt a second method for imposing its will and attaining the identified political aims. In contrast to the first method, which involves the destruction of the adversary's ability to resist, the second method concentrates upon eroding or exhausting the adversary's will to resist (Bassford 1997, Chapter 3).[6] It entails the state imposing costs and pain on the adversary that prove much harder to bear than what is involved in conceding the state's political aims. In effect, the second method enables the state to impose its will by wearing out and exhausting the adversary through 'blows and destruction of all kinds' (Delbrück 1985, 294). Hence the appellation 'strategy of exhaustion'.

Discussing the utility of this approach, Clausewitz had suggested that territory could be captured in order to exact 'financial contributions' or to lay it to waste and 'cause general damage'. He also recommended unleashing military operations that increase 'the enemy's suffering' and brings about 'a gradual exhaustion of his physical and moral resistance' (Clausewitz 1976, 69, 92–93; Delbrück 1985, 294). For his part, Delbrück flagged the importance of exploiting the adversary's vulnerabilities including by occupying a portion of territory, cutting off supplies, causing military setbacks to adversary forces, etc. At the same time, however, he highlighted the importance of safeguarding one's own forces, territory, and population, given the fact that the adversary continued to retain the advantage of his main force remaining intact (Delbrück 1985, 294).

Some studies, including the translation of Delbrück's four-volume history of the art of war referred to here, translate his German term for the second strategy—*Ermattungsstrategie*—as the strategy of attrition (Delbrück 1985, 293–318; Weigley 1973, xxii, 3–17; Inbar and Shamir 2014, 65–90). However, as Lawrence Freedman has explained, Delbrück conceived of the strategy of exhaustion as an extended campaign to wear the adversary down, as against the first method of annihilating the adversary's forces in a decisive battle. Hence, it is more appropriate to describe it as the strategy of exhaustion (Freedman 2013, 108). In addition, we also need to ensure that the strategy of exhaustion is not confused with the land-warfare doctrine of attrition [discussed below].

Consequently, this study employs the term 'strategy of exhaustion' and not 'strategy of attrition'.

Delbrück's categorisation of the two broad strategies of annihilation and exhaustion was drawn from a survey of war on land. It is nevertheless possible to expand the concept to other domains of war. Corbett, for instance, extrapolated the strategy of annihilation to naval war, noting that 'the practical annihilation of the enemy's fleet' is essential to secure 'permanent general control' of the sea (Corbett 1911, 321). In the same vein, command of the air or air superiority in a theatre of war may be obtained by destroying the adversary's air bases and frontline aircraft on the ground, as demonstrated by Nazi Germany during the invasions of Poland and the Soviet Union and by Israel in the 1967 War against Arab states (Singh 1984, 856–858, 860). Air and naval power also play a critical role in executing the strategy of exhaustion. Aerial strikes against carefully selected targets, such as over the terrorist base in Balakot in 2019, as well as the bombing of military targets, civilian areas, industrial centres, and transport hubs inflict cost and pain on the adversary (Pape 2004, 116–130). In the naval realm, blockade of adversary ports and seizure of commercial vessels would similarly inflict cost and pain (Corbett 1911, 185). The overall military objectives suggested by the strategies of annihilation and exhaustion may be broadly termed as 'unlimited' and 'limited' following John Mearsheimer or, better still, 'high-end' and 'limited' following Bassford (Mearsheimer 1983, 29; Bassford 1997, Chapter 3).

Military Doctrines

Doctrine comes into play after strategy lays down the overall military objectives to be attained. It guides the operations of each armed service in individual as well as joint missions, and it provides 'the basis for war plans' (Rajagopalan 2008, 36).[7] If doctrine is about how military operations are conducted by a service either singly or jointly with other services, then it is best defined thus:

> [T]he preferred mode of a group of services, a single service, or a subservice for fighting wars. It reflects the judgements of professional

> military officers, and to a lesser but important extent civilian leaders, about what is and is not militarily possible and necessary. Such judgments are based on appraisals of military technology, national geography, adversary capabilities, and the skills of one's own military organization. Military doctrine, particularly the aspects that relate directly to combat, is strongly reflected in the forces that are acquired by the military organization. (Posen 1984, 14)

Posen and other scholars divide doctrine into the three categories of offensive, defensive, and deterrent. Offensive doctrines seek to destroy the adversary's armed forces. Defensive doctrines endeavour to deny the adversary its objective. Deterrent doctrines punish and impose costs on the adversary (Posen 1984, 14). Such a categorisation goes against the Clausewitzian understanding of war. Clausewitz pointed out that offence and defence are two forms that war may assume, depending upon the political aim. The only difference between them lies in which party initiates war. Despite repeatedly emphasising that defence is the stronger and more effective form of war than offence, Clausewitz cautioned against conceiving of defence as restricted to parrying and enduring the adversary's blows for the limited purpose of defending and maintaining the status quo. Such a conception, in his view, is 'contrary to the idea of war, since it would mean that only one side was waging it'. Instead, defence merely serves to bide time and choose the right opportunity to transition to the counter-offensive—'the flashing sword of vengeance' in Clausewitz's splendid phrase—before finally undertaking the strategic offensive to attain victory (Clausewitz 1976, 357, 370). Or, as Corbett put it, defence only meant 'taking certain measures to defer a decision until military or political developments so far redress the balance of strength that we are able to pass to the offensive' (Corbett 1911, 211). In sum, defence may help avoid defeat but cannot provide victory (Singh 1984, 944).

Given this understanding, there is nothing to stop a commander from employing an offensive doctrine as a counterstroke in an otherwise defensive war or even to deter a potential adversary from initiating war in the first place. For example, NATO's manoeuvre doctrine of the 1980s was essentially conceived of as an armoured counterstroke in what would have been a defensive war aimed at defeating a Soviet invasion of West Germany (Strachan 2013, 65). It may also be argued that this doctrine contributed to deterring the Soviet Union from initiating such an invasion. In the same vein, a defensive doctrine may deter an adversary by convincing it about the great difficulties involved in achieving its objectives. Alternatively, a defensive doctrine may serve the purpose of giving time for mobilisation and an eventual counter-offensive, as was calculated by the French Army while envisaging the Maginot Line (Kier 1997, 39–46). Finally, a deterrent doctrine may involve either a punitive offensive into adversary territory or simply adopting the defensive to avoid the risk of great losses. Thus, during the course of the 1930s, while the Royal Air Force contemplated the idea of punitive aerial offensives for a few years, British military leaders, in general, favoured a defensive war 'in any one of the three critical theaters' in order to ensure that they retained the 'ability to "deter" the outbreak of war elsewhere' (Posen 1984, 152–153).

In the light of these conceptual problems associated with Posen's categorisation, this study adopts a more basic division of doctrines into 'direct' and 'indirect' types by drawing upon and expanding the distinction that Basil Liddell Hart had made between direct and indirect approaches to military strategy (Liddell Hart 1967, 18). Direct military doctrine may be defined as an approach that emphasises force-upon-force action to either completely destroy, or cause varying degrees of damage to, adversary forces, depending upon the war's political and military objectives. In contrast, indirect military doctrine lays stress on dislocating the adversary and throwing it off-balance with a view to either cause its systemic collapse or variously wrest territory and degrade the economy and infrastructure to erode its resistance (Liddell Hart 1967, 339–341).[8]

The meaning of the term 'doctrine' employed in this study is distinct from the official doctrine that is prepared and periodically updated by the armed services. Official doctrine is a foundational document that contains 'broad tenets for the prosecution of operations ... across the entire spectrum of conflict' (Indian Army 2018), generates 'a common language and a uniform understanding' of the relevant concepts (Integrated Headquarters 2015, 6), and provides commanders 'the framework to prepare and fight a war in a coordinated and controlled manner' (Indian Air Force 2012, vii).

Doctrines in Land Warfare

According to the 2004 edition of the Indian Army's doctrine, the goal of combat is the 'strategic dislocation of the adversary' (Army Training Command 2004, 30–31). It may be obtained either by the physical destruction of the adversary's combat capability or by throwing the adversary force off-balance through surprise, strategic penetration and envelopment, and selective attacks on critical assets. This understanding is in broad agreement with the distinction between the direct doctrine of attrition and the indirect approach represented by manoeuvre.

Attrition involves an army advancing along a broad front and fighting a series of set-piece battles to push the other side back. 'Rout and retreat alternate' in this protracted process, which eventually wears down the adversary (Mearsheimer 1983, 34). Artillery plays a critical role in this process of wearing down the defence. Even armour is employed mainly as a platform from which to deliver fire. For instance, the British Army employed armoured forces in an attritional role, with a view to gain 'armoured superiority' in the initial phases of the Second World War (Palit 2000, 81–82). The essence of attrition, thus, lies in bringing to bear superior firepower upon the adversary's forces and supporting infrastructure. Victory is contingent upon destroying that proportion of the adversary forces that breaks their cohesion and causes retreat or defeat. If both sides were to employ the doctrine of attrition, then the side able to absorb greater losses and outlast the other would emerge the victor. In other words, it would be a battle of strengths. Consequently, a fundamental prerequisite for victory is the 'overall superiority in net attritive capacity', that is, a larger force and a superior material base (Luttwak 1980/81, 62–64).

Attrition may also be used in wars of exhaustion to inflict a degree of damage on the opposing army and, thereby, even compel it to abandon some territory. As will be seen in later chapters, the Indian Army's campaigns in the 1947–1948 conflict, the 1965 War, and the Kargil conflict were all marked by the employment of attrition.

In contrast to attrition, manoeuvre is an indirect approach that avoids the adversary's strength. It selectively and precisely applies strength on the adversary's 'identified points of weakness' with the aim of incapacitating the opposition's 'forces or structures' through a process of 'systemic disruption' (Luttwak 1980/81, 64–66).[9] The system to be thus disrupted may be the entire army or only the forces in a particular theatre. Manoeuvre doctrine may assume either a defensive or offensive form. In the defensive form of manoeuvre, an army avoids a frontal confrontation with an invading force and instead concentrates on disrupting the latter's lines of communication. Finland, for example, planned to employ such an operational doctrine during the Cold War in the event of a Soviet invasion (Luttwak 1980/81, 73–76).

Blitzkrieg is the offensive, 20th-century form of manoeuvre. It involves armoured forces piercing the adversary's front and penetrating deep into the rear. The purpose of such a 'strategic penetration' is to destroy the 'central nervous system' of the adversary's army, namely the vulnerable network comprising 'numerous lines of communication, along which supplies as well as information move, and key nodal points at which the various lines intersect'. As Mearsheimer notes, the 'destruction of this central nervous system is tantamount to destruction of the army' (Mearsheimer 1983, 36). Strategic penetration is effected at one or two specific locations to ensure that the necessary superiority of forces may be mobilised at those points. Holes that are punched through the adversary front are kept open by the infantry.[10] After effecting the penetration, armoured forces bypass strong points and drive deep into the rear, disrupting supplies and reinforcements to adversary units and preventing them from coalescing together. This disruption in the rear combines with the continuing pressure exerted by forces along the frontline to unbalance the adversary physically and psychologically, eventually resulting in its systemic collapse (Mearsheimer 1983, 35–43).

Doctrines in Naval Warfare

In war, the navy's main tasks may vary between defeating the enemy fleet and disrupting its maritime trade and sea lines of communication (SLOCs). In accordance with our definition, direct naval doctrine involves drawing or seeking out the enemy fleet and destroying it in a decisive naval battle. In contrast, indirect naval doctrine entails trade warfare and interdiction of sea lines of communication to erode or exhaust adversary resistance.

Historically, decisive naval battle was the means by which navies obtained command of the sea (Corbett 1911, 167–183). While there was some scepticism about the viability of such battles in the nuclear age, it did not last, and both superpowers emphasised the destruction of the other's fleet in their respective naval doctrines during the Cold War. A naval battle is also conceivable in the context of limited war between nuclear-weapon powers, although its objective would be restricted to bringing about 'an early and moderately advantageous end' to the war (Till 1982, 184). Accordingly, the Indian Maritime Doctrine of 2009 notes that it would seek to attain the primary objective of decisive victory through 'proactive, coordinated and joint combat operations' against the adversary's centre of gravity, namely, its naval forces (Integrated Headquarters 2015, 82–83).

There is, however, a crucial difference between the past and present in terms of what is obtained from a decisive naval engagement. Whereas the destruction of the adversary fleet resulted in command of the sea until the 19th century, successive technological developments during the course of the 20th century, such as torpedoes, submarines, land-based aircraft and missiles, have made it impossible for a successful navy to exercise absolute command at sea. It has consequently become more realistic, as Admiral Stansfield Turner acknowledged, to conceive of navies securing sea control 'in limited areas and for limited periods of time' (Till 1982, 189). As defined by the Indian Maritime Doctrine, sea control 'is a condition where one is able to use a defined sea area, for a defined period of time, for one's own purposes, and at the same time deny its use to the adversary' (Integrated Headquarters 2015, 77). That sea area under one's control includes the surface, sub-surface, airspace, and electromagnetic environments.

A related concept is sea denial, which entails denying the use of a defined area to an adversary. However, a precondition to practising sea denial is that one's own side should not also require that area for the duration. In addition to this defensive conception, sea denial may also be used offensively to degrade the adversary's capability by curtailing its freedom of action and interdicting its SLOCs (Integrated Headquarters

2015, 78). Submarines are the preferred medium for performing this mission. Given the hit-and-run nature of submarine attacks, sea denial has been described as 'guerrilla warfare at sea' (Till 1982, 191).

Although not part of the direct doctrine to obtain sea control, one naval mission that may be taken note of is the projection of power through the sea to the territory of the adversary. These amphibious operations include full-fledged invasion, capture of territory, denial of an area, showing presence, creating diversion, and causing damage (Integrated Headquarters 2015, 82–83). The more ambitious of these tasks, especially the capture of territory and full-fledged invasion, would, however, be practical only if sea control has already been obtained.

Like in the case of blitzkrieg in land warfare, indirect doctrine in the naval realm seeks to disrupt the adversary's 'sea' lines of communication. SLOCs are routes that ships normally take to transit between two points. Their length varies according to the geography of the landmass, choke points, reefs, and location of ports and harbours. SLOCs serve as commercial trade routes in times of peace and as strategic pathways during war (Sakhuja 2001, 690). Interdiction of SLOCs, thus, disrupts the adversary's ability to use the sea for both commercial and military purposes. On the one hand, it hinders the availability of commodities necessary for prosecuting the war. On the other, it restricts the adversary's ability to conduct naval operations. Corbett had compellingly noted more than a century ago that command of the sea, or sea control in the contemporary era, 'means nothing but the control of maritime communications, whether for commercial or military purposes' (Corbett 1911, 183). According to the Indian Maritime Security Strategy, SLOCs may be interdicted in ports of embarkation and disembarkation, maritime choke points, and even in the open ocean (Integrated Headquarters 2015, 69–70). Submarines are particularly suited for interdicting SLOCs, although surface and air elements are also effective in many circumstances.

SLOCs may be interdicted either by imposing a blockade or by engaging in trade warfare, depending upon the balance of naval strength. Historically, stronger naval powers have preferred the blockade, while weaker navies have opted for trade warfare. Blockade involves preventing the vessels of all states 'from entering or exiting specified ports or coastal areas, belonging to, or under the control of an enemy nation' (Integrated Headquarters 2015, 85). The aim is to disrupt the availability of or altogether deny commodities, supplies, and reinforcements, thereby degrading the adversary's capacity to continue the war. Blockade also offers the additional advantage of compelling the adversary to either keep its fleet confined at home ports, thereby ceding sea control, or bringing it out to be destroyed in battle and, thus, losing sea control (Corbett 1911, 183).

Trade warfare is the alternative method of interdicting SLOCs and targeting the adversary's merchant trade. Also known as *guerre de course*, or commerce raiding, it has been the method of choice for weaker naval powers, albeit with limited success. When the French *Jeune Ecole* (Young School) re-envisaged the method in the 1870s, its logic was that the use of cruisers to destroy the merchant vessels of a highly import-dependent country like Britain would make its shipping disappear from the seas and quickly induce popular panic and social collapse. The error of that conclusion was most fully demonstrated by the failure of Germany's submarine campaigns against British trade during the two World Wars (Ropp 1948, 446–451). Trade warfare may also be carried out by shore-based aircraft as we saw during the 'Tanker War' phase of the Iran–Iraq War between 1984 and 1987. Although it is historically the choice of weaker naval powers, trade warfare may also be employed by superior naval powers 'to impose commodity denial on the adversary' (Integrated Headquarters 2015, 84).

Doctrines in Air Warfare

Attaining control of the air is the first function of the air force in war. That is what enables the force to go on to degrade or destroy the adversary's war-waging and economic capability. Douhet defined control of the air as preventing the adversary from flying a large number of aircraft to conduct significant operations while at the same time retaining such an ability oneself (Douhet 1998, 24, 97). This is the highest degree to which control of the air may be attained. Now termed 'air supremacy', it ensues when an air force has incapacitated and rendered an adversary incapable of interfering with its own operations. Next in the hierarchy of control of the air is air superiority, in which an air force attains the freedom to conduct operations 'at a given time and place' but faces a certain level of interference from the adversary (*Basic Doctrine of the Indian Air Force 2012*, 40). Favourable Air Situation is the last type of control of the air. Operational in an even more limited time and space, it involves a higher degree of interference by the adversary air force in one's own operations.

Control of the air is obtained through a combination of ground-based targeting of adversary aircraft, engaging them in aerial combat, bombing them and their bases on the ground, and bombing ground-based anti-aircraft systems (*Basic Doctrine of the Indian Air Force 2012*, 42–43). Counter Air, the term currently employed for these operations, is thus a mixed doctrine, involving as it does the targeting of both aircraft and ground-based systems that support or threaten them. The categorisation of Counter Air as a mixed doctrine helps overcome an inconsistency in Jasjit Singh's distinction between direct and indirect approaches to gaining air superiority. Writing in the 1980s, Singh had classified the bombing of aircraft and their support infrastructure on the ground as an indirect approach, and aerial combat as the direct approach. Singh's categorisation, however, overlooked the targeting of adversary aircraft by ground-based anti-aircraft and missile systems, although he considered air defence as an integral part of Counter Air (Singh 1984, 946–48). Taking into account all three aspects of Counter Air—air-to-air combat, air-to-ground bombing, and ground-to-air targeting—it is more appropriate to classify Counter Air as a mixed doctrine.

Counter Air may be broadly divided into defensive and offensive operations.[11] Defensive Counter-Air, or Air Defence, seeks to 'nullify or reduce the effectiveness of an enemy aerial attack or a hostile ballistic/cruise missile attack' (Indian Air Force 2012, 47). Combat air patrols by fighter aircraft and the use of surface-to-air missiles and anti-aircraft artillery barrages constitute the offensive aspects of air defence. Whereas air defence unfolds over one's own airspace, Offensive Counter-Air takes the war to the adversary. Its goal is three-fold: suppress or destroy air defences, attack air bases and airfields, and attrite adversary aircraft. First, suppression or destruction of air defences is achieved by bombing radar installations, anti-aircraft artillery and surface-to-missile sites, and communication nodes. Helicopters may also play a role in neutralising the forward tier of the adversary radar network by either attacking these installations themselves or by inserting Special Forces to attack them. Second, air bases are critical targets because of their role in sustaining the air war. Attacks on air bases disable airfields, damage or destroy aircraft on ground, and disrupt the availability of fuel, ammunition and technical services, thereby degrading the adversary air campaign. Offensive Counter-Air also includes fighter sweeps to draw out and attrite adversary aircraft in aerial combat. Aerial combat, or pursuit as it was known earlier, is a 'direct contest for dominance' between fighter aircraft (Singh 2007, 114). The objective is to vanquish the adversary's fighter fleet and, thus, attain control of the air (Mitchell 2009, 164).

Counter Surface Force operations involve the direct application of air power on targets on land and at sea in coordination with the army and navy, respectively. The Indian Air Force terms these operations 'airland' and 'maritime air'. Airland operations comprise three distinct missions. First, battlefield air strikes target adversary forces engaged in battle with one's own army. Battlefield air interdiction is the second type of airland mission in which air attacks are directed against adversary forces that are poised to enter an ongoing battle. The third airland mission is air interdiction, which involves targeting 'strategic reserves, reinforcements and re-supply of the entire battle space up to several hundred kilometres behind the front line' (*Basic Doctrine of the Indian Air Force 2012*, 58). For their part, maritime air operations involve anti-shipping strikes in conjunction with naval vessels and aircraft as well as independent maritime strike missions against adversary warships and naval facilities. Counter Surface Force operations are, thus, missions that the air force undertakes both independently and in coordination with the other two services. They do not, however, constitute a doctrine per se.

Indirect doctrine in air warfare goes a step further than its continental and maritime counterparts by targeting the entire logistical chain that enables the prosecution of war. Termed strategic bombing, it involves targeting both vital infrastructure (farms, factories, commercial establishments, fuel and oil storage facilities, and transportation arteries and centres) as well as 'certain designated areas of civilian population'[12] (Douhet 1998, 20; Mitchell 2009, 126–127). The underlying logic is that vital infrastructure and popular will together constitute the adversary's centre of gravity and, hence, must be targeted and destroyed. While the destruction of vital infrastructure would make it impossible for the adversary to logistically maintain its armed forces in the field and, thus, continue to prosecute the war, targeting of the civilian population would compel the people to stop supporting the government's war effort. By thus destroying the adversary's moral and material resources, strategic bombing would usher in a swift victory in a full-scale war (MacIsaac 1986, 629–635).[13] Although the United States did employ strategic bombing in the context of limited wars in Vietnam and more recently in Kosovo, the expansive scale and high-intensity nature of strategic bombing make its application inconceivable in the context of limited war between nuclear-weapon powers.

Summary

Strategy is the transmission link between political aims and military objectives. Originally conceived as a term to capture the art of the general, strategy has evolved into a concept that is more political in its connotation. This current meaning of strategy as the use of war for attaining political aims is an extension of the Clausewitzian dictum of war being the continuation of policy by military means, for it is strategy that directs the war towards its political objective. Employing this conception of strategy, this chapter has suggested a tripartite division of war composed of policy, strategy, and doctrine. This is a simple framework for thinking about the application of military force in the context of both the policy aims sought and the military objectives that the armed forces are structured, equipped, and trained to deliver. Thinking about war in this fashion ought to help the political leadership and the military brass bring political aims into better alignment with the use of force. This is also the schema that is being employed in subsequent chapters to analyse India's use of force against Pakistan.

Notes

1 Strachan's portrait of how strategy came to lose its original meaning is the inspiration for the discussion that follows (Strachan 2013, 28).
2 The quoted phrases can be found on pp. 17–18, 51 (Cohen 2002, 15–51).
3 This definition of naval strategy is not that of Mahan but of an unnamed 'recent French author' whom he cites.
4 This was Corbett's paraphrase of Clausewitz's definition.
5 Corbett did, indeed, acknowledge that a close blockade was no longer 'practicable' given technological innovations such as mines, torpedoes, and submarines, which were joined, subsequently during the course of the 20th century, by land-based aircraft and missiles. But he asserted that 'the antithetical ideas' connoted by the two forms of close and open blockade 'can never be eliminated from strategical consideration'.
6 Bassford terms this strategy as erosion.
7 Rajesh Rajagopalan, citing Dale O. Smith (1955).
8 On dislocation as the aim of the indirect approach, see Liddell Hart (1967, 339–341).
9 Luttwak prefers to use the term 'relational-maneuver' for this.
10 For a concise summary of the origins of this idea as an infantry infiltration tactic in the artillery- and machine gun-dominated battlefields of the First World War and its subsequent adaptation for armoured warfare, see Palit (2000, 74–78).
11 This description of the Counter-Air campaign is based on *Basic Doctrine of the Indian Air Force 2012*, 39–56.
12 The quoted phrase is from Douhet.
13 This view was particularly prevalent in the years between the two World Wars.

References

Bassford, Christopher. 1997. *Policy, Politics, War, and Military Strategy*. Washington D.C.: Department of Navy. Available at: http://www.clausewitz.com/readings/Bassford/StrategyDraft/index.htm (accessed on 20 January 2019).

Baylis, John. 2001. 'The Continuing Relevance of Strategic Studies in the Post-Cold War Era'. *Defence Studies*, 1(2): 1–14.

Brodie, Bernard. 1978. 'The Development of Nuclear Strategy'. *International Security*, 2(4): 65–83.

Clausewitz, Carl von. 1976. *On War*. Translated and edited by Michael Howard and Peter Paret. Princeton, NJ: Princeton University Press.

Cohen, Eliot A. 2002. *Supreme Command: Soldiers, Statesmen and Leadership in Wartime*. New York: The Free Press.

Corbett, Julian Stafford. 1911. *Some Principles of Maritime Strategy*. London: Longmans, Green and Co.

Craig, Gordon A. 1986. 'The Political Leader as Strategist'. In *Makers of Modern Strategy: From Machiavelli to the Nuclear Age*, edited by Peter Paret with Gordon A. Craig and Felix Gilbert, 481–509. Princeton, NJ: Princeton University Press.

Creveld, Martin van. 2000. 'Through a Glass, Darkly: Some Reflections on the Future of War'. *Naval War College Review*, 53(4): 25–44.

Delbrück, Hans. 1985. *History of the Art of War, Volume IV: The Dawn of Modern Warfare*. Translated by Walter J. Renfroe, Jr. Lincoln: University of Nebraska Press.

Douhet, Giulio. 1998. *The Command of the Air*. Translated by Dino Ferrari. Washington D.C.: Air Force History and Museums Program.

Freedman, Lawrence. 2013. *Strategy: A History*. New York: Oxford University Press, Kindle Edition.

Freedman, Lawrence. 2017. 'The Meaning of Strategy: Part I: Origins'. *Texas National Security Review*, 1(1). Available at: https://tnsr.org/2017/10/meaning-strategy-part-origin-story/ (accessed on 29 November 2017).

Freedman, Lawrence. 2018. 'The Meaning of Strategy: Part II: The Objectives'. *Texas National Security Review*, 1(2). Available at: https://tnsr.org/2018/01/meaning-strategy-part-ii-objectives/ (accessed on 2 February 2018).

Handel, Michael I. 2001. *Masters of War: Classical Strategic Thought*. London: Frank Cass.

Headquarters Army Training Command. 2004. *Indian Army Doctrine*. Shimla: Headquarters Army Training Command.

Holsti, Kalevi J. 1991. *Peace and War: Armed Conflicts and International Order 1648–1989*. Cambridge: Cambridge University Press.

Howard, Michael. 1957. 'Introduction: The Armed Forces as a Political Problem'. In *Soldiers and Governments: Nine Studies in Civil-Military Relations*, 9–24. London: Eyre and Spottiswoode.

Inbar, Efraim and Eitan Shamir. 2014. '"Mowing the Grass": Israel's Strategy for Protracted Intractable Conflict'. *Journal of Strategic Studies*, 37(1): 65–90.

Indian Air Force. 2012. *Basic Doctrine of the Indian Air Force 2012*. New Delhi: Indian Air Force.

Indian Army. 2018. *Land Warfare Doctrine—2018*. Available at: https://www.indianarmy.nic.in/Site/FormTemplete/frmTempSimple.aspx?MnId=2Rm-2MVYyRENGMg+d6esxYw==&ParentID=nj6p0oG9lIa7QFvaAMg66w== (accessed on 11 March 2021).

Indian Navy. 2015. *Ensuring Secure Seas: Indian Maritime Security Strategy*. New Delhi: Indian Navy.

Integrated Headquarters. 2015. *Indian Maritime Doctrine 2009*. Sivakasi: Standard Press (India) Pvt.

Jomini, Baron Henri de. 1862. *The Art of War*. Translated by G.H. Mendell and W.P. Craighill. West Point, NY: US Military Academy.

Kier, Elizabeth. 1997. *Imagining War: French and Military Doctrine Between the Wars*. Princeton, NJ: Princeton University Press.

Ledwidge, Frank. 2018. *Aerial Warfare: The Battle for the Skies*, Oxford: Oxford University Press.

Liddell Hart, B.H. 1967. *Strategy: The Indirect Approach*. New Delhi: Jupiter Publications.

Luttwak, Edward N. 1980/81. 'The Operational Level of War'. *International Security*, 5(3): 61–79.

MacIsaac, David. 1986. 'Voices from the Central Blue: The Air Power Theorists'. In *Makers of Modern Strategy: From Machiavelli to the Nuclear Age*, edited by Peter Paret with Gordon A. Craig and Felix Gilbert, 624–647. Princeton, NJ: Princeton University Press.

Mahan, Alfred Thayer. 1890. *The Influence of Sea Power Upon History, 1660–1783*. Boston: Little, Brown and Company, 12th edn. Kindle Version.

Mearsheimer, John J. 1983. *Conventional Deterrence*. Ithaca: Cornell University Press.

Mitchell, William "Billy". 2009. *Winged Defense: The Development and Possibilities of Modern Air Power—Economic and Military*. Tuscaloosa, AL: The University of Alabama Press.

Nicolay, John George and John Hay. 1890. *Abraham Lincoln: A History*, Volume 4. New York: The Century Company.

Palit, D.K. 2000. *The Essentials of Military Knowledge*, rev. edn. Dehradun: Natraj Publishers.

Pape, Robert A. 2004. 'The True Worth of Air Power'. *Foreign Affairs*, 83(2): March/April: 116–130.

Posen, Barry Posen. 1984. *The Sources of Military Doctrine: France, Britain, and Germany Between the World Wars*. Ithaca and London: Cornell University Press.

Project Gutenberg EBook #13549. 2004. Available at: http://www.gutenberg.org/files/13549/13549-h/13549-h.htm (accessed 13 on January 2019).

Rajagopalan, Rajesh. 2008. *Fighting Like a Guerrilla: The Indian Army and Counterinsurgency*. New Delhi: Routledge.

Ropp, Theodore. 1948. 'Continental Doctrines of Sea Power'. In *Makers of Modern Strategy: Military Thought from Machiavelli to Hitler*, edited by Edward Mead Earle. Princeton: Princeton University Press.

Sakhuja, Vijay. 2001. 'Indian Ocean and the Safety of Sea Lines of Communication'. *Strategic Analysis*, 25(5): 689–702.

Schelling, Thomas. 1966. *Arms and Influence*. New Haven: Yale University Press.

Shy, John. 1986. 'Jomini'. In *Makers of Modern Strategy: From Machiavelli to the Nuclear Age*, edited by Peter Paret with Gordon A. Craig and Felix Gilbert, 143–185. Princeton, NJ: Princeton University Press.

Silove, Nina. 2018. 'Beyond the Buzzword: The Three Meanings of "Grand Strategy"'. *Security Studies*, 27(1): 27–57.

Singh, Jasjit. 1984. 'Air Superiority: A New Look at an Old Doctrine—I'. *Strategic Analysis*, 7(10): 852–864.

Singh, Jasjit. 1984. 'Air Superiority: A New Look at an Old Doctrine—II'. *Strategic Analysis*, 7(11): 941–955.

Singh, Jasjit. 2007. *Defence from the Skies: 80 Years of the Indian Air Force*. New Delhi: KW Publishers Pvt. Ltd.

Smith, Dale O. 1955. *U.S. Military Doctrine*. New York: Duell, Sloan and Pearce.

Spears, Edward Louis. 1939. *Prelude to Victory*. London: Jonathan Cape.

Strachan, Hew. 2013. *The Direction of War: Contemporary Strategy in Historical Perspective*. Cambridge, UK: Cambridge University Press.

Strachan, Hew. 2019. 'Strategy in Theory; Strategy in Practice'. *Journal of Strategic Studies*, 42(2): 171–190.

Till, Geoffrey. 1982. *Maritime Strategy and the Nuclear Age*. London: Macmillan.

Weigley, Russell F. 1973. *The American Way of War: A History of United States Military Strategy and Policy*. New York: Macmillan.

2

The Politics of India–Pakistan Conflict

Since Partition and Independence, India–Pakistan relations have been marked by a series of wars, armed confrontations short of war, diplomatic and military crises, and periodic firefights along the Line of Control in Jammu and Kashmir. This history has led to the relationship being variously characterised as deadly impasse (Ganguly 2016), unending conflict (Ganguly 2020), enduring rivalry (Paul 2006), eternal rivalry between paired minorities (Cohen 2013, 138–141), and strategic rivalry (Colaresi et al. 2007, 7–9). Whatever be the descriptor applied to the relationship, three inter-related factors have sustained rivalry and conflict: incompatible conceptions of national identity, Pakistan's quest for parity with India, and the conflict over 'Kashmir'.

National Identity

Pakistan was conceived of as 'a homeland' for the Muslims of British India where they would be free from 'Hindu domination' (Jalal 2014, 47, 16). Lacking 'a positive national identity' that is sui generis and distinct from Indian culture, Pakistan defined itself negatively in terms of opposition to India (Jaffrelot 2002, 7). Since Pakistan was established to prevent the 'Hindu Congress' from dominating Indian Muslims, hostility to 'Hindu India' became one of the cornerstones of Pakistan's national ideology, alongside Islam and the Urdu language. As a result, 'Islamic Pakistan' began to define itself 'through the prism of resistance to "Hindu India"' (Haqqani 2010, 15). Resistance to India has been accompanied by irredentist ambition. While Pakistan's efforts to wrest Jammu and Kashmir are well known, 'Pakistani lament over the "lost" Muslim brethren held captive by India'—namely, the one-third of British India's Muslims left behind in India after Partition—'implies that Pakistan has irredentist concerns about *all* Indian Muslims' [emphasis in original] (Cohen 2013, 125). This is reinforced by the complementary conception of Islamic Pakistan as a New Medina that would become 'the instrument for the *ummah*'s unification and propel its triumphal rise on the global stage as a great power' and, as part of that project, pave the way for 'Islam's return as the ruling power in the subcontinent' (Dhulipala 2015, 5).

In contrast, India was conceived of and established as an inclusive polity, composed of multiple religious, linguistic, and racial groups mixing and fusing together to form a modern state. Citizenship has consequently been defined in civic and universal terms rather than through ethnic, linguistic, religious, or racial markers. Indian national identity is, thus, not defined in an exclusive manner. Instead, it is a layered identity, composed of linguistic, religious, and cultural elements (Khilnani 2003). This commitment to unity in diversity is also emphasised by advocates of Hindutva (Vaidya 2019). The original conception of Hindutva had excluded from its ambit communities that did not consider India as their holy land (Savarkar 1922). However, a recent explication by Mohan Bhagwat, the *sarsanghchalak* of the Rashtriya Swayamsevak Sangh (RSS), emphasises that the term 'Hindutva' merely expresses the identity, traditions, and value system of 'the land of Bharat' and is, thus, applicable 'to all the 1.3 billion people who call themselves the sons and daughters of Bharatvarsh', none of whom is required to give up their 'faith, language, land or any other identity marker' (RSS 2020, 5). Earlier, Bhagwat had highlighted one of Hindutva's special characteristics as being assimilation and acceptance of the plurality of languages, faiths, and traditions in keeping with the philosophy of *Vasudhaiva Kutumbakam* (*The Times of India* 2014). Prime Minister Narendra Modi has also repeatedly invoked this *mantram* to emphasise that all of creation is a single family (PM India 2019; PM India 2020).

Both conceptions of Indian national identity, thus, emphasise civilisational attributes and inclusiveness despite varying levels of empathy towards minorities, particularly Muslims. Neither, however, lends itself to legitimising the idea of Pakistan. The modernist conception of India tends to question the rationale of Pakistan by asserting the multi-religious character of India and highlighting the fact that nearly as many Muslims live in India as in Pakistan (Pew Research Centre 2010). For its part, the Hindutva conception is committed to the notion of *Akhand Bharat* or Undivided India, which includes the territory and people of Pakistan. As recently as February 2021, Bhagwat asserted that '*Akhand Bharat*' is a necessity and that it can be established with Hindu dharma. He went on to note, 'We consider countries like Pakistan and Afghanistan as ours. Once they are with us, it does not matter what they practice or what they eat. It is not colonialism. India believes in *Vasudhaiva Kutumbakam* (the world is one family)' (Times News Network 2021).

In effect, Pakistan's conception of itself as a political community that is inveterately opposed to India and India's conception of itself as a civilisational entity embracing or encompassing Muslims sustain India–Pakistan rivalry and conflict.

Pakistan's Quest for Parity

A second related factor that has contributed to the persistence of India–Pakistan rivalry and conflict is Pakistan's quest for parity with India. The asymmetry in national power indices between the two countries is widely recognised, and its impact on the structure of the conflict has been well analysed (Paul 2006). Previous evaluations of the military balance have taken into consideration both the qualitative and quantitative aspects of India and Pakistan's conventional and nuclear capabilities as they existed in the mid-1980s, early 2000s, and early 2010s, concluding that while India does enjoy an advantage, the degree of imbalance in its favour is not that stark (Elkin and Ritezel 1986, 518–538; Cordesman 2002; Clary 2013). Broadly agreeing with this conclusion, the comparison of India and Pakistan's military capabilities adopts a longer timeframe, starting in the 1960s and ending in 2020. With a view of providing as comprehensive a picture as possible, the comparison considers total population, gross domestic product (GDP), defence expenditure, and military manpower of the countries, as well as the offensive capabilities of each armed service.

Extent of Asymmetry

India dwarfs Pakistan when it comes to the size of the population. As can be seen in Table 2.1, the differential between the total population of the two countries widened from 4.7 times in 1963, when Bangladesh was still a part of Pakistan, to nearly nine times in 1980. Although the gap narrowed thereafter, the differential still stood at 6.3 times in 2019.

The differential in economic power between India and Pakistan is even wider. India's GDP was nearly 11 times larger than that of

TABLE 2.1: Total Population of India and Pakistan: Select Years between 1963 and 2019

[in hundreds of millions]

Year	India	Pakistan	Differential
1963	462	98.57	4.69 times
1965	470	101	4.65 times
1970	550	128.4	4.28 times
1971	557	126.3	4.41 times
1975	623.102897	66.816877	9.33 times
1980	698.952844	78.054343	8.95 times
1985	784.360008	92.191510	8.51 times
1990	873.277798	107.647921	8.11 times
1995	963.922588	123.776839	7.79 times
1999	1,038	138.624621	7.49 times
2000	1,057	142.343578	7.43 times
2005	1,148	160.304008	7.16 times
2010	1,234	179.424641	6.88 times
2015	1,310	199.426964	6.57 times
2019	1,366	216.565318	6.31 times

Source: *The Military Balance* (The International Institute for Strategic Studies, London, 1963, 1965, 1970, 1971); 'Total Population of India and Pakistan', World Bank Group, available at: https://data.worldbank.org/?locations=IN-PK (accessed on 23 December 2020).

Note: Data for the years 1963, 1965, 1970, and 1971 are from the IISS Military Balance, which takes into account the population of both East and West Pakistan. Data for the rest of the years are from the World Bank.

Pakistan's in 1960. Even after Pakistan reduced the asymmetry in the next three decades, Indian GDP was still more than six times larger in 1987. Thereafter, the differential steadily widened to nearly 7.5 times in 2000, 9.5 times in 2010, and 11.5 times in 2019. Table 2.2 provides a full picture of the GDPs of India and Pakistan as well as the differential between them for select years between 1960 and 2019.

TABLE 2.2: Gross Domestic Products of India and Pakistan: Select Years between 1960 and 2019

[in billions of constant 2010 US dollars]

Year	Pakistan	India	Differential
1960	13.591	148.773	10.95 times
1962	15.05	158.835	10.55 times
1965	19.43	176.135	9.07 times
1970	27.294	219.862	8.06 times
1971	27.422	223.474	8.15 times
1975	31.936	253.536	7.94 times
1980	43.134	295.59	6.85 times
1985	59.862	380.135	6.35 times
1987	67.23	414.086	6.16 times
1989	75.946	480.952	6.33 times
1990	79.332	507.565	6.4 times
1995	99.464	650.281	6.54 times
1998	108.029	772.701	7.15 times
1999	111.983	841.053	7.27 times
2000	116.754	873.357	7.48 times
2001	120.904	915.488	7.57 times
2002	123.936	950.313	7.67 times
2005	150.181	1,194	7.95 times
2008	169.563	1,432	8.45 times
2010	177.166	1,676	9.46 times
2014	205.898	2,125	10.32 times
2015	215.639	2,295	10.64 times
2016	227.557	2,484	10.92 times
2017	240.196	2,659	11.07 times

Year	Pakistan	India	Differential
2018	254.215	2,822	11.1 times
2019	256.729	2,964	11.55 times

Source: World Bank Group, available at: https://data.worldbank.org/indicator/NY.GDP.MKTP.KD?locations=IN-PK (accessed on 22 November 2020).

In the military sphere, however, the asymmetry between India and Pakistan has not been as wide as in the economic arena. To take the metric of defence expenditure first, India's defence expenditure in the mid-1950s was about 4.5 times larger. In subsequent years, the gap widened to an extent owing to the Indian build-up in the wake of the 1962 War with China. As a result, India ended up spending 5.8 times more than Pakistan in 1965 and 5.4 times more in 1971. As Table 2.3 details, the 1970s, 1980s, and the first half of the 1990s saw the gap gradually narrowing. India spent 4.9 times more than Pakistan on defence in 1980, which declined to less than four times more in 1995. Since then, however, there has been a steady increase in the gap between Indian and Pakistani defence expenditure. India spent 5.6 times more in 1999. The differential increased to 7.5 times more in 2010, before declining to six times larger in 2019.

TABLE 2.3: Defence Expenditures of India and Pakistan, 1956–2019
[in millions of constant 2018 US dollars and exchange rates]

Year	India	Pakistan	Pakistan Defence Expenditure Smaller by
1956	2,745	619 [est]	4.43 times
1957	3,283	514 [est]	6.39 times
1958	3,289	533 [est]	6.17 times
1959	3,036	629 [est]	4.83 times
1960	3,066	655 [est]	4.68 times
1961	3,307	648 [est]	5.10 times
1962	4,546	621 [est]	7.32 times
1963	7,442	671 [est]	11.09 times
1964	7,264	757 [est]	9.60 times
1965	7,100	1,222 [est]	5.81 times

Year	India	Pakistan	Pakistan Defence Expenditure Smaller by
1966	6,686	1,425 [est]	4.69 times
1967	6,247	1,161 [est]	5.38 times
1968	6,469	1,193 [est]	5.42 times
1969	6,856	1,298 [est]	5.28 times
1970	7,070	1,416 [est]	4.99 times
1971	8,429	1,573 [est]	5.36 times
1972	8,887	1,764 [est]	5.04 times
1973	7,850	1,648 [est]	4.76 times
1974	7,310	1,644 [est]	4.45 times
1975	8,205	1,721 [est]	4.77 times
1976	9,420	1,735 [est]	5.43 times
1977	8,950	1,728 [est]	5.18 times
1978	9,359	1,838 [est]	5.09 times
1979	10,086	1,945 [est]	5.19 times
1980	10,350	2,101 [est]	4.93 times
1981	10,928	2,283 [est]	4.79 times
1982	11,857	2,751 [est]	4.31 times
1983	12,270	3,069 [est]	3.998 times
1984	12,980	3,299 [est]	3.93 times
1985	14,560	3,591 [est]	4.05 times
1986	17,211	3,861 [est]	4.46 times
1987	18,540	4,222 [est]	4.39 times
1988	18,983	4,369 [est]	4.34 times
1989	20,004	4,382 [est]	4.57 times
1990	19,704	4,625 [est]	4.26 times
1991	18,398	4,951 [est]	3.72 times
1992	17,583	5,265 [est]	3.34 times
1993	19,859	5,238 [est]	3.79 times
1994	19,948	5,087 [est]	3.92 times
1995	20,546	5,175 [est]	3.97 times
1996	20,918	5,174 [est]	4.04 times
1997	23,156	4,954 [est]	4.67 times

Year	India	Pakistan	Pakistan Defence Expenditure Smaller by
1998	24,159	4,954 [est]	4.88 times
1999	28,077	5,003 [est]	5.61 times
2000	28,972	5,013 [est]	5.78 times
2001	29,981	5,363 [est]	5.59 times
2002	29,888	5,768 [est]	5.18 times
2003	30,555	6,163 [est]	4.96 times
2004	35,493	6,417 [est]	5.53 times
2005	37,772	6,679 [est]	5.66 times
2006	38,078	6,789 [est]	5.61 times
2007	38,538	6,836	5.64 times
2008	43,712	6,445	6.78 times
2009	51,464	6,642	7.75 times
2010	51,671	6,888	7.50 times
2011	52,171	7,261 [est]	7.19 times
2012	51,986	7,700	6.75 times
2013	51,603	7,954	6.49 times
2014	54,276	8,357	6.49 times
2015	54,292	9,078	5.98 times
2016	59,833	9,382	6.38 times
2017	64,572	10,391	6.21 times
2018	66,258	11,529	5.75 times
2019	70,794	11,740	6.03 times

Source: Stockholm International Peace Research Institute, *Military Expenditure Database, 1949–2019*, available at: https://www.sipri.org/sites/default/files/SIPRI-Milex-data-1949-2019.xlsx (accessed on 23 November 2020).

Much of the increase in defence expenditure in recent years has, however, been due to increases in pay, allowances, and pensions. The share of these items in the defence budget has shot up from 49 per cent in 2011–2012 to 60 per cent in 2020–2021. In the process, expenditure on new equipment and stores has dwindled from 36 per cent in 2011–2012 to 25 per cent in 2020–2021 (Behera and Kaushal 2020, 3–4). In effect, the asymmetry in defence expenditure between India and Pakistan is likely to be lesser than what the actual expenditures indicate.

A more accurate picture of relative military capabilities emerges from a comparison of the total numbers of military personnel as well as army personnel. As Tables 2.4 and 2.5 indicate, India consistently had more military personnel than Pakistan throughout these decades. But the Indian advantage was only a modest one. India's advantage in the total force ratio increased marginally from 2.3-to-1 in 1963 to 2.5-to-1 in 1971 and 2.52-to-1 in 1980. Thereafter, it declined to less than 2-to-1 in 1999 and then recovered to about 2.23-to-1 in 2020. The force ratio between the two armies was synchronous with the above trend, given that ground forces constitute the bulk of military manpower. Thus, from a high of nearly 2.4-to-1 in 1963, the force ratio between the armies of India and Pakistan declined to less than 1.88-to-1 in 1999, and thereafter went up to 2.21-to-1 by 2020.

While there is no denying the Indian advantage in terms of maintaining double the number of military personnel, the fact that India has dedicated 10 mountain divisions (12 in recent years) to the China border after the 1962 War means that the differential in troop strength between India and Pakistan is actually much lower.[1] Given that a typical infantry division has about 15,500 combat troops, a total of about 155,000 troops (186,000 in the last few years) need to be taken out of consideration while calculating the differential in troop numbers between India and Pakistan (Global Security 2016). Accordingly, the personnel ratio between the Indian and Pakistani armies stood at 1.93-to-1 in 1971. After declining over the next decade to 1.64-to-1 in 1980, it rose to 1.89-to-1 in 1990. It again declined in the next 10 years to reach the low of 1.59-to-1 in 1999, but it has thereafter recovered to reach a ratio of 1.88-to-1 in 2020.

TABLE 2.4: Number of Military Personnel in India and Pakistan: Select Years between 1963 and 2020

Year	Army Personnel		Navy Personnel		Air Force Personnel		Total Military Personnel	
	India	Pakistan	India	Pakistan	India	Pakistan	India	Pakistan
1963	550,000	230,000	16,000	7,700	18,000	15,000	585,000	253,000
1964	825,000 [sanctioned]	230,000	16,000	7,700	28,000	17 to 25,000	867,000 [sic] minus	253,000
1965	825,000 [sanctioned]	160 to 180,000	16,000	8,000	28,000	20,000	869,000 minus	188 to 208,000
1966	807,000	250,000 including 25,000 militia	17,000	8,350	55,000	20,000	879,000	278,350
1967	900,000	300,000 including 25,000 militia	17,000	9,000	60,000	14,000	977,000	323,000
1968	950,000	300,000 including 25,000 'Azad Kashmir' (AK) troops	25,000	9,000	58,000	15,000	1,033,000	324,000
1969	848,000	300,000 including 25,000 AK troops	20,000	9,000	57,000	15,000	925,000	324,000
1970	800,000	300,000 including 25,000 AK troops	40,000	9,500	90,000	15,000	930,000	324,500
1971	860,000	365,000 including 25,000 AK troops	40,000	10,000	80,000	17,000	980,000	392,000

Year	Army Personnel		Navy Personnel		Air Force Personnel		Total Military Personnel	
	India	Pakistan	India	Pakistan	India	Pakistan	India	Pakistan
1972	840,000	278,000 including 25,000 AK troops	28,000	10,000	92,000	17,000	960,000	395,000 including some 90,000 prisoners of war
1975	826,000	365,000 including 25,000 AK troops	30,000	10,000	100,000	17,000	956,000	392,000
1980	944,000	408,000 including 29,000 AK troops	47,000	13,000	113,000	17,600	1,104,000	438,600
1985	1,100,000	450,000	47,000	15,200	113,000	17,600	1,260,000	482,800
1986	1,100,000	450,000	47,000	13,000	113,000	17,600	1,260,000	480,600
1990	1,100,000	500,000	52,000	20,000	110,000	30,000	1,262,000	550,000
1995	980,000	520,000	55,000	22,000	110,000	45,000	1,145,000	587,000
1999	980,000	520,000	53,000	22,000	140,000	45,000	1,173,000	587,000
2000	1,100,000	550,000	53,000	22,000	150,000	40,000	1,303,000	612,000
2001	1,100,000	550,000	53,000	25,000	110,000	45,000	1,263,000	620,000
2005	1,100,000	550,000	55,000	24,000	170,000	45,000	1,325,000	619,000

2010	1,129,900	550,000 including Strategic Forces Command–12 to 15,000	58,350	22,000	127,200	45,000	1,325,000 including Coast Guard–9,550	617,000
2015	1,150,900	550,000 including Strategic Forces Command–12 to 15,000	58,350	23,800	127,200	70,000	1,346,000 including Coast Guard–9,550	643,800
2020	1,237,000	560,000 including Strategic Forces Command–12 to 15,000	66,100	23,800	139,850	70,000	1,455,550 including Coast Guard–12,600	653,800

Source: *The Military Balance* (London: The International Institute for Strategic Studies, 1963–2020).

TABLE 2.5: Ratios of India and Pakistan Armies and Total Military Personnel: Select Years

Year	Armies	Armies minus India's Mountain Divisions	Total Military Personnel
1963	2.39:1	NA	2.31:1
1971	2.36:1	1.93:1	2.5:1
1980	2.31:1	1.64:1	2.52:1
1990	2.2:1	1.89:1	2.29:1
1999	1.88:1	1.59:1	1.99:1
2010	2.05:1	1.77:1	2.15:1
2020	2.21:1	1.88:1	2.23:1

Source: *The Military Balance* (London: The International Institute for Strategic Studies, 1963–2020).

An even more fine-grained picture of asymmetry emerges when the offensive capabilities of the two armies are compared. For instance, as can be seen from Table 2.6, the two armies possessed equal numbers of divisions and brigades of heavy and medium tanks in 1965. Historians of the Indian Ministry of Defence have recorded that the Pakistani Army actually possessed 45 tanks more than the Indian Army on the eve of the 1965 War (Prasad and Thapliyal 2011, 10). By 1971, the Indian Army had gained an advantage of 1.7-to-1 by fielding 1,450 main and medium battle tanks compared to the Pakistani Army's 850. The Indian Army maintained this advantage in the subsequent decades as well. By 1980, the ratio had gone up to 2.12-to-1 but declined thereafter to 1.47-to-1 in 1999. In 2020, it stands at 1.46-to-1. In a similar vein, a comparison of the number of towed and self-propelled artillery guns each army possessed indicates that India had an advantage of 2.8-to-1 in 1966, which increased to 3.35-to-1 in 1980, but subsequently declined to 2.4-to-1 in 1999 and to 1.4-to-1 in 2020.

TABLE 2.6: The Armies of India and Pakistan in Numbers: Select Years between 1963 and 2020

Year	Armour		Infantry		Artillery, Missiles		Aviation	
	India	**Pakistan**	**India**	**Pakistan**	**India**	**Pakistan**	**India**	**Pakistan**
1963	Divs - 1 MBT Bdes - 1 Med Tk Rgts - 4 Lt Tk	NA	Divs - 13 [Inf 10; Mtn 3]	Divs - 8	NA	NA	NA	NA
1964	Divs - 1 MBT Bdes - 1 Med Tk Rgts - 4 Lt Tk	NA	Divs - 16 [Inf 7; Mtn 9]	Divs - 8	NA	NA	NA	NA
1965	Divs - 1 MBT Bdes - 1 Med Rgts - 4 Lt Tk	Divs - 1 Bdes - 1	Divs - 16 [Inf 7; Mtn 9]	Divs - 6 [sic]	NA	NA	NA	NA
1966	Divs - 1 MBT Bdes - 1 Med Rgts - 6 Lt Tk	Divs - 2 [MBT & Med] Rgts - Lt Tk	Divs - 20 [Inf 9; Mtn 11] Para Bdes - 1	Divs - 8	Guns etc - 2500	Guns etc - 900	NA	NA

Year	Armour		Infantry		Artillery, Missiles		Aviation	
	India	Pakistan	India	Pakistan	India	Pakistan	India	Pakistan
1967	Divs - 1 MBT Rgts - 1 Med some Lt Tk Total Tks - 800 Armd Cars - 200	Bdes - 4 [MBT & Med] Rgts - Lt Tk	Divs - 21 [Inf 12; Mtn 9] Bdes - 1 para	Divs - 13 (= 32 Bdes)	Guns etc. - 2,500	Guns etc. - 900 ATk Msls	NA	NA
1968	Divs - 1 Indep Bdes - 2 Tks - 760 [MBT & Med 520; Lt 240]	Bdes - 4 [MBT & Med] Rgts - Lt	Divs - 23 [Inf 13; Mtn 10] Indep Bdes - 6 Para Bdes - 2	Divs - 12 [32 Bdes]	Guns etc. - about 3,000	Guns etc. - 900 ATk Msls	NA	NA
1969	Divs - 1 Indep Bdes - 2 Tks - 1320 [MBT + Med 980; Lt 340]	Bdes - 4 [MBT & Med] Rgts - Lt	Divs - 23 [Inf 13; Mtn 10] Indep Bdes - 6 Para Bdes - 2	Divs - 12 [32 Bdes]	Guns etc. - About 3,000	Guns etc. - 900 ATk Msls	NA	Obs & Lt Hel - 60

1970	Divs - 1 Indep Bdes - 1 MBT & Med - 1150 Armd Cars - 350	Divs - 2 Indep Bdes - 1 MBT & Med- 400 Lt Tks & APC	Divs - 23 [Inf 13; Mtn 10] Indep Bdes - 6 Para Bdes - 2	Divs - 11	Guns etc. - About 3,000	Guns- 900 SP Arty - 200 Total - 1100 ATk Msls	NA	Lt Hel - 20
1971	Divs - 1 Indep Bdes - 2 Tks – 1450 [MBT & Med 1200; Lt 250] APC	Divs - 2 Indep Bdes - 1 Tks - 870 [MBT & Med 850; Lt 20] APC- 300	Divs - 23 [Inf 13; Mtn 10] Indep Bdes - 6 Para Bdes - 2	Divs - 12	Guns etc. - About 3,000	Guns etc. -About 1,100 ATk Msls	NA	Lt Hel - 20
1972	Divs - 2 Indep Bdes - 3 Tks - 1490 [MBT & Med 1200; Lt 290] APC	Divs - 2 Indep Bdes – 1 Tks - 660 [MBT & Med 450; Lt 210] APC - 250	Divs - 23 [Inf 13; Mtn 10] Indep Bdes- 6 Para Bdes - 2	Divs - 10	Guns etc. - 3,000 ATGW	Guns etc. - About 1,100	NA	NA
1975	Divs - 2 Indep Bdes - 5 Tks - 1800 [MBT & Med 1680; Lt 120] APC - 500	Divs – 2 Indep Bdes - 2 Tks – 1050 [MBT & Med 950; Lt 100] APC - 350	Divs – 25 [Inf 15; Mtn 10] Indep Bdes - 6 Para Bdes - 2	Divs - 13	Indep Bdes - 9 Guns, etc. - 3,000	Guns etc. - about 1,100	Lt AC - 75.	Sqns - 3 Lt Hel - 47

Year	Armour		Infantry		Artillery, Missiles		Aviation	
	India	Pakistan	India	Pakistan	India	Pakistan	India	Pakistan
1980	Divs - 2 Indep Bdes - 5 Tks - 2170 [MBT & Med 2120; Lt 50] APC - 700	Divs - 2 Indep Bdes - 4 Recce Rgts - 6 Tks - 1065 [MBT & Med 1000; Lt 65] APC 550	Divs - 27 [Inf 17; Mtn 10] Indep bde - 1 Para bde - 2	Div - 16 Indep Bdes - 4 Btn - 3 SSG	Indep Bdes - 14 Guns etc. - 3,350	Bdes - 6 Guns etc. - about 1,000	Obs Sqns & Indep Flts - 4 Lt AC - 60 Lt Hel - 38+	Sqns - 5 Lt AC - 70 Lt Hel - 94
1986	Divs - 2 Indep Bdes - 7 Tks - 2790 [MBT & Med 2640; Lt 150 AFV - 1000	Divs - 2 Indep Bdes - 4 Recce Rgts - 6 Tks - 1600 APC - 645	Divs - 30 [Inf 22; Mech 1; Mtn 7] Indep Inf Bdes - 10 Indep Mtn Bde - 1 Indep Para Bde - 1	Divs - 17 Indep Bdes - 8 Btns - 3 SSG	Bdes - 4 Guns - 2,230 Hows - 1,658 MRL - 120 Mor - 550 Total - 4,558	Bdes - 8 Guns - 1,180 Hows - 267 Total - 1,447	Flights (Obs & Fire control) - 29	Sqns - 5 AC Lias Sqn - 1 [with 55 AC] Hel Lias Sqn - 4 Obs Flts - 95 AC, 97 Hel

1990	Divs - 2 Indep Bdes - 5 Tks - 3,250 [MBT 3,150; Lt 100] AFV - 1,250+	Divs - 2 Indep Bdes - 7 Recce Rgts - 3 MBT - 1850+ APC - 800	Divs - 31 [Inf 19; Mech 1; Mtn 11] Indep Inf Bdes - 7 Indep Mtn Bdes - 1 AB/ Cdo Bdes - 1	Divs - 19 Indep Bdes - 4 Btns - 3 SSG	Indep Bdes - 3 Towed Arty - some 3,860 SP Arty - 180 MRL - 80 Mor - 1,200+	Bdes - 7 Towed Arty - 1,230 SP Arty - 215	Hel - 13 Sqns, 280 Craft	Sqns - 5 [AC - 1; Hel - 4] Total AC - 169 [Survey, Lias, Obs] Total Hel - 122 [Atk 20, Tpt 102]
1995	Divs - 3 Indep Bdes - 5 Recce Rgts - 3 MBT - 2,400 AIFV & APC - 1057	Divs - 2 Indep Bdes - 7 Recce Rgts - 3 MBT - 2,050+ APC - 1019	Divs - 31 [Inf 17; RAPID 4; Mtn 10] Indep Inf Bdes - 7 Indep Mtn Bdes - 1 Indep AB/ Cdo Bdes - 1	Divs - 20 [Inf 19; Area Command 1] Indep Bdes - 9 Btns - 3 special forces [SSG]	Indep Bdes - 3 Towed Arty - 4,075 SP Arty - 180 MRL - 80 Mortar - 1,200+ SSM - 3-5 Prithvi launchers ATGW RCL - 1,000+	Bdes - 8 Towed Arty - 1,566 SP Arty - 240 MRL - 45 Mor - 725 SSM - 18 [Hatf 1 & 2] ATGW - 800	Hel Sqns - 14 [Atk 6, Obs Serva-tion 8] Hel - 199	Sqns - 17 [AC 7; Hel 8; VIP 1; Obs Flt 1] Aircraft - 175 [Survey 1, Lias 84, Obs 90] Helicopter - 134 [Atk 20; Tpt 114]

Year	Armour		Infantry		Artillery, Missiles		Aviation	
	India	Pakistan	India	Pakistan	India	Pakistan	India	Pakistan
1999	Divs - 3 Indep Bdes - 7 Tanks - 3,504 [MBT - 3,414, Lt - 90] AIFV, APC - 1507 Armd Car - 100	Divs - 2 Indep Bdes - 7 Recce Rgts - 3 MBT - 2,320+ APC - 850	Divs - 31 [Inf 18, RAPID 4, Mtn 9] Indep Inf Bdes - 5 Indep Mtn Bdes - 2 Indep AB/ Cdo Bdes - 1	Divs - 20 [Inf 19, Area Command 1] Indep Bdes - 9 Btns - 3 SSG	Divs - 1 [3 Bdes, 190 Rgts] Towed - 4175 SP - 180+ MRL - 150 Mor - 1200 SSM - 1 Prithvi Rgt ATGW RCL - 1,000+	Bdes - 9 Towed - 1590 SP - 240 MRL - 45 Mor - 725 SSM - 18 [Hatf 1&2, Shaheen 1] ATGW - 800 RL, RCL	Hel Sqns - 14 [Atk 6, Air Obs 8 Sqns] Hel - 199 UAV	Sqns - 17 [AC 7; Hel 8; VIP 1; Obs Ft 1] AC - 175 [Sur 1, Lias 84, Obs 90] Hel - 134 [Atk 20, Tpt 114]

2001	Divs - 3 Indep Bdes - 7 Tanks - 3,504 [MBT 3,414, Lt 90] AIFV, APC - 1,667 Armd Cars - 100	Divs - 2 Indep Divs - 7 Recce Rgts - 3 MBT - 2,300+ APC - 1,150+	Divs - 31 [Inf 18, RAPID 4, Mtn 9] Indep Inf Bdes - 5 Indep Mtn Bdes - 2 AB/Cdo Bdes - 1	Divs - 20 [Inf 19, Area Command 1] Indep Mech Bdes - 6 Indep Inf Bdes - 9 Btns - 3 SF	Divs - 1 [3 Bdes, 190 Rgts] Towed - 4175 SP - 180+ MRL - 100 Mor - 1,000+ SSM - 3-5 Prithvi launchers ATGW RCL - 1,000+	Bdes - 9 Towed - 1,467 SP - 240 MRL - 45 Mor - some 1,200 SSM - 122 [80 Hatf 1; 30 Hatf 3, Shaheen1; Ghauri 12] ATGW - 800 RCL - 3,700	Hel Sqns - 22 [Atk 5 Sqns] Utility Hel - 150 UAV	Sqns - 17 [AC 7, Hel 8, VIP 1, Obs Flt 1] AC - 132 [Sur 1; Lias 56; Obs 75] Hel - 137 [Atk 20; Tpt 117] UAV

Year	Armour		Infantry		Artillery, Missiles		Aviation	
	India	Pakistan	India	Pakistan	India	Pakistan	India	Pakistan
2005	Divs - 3 Indep Bdes - 8 Tks - 4,168 [MBT 3,978, Lt 190] AFV - 2,517 [AIFV 1,700, APC 817+] Armd Cars - 110 Casspir - 160	Divs - 2 Indep Bdes - 7 MBT - 2,461+ APC - 1,266	Divs - 32 [Inf 18, RAPID 4, Mtn 10] Indep Inf Bdes - 8 Indep Mech Bdes - 2 [25 Btns] Indep Mtn Bdes - 2 Indep AB/ Cdo Bdes - 1 [3 Cdo btns, 8 Airborne Btns]	Divs - 19 [Inf 18, Area Cmd 1] Indep Mech Bdes - 1 Indep Inf Bdes - 6 Btns - 3 SF	Divs - 2 [6 Bdes] Arty pieces - 12,675+ [Towed 5,625+; SP 150+; MRL 180; Mor 6,720+] ATk Msls RCL 3,000+	Bdes - 14 [Corps 9, Indep 5] Arty pieces - 4,291+ [Towed 1,629, SP 260, MRL 52, Mor 2,350+] ATk - 14,400+ [Msls 10,500; RCL 3,700; RL; Guns 200]	Hel Sqns - 22 [Atk 5] Atk Hel - 12 Utility Hel - 150 UAV	AC Sqns - 6 [1 VIP, 5 Comp] AC - 124 [Recce 30; Tpt 4; Obs & Lias 90] Hel Sqns - 10 Hel - 153 [Atk 22; Spt 54; Utility 55; Trng 22] UAV

2010	Divs - 3 Indep Bdes - 8 MBT - 4,047+ AIFV - 1,455 APC - 317+ Armd Cars - 110	Divs - 2 Indep Bdes - 7 MBT - 2,461+ APC - 1,266	Divs - 32 [Inf 18, RAPID 4, Mtn 10] Indep Inf Bdes - 6 Indep Mech Bdes - 2 [25 Btns] Indep Mtn Bdes - 2 SF Btns - 5-7 Airborne Bde - 1 para [5 Btns]	Divs - 19 [Inf 18, Area Cmd 1] Indep Mech Bde - 1 Indep Inf Bdes - 6 SF Btns - 3	Divs - 2 [each 2 Bdes] Arty pieces - 11,258+ [SP 20+; Towed 4,510+; MRL 208; Mor 6,520+] ATk Msls RCL 3,000+ SSM: Brahmos (8-10); Agni I (70-90); Agni II (15-20); Agni III; Prithvi I & II	Bdes - 14 [9 Corps, 5 Indep] Arty pieces - 4,291+ [SP 260, Towed 1,629, MRL 52, Mor 2,350+] ATk Msls - 10,000+ RCL - 3,700 RL ATk Guns - 200 SSM - 166 [95 Hatf 1; Hatf 2/ Abdali; 50 Hatf 3/M11; 6 Shaheen 1/ Hatf 4; up to 20 Hatf 5/ Ghauri	Hel - 14 Sqns; 12 Atk Hel; 210 Util Hel UAV - 26	AC - 6 Sqns [VIP 1, Composite 5]; 124 Craft [Recce 30, Tpt 4, Util 90] Hel - 10 Sqns, 183 Craft [Atk 26, Spt 54, Util 81, Trng 22] UAV

Year	Armour		Infantry		Artillery, Missiles		Aviation	
	India	**Pakistan**	**India**	**Pakistan**	**India**	**Pakistan**	**India**	**Pakistan**
2015	Divs - 3 Indep Bdes - 8 MBT - 2,874+ AIFV - 1,455+ APC - 336+ Armd Cars - 110	Divs - 2 Indep Bdes - 7 MBT - 2,531+ APC - 1,390	Divs - 33 [Inf 15, RAPID 6, Mtn 12] Indep Mech Bdes - 2 Indep Inf Bdes - 7 Indep Mtn Bdes - 2 Para Bdes - 1	Divs - 20 [Inf 18, Mech Inf 2] Indep Mech Bdes - 1 Indep Inf Bdes - 5 SF Btns - 4	Divs - 3 SSM Rgts - 2 Brahmos Arty pieces - 9,702+ [SP 20+, Towed 2,970+, MRL 192, Mor 6,520+] ATk Msls RCL - 3,000+ SSM - 30 Prithvi SRBM; 8-10 Brahmos LACM;	Bdes - 14 [9 Corps, 5 Indep] Arty piees - 4,472+ [SP 375; Towed 1,659; MRL 88+; Mor 2,350+] ATk - Msls, RCL, RL, 200 Guns SSM - 30 Ghauri MRBM; 30 Ghaznavi SRBM; some Babur LACM; 105 Hatf 1 tactical SRBM	Hel - 14 Sqns, 275+ MRH UAV - 26	AC - 5 Sqns [VIP 1, Avn 4]; 102 craft [LT Tpt 14, Trng 88] Hel - 10 Sqns [Atk 3, ISR 2, SAR 2, Tpt 2, Spl Ops 1]; 278 Craft [Atk 38, Multi-role 114+, Med Tpt 76, Lt Tpt 40, Trng 10] UAV

2020	Divs - 3 Indep Bdes - 8 MBT - 3,565+ AIFV - 3,100 APC - 336+	Divs - 2 Indep Bdes - 7 MBT - 2,433 APC - 3,545	Divs - 23 [Inf 15, RAPID 6, Mtn 12] Indep Mech Bdes - 2 Indep Inf Bdes - 7 Indep Mtn Bdes - 2 Para Bdes - 1	Divs - 21 [Inf 18, Mech 2, Sy 1] Indep Mech Bdes - 1 Indep Inf Bdes - 5	Divs - 3 Indep Bdes - 2 ATk - Missiles & 3,000+ RCL Arty pieces - 9,719+ [SP 10; Towed 2,975+; MRL 214; Mor 6,520+] SSM - Brahmos GLCM 15.	Divs - 1 [14 Arty Bdes]. ATk - 30+ Msls; RCL; 200 Guns Artypiees - 4,595+ [SP 498; Towed 1659; MRL 88+; Mor 2,350+] SSM - 105 Hatf 1	Hel - 23 Sqns; 320+ MRH UAV - 25	AC Sqns - 5 [VIP 1, 4 Avn] AC - 100 [Lt Tpt 13; Trng 87] Hel Sqns - 10 [Atk 3, ISR 2, SAR 2, Tpt 2, Spl Ops 1] Hel - 243 [Atk 42, MRH 115+, Tpt 76, Trng 10] UAV

Source: *The Military Balance* (London: International Institute for Strategic Studies, 1963–2020).

Abbreviations

AB – Airborne
AC – Aircraft
AFV – Armoured Fighting Vehicle
AIFV – Armoured Infantry Fighting Vehicle
APC – Armoured Personnel Carrier
Area Cmd – Area Command
Armd - Armoured
Arty – Artillery
ATGW – Anti-Tank Guided Weapon
Atk Hel – Attack Helicopter
ATk Msl – Anti-Tank Missile
Bde – Brigade
Btn – Battalion
Cdo – Commando
Div – Division
Flt – Flight
GLCM – Ground Launched Cruise Missile
Hel – Helicopter
How – Howitzer
Indep Bde – Independent Brigade
Inf – Infantry
ISR – Intelligence Surveillance and Reconnaissance
LACM – Land Attack Cruise Missile
Lias – Liaison
Lt AC – Light Aircraft
Lt Hel – Light Helicopter
Lt Tk – Light Tank
Mech – Mechanised
Med Tk – Medium Tank
MBT – Main Battle Tank
Mor – Mortar
MRBM – Medium Range Ballistic Missile
MRH – Multi Role Helicopter
MRL – Multiple Rocket Launcher
Msl – Missile
Mtn – Mountain
Obs Hel – Observation Helicopter
Para – Paratroop
RAPID – Reorganised Army Plains Infantry Division
RCL – Recoilless Rifle
Recce – Reconnaissance
Rgt – Regiment
RL – Rocket Launcher
SAR – Search and Rescue
SP arty – Self-Propelled Artillery
Spl Ops – Special Operations
Sqn – Squadron
SRBM – Short-Range Ballistic Missile
SSG – Special Service Group
SSM – Surface-to-Surface Missile
Sy div – Special Security Division
Tk – Tank
Tpt – Transport
Trng – Training
UAV – Unmanned Aerial Vehicle
VIP – Very Important Person

In the domain of air power, the Indian Air Force (IAF) has consistently fielded a larger number of fighters and fighter bombers than its Pakistani counterpart. The IAF held a 2.6-to-1 advantage in 1963, which declined to 1.8-to-1 in 1971 and remained at the same level in 1985. In the next 25-year period, the IAF enjoyed a force ratio of 2.2-to-1 during the Kargil conflict of 1999 and 2.5-to-1 in 2010. But during the last decade, with the retirement of older aircraft from the IAF fleet, the ratio has declined to 1.88-to-1 by 2020. Table 2.7 provides a complete break-up of the differential in the force levels of the Indian and Pakistani air forces with respect to fighters, fighter bombers, early warning and surveillance aircraft, attack helicopters, and missiles.

TABLE 2.7: The Air Forces of India and Pakistan in Numbers: Select Years between 1963 and 2020

Year	Fighters		Bombers, Fighter Bombers, Ground Attack		AEW, ISR, UAV		Attack Helicopters		Missiles	
	India	Pakistan	India	Pakistan	India	Pakistan	India	Pakistan	India	Pakistan
1963	8 Sqns, 200 AC	1 Sqn	Lt B - 4 Sqns, 80 AC FB - 6+ Sqns, 150+ AC	Lt B - 2 Sqns FB - 4 Sqns	NA	NA	NA	NA	NA	NA
1964	8 Sqns, 200 AC	1 Sqn	Lt B – 4 Sqns, 80 AC FB - 10+ Sqns, 150+ AC	Lt B - 2 Sqns, 30 AC FB - 4 Sqns	Recce - 1 Sqn, 8 AC	Recce AC	NA	NA	NA	NA
1965	9 Sqns, 212 AC [incl 1 MiG21 Sqn of 12 AC]	1 Sqn	Lt B - 4 Sqns, 80 AC FB - 10+ Sqns, 150+ AC	Lt B - 2 Sqns FB - 4 Sqns	Recce - 1 Sqn, 8 AC	Recce AC	NA	NA	NA	NA

1966	12 Sqns	2 Sqns	Lt B - 3 Sqns FB - 9 Sqns	Lt B - 3 Sqns FB - 6 Sqns	PR - 1 Sqn MR - 1 Sqn	Recce - 1 Sqn	NA	NA	SAM btys.	NA
1967	240 AC	6 Sqns, 100 AC	Lt B - 45 AC FB - 200 AC	Lt B - 3 Sqns, 28 AC FB - 5 Sqns, 100 AC	PR - 8 AC MR - 16 AC	Recce - 2 Units		NA	SAM btys.	NA
1968	230 AC	52 AC	Lt B - 45 AC FB - 260 AC	Lt B - 24 AC FB - 154 AC	PR - 8 AC MR - 7 AC	Recce - 20 AC	NA	NA		NA
1969	270 AC	5 Sqns	Lt B - 50 AC FB - 285 AC [50 in reserve]	Lt B - 3 Sqns FB - 10 Sqns	PR - 8 AC MR - 8 AC	Recce - 10 AC	NA	NA	SAM – 50 launchers	NA
1970	14 Sqns	6 Sqns	Lt B - 3 Sqns FB - 12 Sqns	Lt B - 3 Sqns FB - 8 Sqns	PR - 1 Sqn Tactical Recce - 2 Sqns MR - 1 Sqn	Recce - 5 AC	NA	NA	SAM - about 50 launchers	NA

Year	Fighters		Bombers, Fighter Bombers, Ground Attack		AEW, ISR, UAV		Attack Helicopters		Missiles	
	India	Pakistan	India	Pakistan	India	Pakistan	India	Pakistan	India	Pakistan
1971	15 Sqns	5 Sqns, 80 AC	Lt B - 3 Sqns FB - 15 Sqns	Lt B - 3 Sqns, 48 AC FB - 10 Sqns, 160 AC	PR - 1 Sqn MR - 1 Sqn	Recce - 1 Sqn, 6 AC	NA	NA	SAM - about 50 complexes	NA
1972	16 Sqns	5 Sqns, 60 to 80 AC	Lt B - 4 Sqns FB - 17 Sqns	Lt B - 2 Sqns, 24 to 32 AC FB - 8 Sqns, 96 to 128 AC	PR - 1 Sqn MR - 1 Sqn	Recce - 1 Sqn, 10 AC	NA	NA	SAM - about 20 sites	NA
1975	18 Sqns, 400 AC	NA	Lt B - 3 Sqns, 50 AC. FGA - 14 Sqns, 267 AC	Lt B - 1 sqn, 10 AC FB - 5 Sqns, 70 AC FGA - 10 Sqns, 189 AC	Recce - 1 Sqn, 8 AC	Recce - 1 Sqn, 9 AC	NA	NA	SAM - 20 sites	NA

1980	14 Sqns, 252 AC	NA	Lt B - 3 Sqns, 60 AC FGA - 18 Sqns, 298 AC [incl 1 OCU Sqn of 24 AC]	Lt B - 1 Sqn, 11 AC FGA - 12 Sqns, 235 AC	Recce - 1 Sqn, 18 AC	Recce - 1 Sqn, 10 AC	NA	NA	AAM ASM SAM - 2 Sqns, 120 Msls	AAM
1985	20 Sqns, 392 AC	11 Sqns, 200 AC.	Lt B - 3 Sqns, 35 AC FGA - 12 Sqns, 200 AC	FGA - 8 Sqns, 108 AC	Recce - 2 Sqns, 20 AC	Recce - 1 Sqn, 13 AC	60 Hel	NA	AAM ASM SAM - 30 Btns, 180 Msls	AAM
1990	22 Sqns, 361 AC	12 Sqns, 229 AC.	Lt B - 1 Sqn, 9 AC FGA - 26 Sqns, 400 AC Maritime Attack - 8 AC	FGA - 14 Sqns, 214 AC	Recce - 3 Sqns, 20 AC MR/Survey - 4 AC	Recce - 1 Sqn, 12 AC	12 Hel	NA	AAM ASM SAM - 30 Btns, 280+ Msls	AAM ASM SAM - 7 Btys
1995	20 Sqns, 372 AC	10 Sqns, 243 AC.	FGA - 22 Sqns, 443 AC Mar Atk - 8 AC	FGA - 7 Sqns, 123 AC	ECM - 5 AC ELINT - 2 AC AWAC - 2 AC Recce - 2 Sqns, 16 AC MR/Sur - 4	Recce - 1 Sqn, 12 AC ASW/MR - 1 Sqn, 4 AC	2 Sqns, 32 Hel	NA	AAM ASM SAM - 30 Sqns, 280 Msls	AAM ASM SAM - 7 Btys

Year	Fighters		Bombers, Fighter Bombers, Ground Attack		AEW, ISR, UAV		Attack Helicopters		Missiles	
	India	Pakistan	India	Pakistan	India	Pakistan	India	Pakistan	India	Pakistan
1999	20 Sqns, 368 AC	10 Sqns, 195 AC	FGA - 18 Sqns, 365 AC Mar Atk - 6 AC	FGA - 7 Sqns, 113 AC	ECM - 6 AC ELINT - 4 AC AEW - 4 AC Recce - 2 Sqns, 16 AC MR/Sur - 4 AC	Recce - 1 Sqn, 11 AC	3 Sqns, 32 Hel		AAM ASM SAM - 38 Sqns, 280 Msls	AAM ARM ASM SAM - 7 Btys
2005	5 Sqns, 137 AC	10 Sqns, 3 OCU Sqns, 143 AC	FGA - 33 Sqns, 610 AC Mar Atk - 1 Sqn, 16 AC	FGA - 5 Sqns, 91 AC 1 OCU Sqn	ELINT - 9 AC Recce - 1 Sqn, 5 AC MR/Sur - 9 AC ECM - 3 Sqns, 60 AC UAV	ELINT/ECM - 2 AC Recce - 1 Sqn, 15 AC	3 Sqns, 40-60 Hel	NA	AAM ASM SSM SAM - 38 Sqns & 4 Flts	AAM ASM SAM - 7 Btys, 150+ Msls
2010	6 Sqns, 96 AC	10 Sqns, 234 AC	FGA - 31 Sqns, 520 AC Mar Atk. - 1 Sqn, 16 AC	FGA - 5 Sqns, 104 AC	AEW&C - 1 Sqn, 1 AC Recce - 1 Sqn, 3 AC UAV - 5 Sqns	ELINT/ECM - 1 Sqn, 2 AC Recce - 1 Sqn, 15 AC	2 Sqns, 20 Hel	NA	AAM ARM ASM SAM - 31 Sqns & 10 Flts	AAM ASM SAM - 7 Btys, 150+ Msls

2015	3 Sqns, 62 AC	8 Sqns, 211 AC	FGA - 33 Sqns, 743 AC Mar Atk - 1 Sqn, 10 AC	7 Sqns, 190 AC	AEW&C - 1 Sqn, 5 AC ISR - 1 Unit, 3 AC UAV - 5 Sqns	EW/ELINT - 1 Sqn, 2 AC AEW - 2 Sqns, 3 AC ISR - 10 AC	2 Sqns, 20 Hel	NA	AAM ARM Anti-Ship Missiles ASM ALCM SAM - 33 Sqns & 10 Flts	SAM - 17 btys, 190+ Msls AAM ASM ALCM
2020	3 Sqns, 62 AC	6 Sqns, 153 AC	FGA - 26 Sqns, 605 AC Mar Atk - 1 Sqn, 8 AC	10 Sqns, 203 AC	AEW&C - 1 Sqn, 5 AC ISR - 1 unit, 3 AC UAV - 5 Sqns, 9 AC	EW/ELINT 1 Sqn, 2 AC AEW 2 Sqns, 10 AC ISR - 10 AC UAV	2 Sqns, 25 Hel	NA	AAM ASM ALCM SAM - 33 Sqns & 10 Flts	AAM ASM ALCM SAM - 17 Btys 150+ Msls

Source: *The Military Balance* (London: International Institute for Strategic Studies, 1963–2020).

Abbreviations

AAM – Air-to-Air Missile
AC – Aircraft
AD – Air Defence
AEW – Airborne Early Warning
AEW&C – Airborne Early Warning and Control
ALCM – Air Launched Cruise Missile
ARM – Anti-Radiation Missile.
ASM – Air-to-Surface Missile
AWACS – Airborne Warning and Control System
Btn – Battalion
Bty – Battery
ECM – Electronic Counter Measures
ELINT – Electronic Intelligence
F – Fighter
FB – Fighter Bomber
FGA – Fighter/Ground Attack
Flt – Flight
ISR – Intelligence, Surveillance, Reconnaissance
Lt B – Light Bomber
MR – Maritime Reconnaissance
Msl - Missile
OCU – Operational Conversion Unit
PR – Photo Reconnaissance
SAM – Surface-to-Air Missile
Sqn – Squadron
SSM – Surface-to-Surface Missile
Sur – Survey
TR – Tactical Reconnaissance
UAV – Unmanned Aerial Vehicle

The one traditional domain of war in which India has maintained a clear advantage in force levels is the naval sphere. In terms of principal surface combatants, the Indian Navy's force levels were more than twice as large as the Pakistan Navy's in 1963 (Table 2.8). For nearly the next three decades, the Indian Navy expanded its lead. It had three times more principal surface combatants than the Pakistan Navy in 1971 and five times more such ships in 1980. While the gap narrowed to 2.8 times by 1990, it soon climbed back to 5.6 times by 1999 and to 6.4 times by 2010. In 2020, the Indian Navy had nearly four times more principal surface combatants than the Pakistan Navy. In the sub-surface realm too, the Indian Navy has maintained a larger fleet of diesel submarines than the Pakistan Navy. While both navies fielded just one submarine apiece during the 1971 War, the Indian Navy built up a larger fleet in the next two decades, possessing three times more submarines than the Pakistan Navy in 1990. The dip in the advantage witnessed during the 1990s, when the favourable ratio declined to 2.3-to-1 by 1999, was subsequently reversed. In 2010, the Indian Navy possessed a submarine fleet that was 3.4 times larger, which declined marginally to 3.2 times larger in 2020.

TABLE 2.8: The Navies of India and Pakistan in Numbers: Select Years between 1963 and 2020

Year	Principal Surface Combatants		Submarines		Combat Aircraft, Missiles		Amphibious	
	India	**Pakistan**	**India**	**Pakistan**	**India**	**Pakistan**	**India**	**Pakistan**
1963	Total - 17: CV - 1 Escort ships - 16.	Total - 8: CL - 1 DD & Fr - 7	NA	NA	Total Aircraft - 39: [F - 24 ASW - 15]	NA	2	NA
1964	19 [CV - 1, CL - 2, DD - 3, Fr - 8, Other Escort - 5]	8 [CL - 1, DD - 5, Fr - 2]	NA	NA	39 AC [F - 24; ASW– 15]	NA	2	NA
1965	20 [CV - 1, CL - 2, DD - 3, Fr - 8, Other Escort - 6]	8 [CL - 1, DD - 5, Fr - 2]	NA	1 [SS]	39 AC [F - 24; ASW– 15]	NA	2	NA
1966	19 [CV - 1, CL - 2, DD - 6, Fr - 8, Oth Esc- 2]	7 [DD - 5, Fr - 2]	NA	1 [SS]	F - 2 Sqns ASW AC - 2 Sqns	NA	2	NA
1967	19 [CV -1, CL - 2, DD - 3, Fr - 13]	7 [DD - 5, Fr -2]	2 [SS]	1 [SS]	72 AC [F - 60, ASW - 12] Some Hel	NA	1	NA

Year	Principal Surface Combatants		Submarines		Combat Aircraft, Missiles		Amphibious	
	India	Pakistan	India	Pakistan	India	Pakistan	India	Pakistan
1968	19 [CV - 1, CL - 2, DD - 6, Fr - 8, Oth Esc - 2]	7 [DD- 5, Fr - 2]	1 [SS]	1 [SS]	42 AC [F - 30, ASW - 12] Some Hel	NA	4 [LS - 1; LC - 3]	NA
1969	21 [CV - 1, CL - 2, DD - 7, Fr - 8, Oth Esc - 3]	7 [DD- 5, Fr - 2]	2 [SS]	1 [SS]	62 AC [F - 50, ASW - 12]	NA	3 [LS - 1; LC - 2]	NA
1970	22 [CV - 1, CL - 2, DD - 11, Fr - 8]	7 [DD- 5, Fr - 2]	4 [SS]	1 [SS]	47 AC [F - 35, ASW - 12] Some 10 Hel	NA	4 [LS - 1; LC - 3]	NA
1971	24 [CV - 1, CL - 2, DD - 12, Fr - 9]	8 [CL - 1, DD - 5, Fr - 2]	4 [SS]	4 [SS]	47 AC [F - 35, ASW - 12] 12 Hel [ASW - 2, MRH - 10]	NA	3 [LS - 1; LC - 2]	NA
1972	22 [CV - 1, CL - 2, DD - 11, Fr - 8]	7 [CL - 1, DD - 4, Fr - 2]	4 [SS]	3 [SS]	50 AC [F - 33, ASW - 17] 12 Hel [ASW - 2, MRH - 10]	NA	3 [LS - 1; LC - 2]	NA

1975	32 [CV - 1, CL - 2, DD - 3, Fr - 26]	9 [CL - 1, DD - 4, Fr - 4]	8 [SS]	9 [SS – 3; Midget (SSI) -6]	51 AC [F - 33, ASW - 12, MR - 6] 28 Hel [MRH - 18, ASW - 10].	NA	4 [LS - 1; LC - 3]	NA
1980	35 [CV - 1, CL - 1, Fr - 29, Cor - 4]	7 [CL - 1, DD - 6, Fr - 1]	8 [SS]	11 [SS – 6; SSI - 5]	50 AC [F - 25, ASW - 17, MR - 8] 20 Hel [ASW] Missiles – SSM, SAM	5 AC [ASW & MR] 9 Hel [MRH - 3, ASW/ SAR - 6] Missiles - ASM	7 [LST - 1; LCT - 6]	NA
1985	31 [CV - 1; CL - 1; DD - 3; Fr - 23; Cor - 3]	8 [DD]	8 [SS]	11 [SS - 6; SSI - 5]	36 AC: [F - 23; ASW - 5; MR - 8] 26 Hel [ASW]	3 AC [ASW/ MR] 10 Hel [ASW/SAR - 6; MRH - 4].	13 [LCT - 9; LCU - 4]	NA
1990	37 [CV - 2; DD - 5; Fr - 20; Cor - 10]	13 [DD - 3; Fr - 10]	19 [SSGN - 1; SS - 18]	9 [SS - 6; SSI - 3]	41 AC [F - 20; ASW - 4; MR - 17] 73 Hel [ASW]	5 AC [ASW/ MR] 10 Hel [ASW] Missiles - ASM	19 [LST - 1; LSM - 9; LCU - 9]. Marines - 1,000 personnel	NA

Year	Principal Surface Combatants		Submarines		Combat Aircraft, Missiles		Amphibious	
	India	Pakistan	India	Pakistan	India	Pakistan	India	Pakistan
1995	44 [CV - 2; DD - 7; Fr - 18; Cor - 17]	11 [DD - 3; Fr - 8]	15 [SS]	9 [SS - 6; SSI - 3]	68 AC [F - 22; MR - 46] 75 Hel [ASW] Missiles - AAM, ASM	4 AC [ASW/ MR] 13 Hel [ASW/SAR] Missiles - ASM	16 [LST - 1; LSM - 8; LCU - 7] Marines - 1,000	Marine Commandos - 1,200
1999	45 [CV - 1; DD - 7; Fr - 13; Cor - 24]	8 [Fr]	16 [SSK]	10 [SSK - 7; SSI - 3]	77 AC [F - 21; MR - 56] 82 Hel [ASW] Missiles - AAM, ASM	7 AC [ASW/ MR] 12 Hel [ASW/SAR] Missiles - ASM	19 [LST - 2; LSM - 7; LCU - 10] Marines - 1,200	Marine Commandos - 1,200
2005	54 [CV - 1; DDG - 8; Fr - 17; Cor - 28]	7 [Fr]	19 [SSK]	11 [SSK - 8; SSI - 3]	67 AC [FGA - 15; MR - 52] 95 Hel [ASW] Missiles - ASM, AAM	9 AC [MR] 12 Hel [ASW]	17 [LSM - 5; LST - 2; LCU - 10] Marines - 1,200	Marine Commandos - 1,400

2010	45 [CV - 1; DDG - 8; Fr - 12; Cor - 24]	7 [Fr]	17 [SSN - 1; SSK - 16]	8 [SSK - 5; SSI - 3]	35 AC [FGA - 11; ASW - 4; MP - 20] 63 Hel [ASW - 54; AEW - 9] 12 UAV Missiles - ASM, ASCM, AAM	12 AC [MP] 6 Hel [ASW] Missiles - ASM	17 [LPD 1; LSM 5; LST 5; LCU 6] Marines - 1,200	1 [LC] Marine Commandos - 1,400
2015	51 [CV - 2; DD - 12; Fr - 13; Cor - 24]	10 [Fr]	14 [SSN - 1; SSK - 13]	8 [SSK - 5; SSI - 3]	61 AC [F - 23; FGA 10; ASW - 14; MP - 14] 114 Hel [ASW - 47; MRH - 58; AEW - 9] 11 UAV Missiles - ASM, ASCM, AAM	16 AC [ASW - 10; MP - 6] 18 Hel [ASW - 12; MRH - 6] Missiles - ASM	42 [LPD - 1; LSM - 4; LST - 5; LC - 32] Marines - 1,200	3,200 Marines
2020	35 [CV - 1; DD - 13; Fr - 13; Cor - 8]	9 [Fr]	17 [SSBN - 1; SSN - 1; SSK - 15]	8 [SSK - 5; SSI - 3]	70+ AC [F/FGA - 44; ASW - 13; MP - 13+] 98 Hel [ASW - 30; MRH - 57; AEW - 11] Missiles - AAM, ASM	15 AC [ASW - 9; MP - 6]. 17 Hel [ASW - 11; MRH - 6] Missiles - ASM	19 [LPD - 1; LSM - 3; LST - 5; LC - 10] Marines - 1,200	8 [LC] 3,200 Marines

Source: *The Military Balance* (London: International Institute for Strategic Studies, 1963–2020).

Abbreviations

AAM – Air-to-Air Missile
AC – Aircraft
AEW – Airborne Early Warning
ASCM – Anti-Ship Cruise Missile
ASM – Anti-Ship Missile
ASW – Anti-Submarine Warfare
CV – Aircraft Carrier
CL – Cruiser Light
Cor. – Corvette
DD – Destroyer
DDG – Destroyer Guided Missile
F – Fighter Aircraft
FGA – Fighter Ground Attack
Fr. – Frigate
Hel. – Helicopter
LC – Landing Craft
LCT – Landing Craft Tank
LCU – Landing Craft Utility
LPD – Landing Platform Dock
LS – Landing Ship
LSM – Landing Ship Medium
LST – Landing Ship Tank
MP – Maritime Patrol
MR – Maritime Reconnaissance
MRH – Multi-Role Helicopter
SAM – Surface-to-Air Missile
SS – Submarine
SSGN –Submarine Guided [Missile] Nuclear
SSK – Submarine [attack]
SSM – Surface-to-Surface Missile
SSN – Submarine Nuclear [attack]

Why Pakistan Challenges India?

Despite being smaller in terms of territory, population, and economy, Pakistan has consistently sought parity with India. Indeed, Pakistani leaders have stated that India's acceptance of Pakistan 'as an equal' is 'a precondition for peace' (Fair 2014, 1).[2] The origins of Pakistan's quest for equality with India lie in pre-Partition India, in the Muslim League's demand for parity with the Indian National Congress (Haqqani 2015). This quest was partly driven by the fear of a 'Hindu Raj' and partly by the perception that Britain 'should restore power to those from whom they had taken it, that is the Muslims' (Gandhi 1991, 351).

Although, until recently, Pakistan's demand for parity of status with India found favour with most countries of the world, India has been loath to concede such a proposition given the vast differential in various indices of national power, which place it in the league of potential great powers (Tellis 1997). In addition, there is no denying the fact that India is the geographic, political, economic, and cultural core of South Asia. The self-perception and aspiration to become a great power and the reality of being the regional power have reinforced in Indian minds the importance of preserving the British Raj's legacy of a geopolitically unified subcontinent. Together, these factors have impelled India to seek to establish its predominance in South Asia and define the 'broad parameters within which' all other countries of the region would formulate and implement their foreign policies in general and security policies in particular (Ayoob 1989/90, 108–109).

Pakistan has determinedly contested India's ambitions in this regard by both maintaining a robust military capability backed by nuclear deterrence and borrowing power (in B.R. Ambedkar's apt phrase) from other sources such as Britain, the United States, and China.[3] In other words, Pakistan refuses to reduce itself into 'a West Bangladesh—a state denuded of its military power and politically and economically subordinated to a hegemonic India' (Cohen 2003, 19)—and thereby seeks to deny India uncontested predominance in the subcontinent. As Sartaj Aziz, a former Foreign Minister of Pakistan and Adviser to the Prime Minister on National Security and Foreign Affairs, asserted a few years ago, Pakistan would not allow India to realise its desire for regional hegemony. He went on to add that Pakistan's acquisition of nuclear weapons has already 'smashed India's dreams' in this regard (Haider 2015).

Imran Khan also articulated a similar view in July 2018 in the run-up to his election as prime minister by calling attention to 'India's *thaanedaari*' (highhandedness), albeit as part of his criticism of Nawaz Sharif, who was then vying with the Pakistan Army for supremacy. Khan observed that Sharif's 'fight against the Army' was 'not about democracy' but 'about telling the international community' that he 'can control the Army so that Pakistan can accept India's *thaanedaari*'. He went on to add that India wants Pakistan to accept its *thaanedaari*, just as Bangladesh, Bhutan, and Nepal have already done. Since the Pakistan Army is standing in the way, India is attempting to weaken and defame the former (Singh and Roy 2018).

For its part, the Pakistan Army, the ultimate arbiter of the country's defence and foreign policies, equates victory in war with 'simply retaining the ability to challenge India' while considering defeat to be 'simply giving up and accepting the [territorial] status quo and India's supremacy' (Fair 2014, 6). This 'way of war', according to Christine Fair, is the product of a strategic culture whose integral elements include resisting India's rise, restricting its 'presence and ability to harm Pakistan', and overturning 'the territorial status quo at all costs'. The pursuit of these objectives is seen as essential for protecting Pakistan's ideology, defined as Islam, the country's 'ideological frontiers' and its 'Islamic identity'—another task that the Pakistan Army has arrogated to itself. Abandoning them and acquiescing to Indian supremacy, it is believed, would erode the very 'legitimacy of the Pakistani state' (Fair 2014, 5–7).

Kashmir Conflict

Closely related to Pakistan's national identity-driven opposition to India and its compulsive quest for parity is its refusal to agree to a compromise solution on the issue of Jammu and Kashmir. The origins of this conflict are well known and are briefly reprised in chapter 3. Here, it would suffice to note the most basic aspects of the issue and India and Pakistan's irreconcilable approaches to a solution to the issue. For Pakistan, the incorporation of 'Kashmir' remains the unfinished business of Partition. In the Pakistani view, Kashmir should be a part of Pakistan in accordance with both the rationale of Partition and the guidelines to be considered by the princely states while deciding which dominion to accede to. Since Partition was effected on the basis of the two-nation theory that Hindus and Muslims constitute two distinct nations, Muslim-majority Kashmir should logically accede to Pakistan. Kashmir also belongs with Pakistan because of territorial contiguity and the fact that most of Kashmir's communications are through Pakistani territory.[4] Driven by the quest to incorporate Kashmir within itself, successive civilian and military governments have made determined efforts to wrest the state, the 'jugular vein' without which Pakistan is neither complete nor can exist.[5]

From the Indian point of view, Jammu and Kashmir is an essential component of its composite national identity. Further, the decision of the Maharaja of Jammu and Kashmir to sign the Instrument of Accession and accede to the Indian Union, as well as the subsequent endorsement of this decision by the state's popularly elected constituent assembly and the Constitution it adopted declaring the state as an integral part of India, have settled the matter (Ministry of External Affairs 2004, 1–4; The Constitution of Jammu and Kashmir 1956). Jammu and Kashmir, Indian leaders have repeatedly emphasised, is an 'integral part' of national territory (Singh 2013). In August 2019, the Indian Parliament abrogated Article 370 of the Constitution, thus removing the distinct status and autonomy afforded to Jammu and Kashmir and fully integrating it within the Union.

Indian Advocacy of Territorial Status Quo

From 1948, the Indian leadership consistently proposed that the Kashmir issue be settled on the basis of the extant status quo, albeit with minor territorial adjustments to establish a rational border. Such a settlement has, however, been unacceptable to Pakistani leaders, who have repeatedly sought, both during negotiations as well as through war and support for insurgent and terrorist groups, to wrest some or all portions of Jammu and Kashmir from India. In essence, India advocates the territorial status quo as a solution and Pakistan the revision of the territorial status quo. The following paragraphs recapitulate the successive efforts made to forge a compromise solution.

The first such effort was made as early as October 1948. On the sidelines of the Commonwealth Prime Minister's Conference held in London, Prime Minister Jawaharlal Nehru proposed to his Pakistani counterpart Liaquat Ali Khan that the issue be settled by both countries accepting the territorial status quo. He added that such a settlement could also include 'certain areas in western Poonch and the north-western part of the State [under Indian control] being allotted to Pakistan' (Nehru 1996, 324). Nehru's rationale for advocating such a settlement was as follows: India had referred the issue of Jammu and Kashmir to the United Nations (UN) mainly to prevent the outbreak of 'an all-out war' with Pakistan. But the experience at the UN compelled him to conclude that 'nothing substantial could be expected' from the world body, especially given India's determination not to concede on 'any basic point' as well as Pakistan's disinclination to 'revert to the *status quo ante*-war'. Under these circumstances, India had two options. One was to continue what was likely to prove to be 'a long drawn-out' war for regaining those territories of Jammu and Kashmir that were under the control of Pakistan and its irregular proxies. But such a step involved the risk of 'an all-out war' with Pakistan as well as international intervention given that the UN Security Council remained seized of the issue. The second option was to reach a settlement with Pakistan 'on the basis of the existing military situation' (Nehru 1996, 323–324). This line of thought led Nehru to propose, in his personal capacity, a settlement along the existing status quo, albeit with minor territorial adjustments in favour of Pakistan. But Liaquat Ali Khan 'refused to consider this matter on this basis' (Nehru 1996, 324; Nehru 2001, 249).

Nehru offered a similar proposal in May 1955 during his conversations in Delhi with the visiting prime minister and interior minister of Pakistan, Mohammad Ali Bogra and General Iskander Mirza, respectively. On this occasion as well, Nehru indicated his willingness 'to consider the transfer of a certain part of the Poonch area' to Pakistan and pointed to the desirability of the Kishanganga River serving as 'a suitable line' in the north (Nehru 2001, 255). During the course of this conversation, he also referred to the impracticality of the informal proposals that Pakistan's then Governor-General Ghulam Mohammed had made through emissaries: India transferring to Pakistan 'a large piece of territory in Jammu, north of Chenab' and 'Kashmir proper' coming under 'some kind of a joint control of a joint army' (Nehru 2001, 254). But Bogra and Mirza also expressed their inability to accept Nehru's proposal of an agreement based largely on the status quo because of three related reasons: public opinion would oppose it, Pakistan would not get anything out of it, and India would be able to free itself from 'entanglements' with the UN Security Council and other international organisations. Instead, they advocated 'major adjustments', which involved India retaining only 'some districts' around Jammu while the rest of the territory went to Pakistan (Nehru 2001, 257–258, 260).

India restated a similar proposal for settling the Jammu and Kashmir issue along the extant status quo, albeit with minor territorial adjustments, during the Swaran Singh–Zulfiqar Bhutto talks. Six rounds of these talks were held in 1962 and 1963 under the urging, pressure, and behind-the-scenes role played by the US. The United States hoped, in the words of the then Secretary of State Dean Rusk, to not only bring about a settlement of the Kashmir issue but also a reconciliation between India and Pakistan, as well as induce India to join America in containing China (Crawford 2002, 7–8). During the negotiations, the then Minister for Railways Sardar Swaran Singh proposed that, in addition to retaining all the territory it then controlled in Jammu and Kashmir, Pakistan would be allotted 'small sections under Indian control to the west and north of the Valley, but nothing in the Valley itself' (Crawford 2002, 13). According to D.K. Palit, the then director of military operations and a member of the Indian negotiating team, Singh was even prepared to offer some portions of the Kashmir Valley. Indeed, Palit records that he was informed by the then Commonwealth Secretary Y.D. Gundevia that the Cabinet had 'unhesitatingly approved the Prime Minister's proposal about a partition of Kashmir' (Palit 1991, 392–393). But Bhutto's counterproposal demanded that Pakistan be allotted almost the whole of Jammu and Kashmir—Kashmir Valley, Chenab Valley, and Ladakh—with India retaining only 'a small part of Jammu' (Crawford 2002, 14). In the absence of a viable meeting point, these talks went nowhere and were eventually suspended.

It was only in the immediate aftermath of the 1971 War that a Pakistani leader was even willing, albeit tactically as it later proved, to consider a settlement along the territorial status quo. Convinced by P.N. Haksar's argument about the possible adverse consequences of imposing a harsh peace on Pakistan, Prime Minister Indira Gandhi emphasised to President Zulfiqar Ali Bhutto the merits of such a settlement and the transformation of the renamed Line of Control into a de jure border at the 1972 Simla Conference (Bass

2016, 164–166). For his part, Bhutto conceded that it was 'the only feasible' solution but expressed his inability to formalise such an agreement at that juncture (Dhar 2000, 192–193). Subsequent Pakistani leaders disowned Bhutto's admission however, with one former official crowing that Bhutto 'fooled' Gandhi at Simla (Dhar 2000, 199).

The most recent effort, undertaken in the mid-2000s, to find a mutually acceptable solution on a 'status quo plus' basis did not also bear fruit, although the top leadership on both sides did make a sincere effort in subtly altering established national positions to bridge the gulf (Tellis 2017, 58–59). In essence, what the top leaders of the two countries sought was to make the Line of Control 'irrelevant ... just lines on a map' so that people and goods could move freely between the two sides (Singh 2006; Tellis 2017, 57).[6] But 'the essential prerequisite' for achieving the goal was 'an end to hostility, violence and terrorism' (Lambah 2014). Only that would pave the way for establishing an open border, especially between the Kashmir Valley and Azad Jammu and Kashmir, considerably thinning down the number of troops deployed on both sides and evolving a joint mechanism to 'look into socio-economic issues like Tourism, Travel, Pilgrimages to Shrines, Trade, Health, Education, and Culture' so that 'self-governance' could be ensured 'for internal management in all areas on the same basis on both sides of the LoC' (Lambah 2014).

That an agreement along these lines was largely worked out to mutual satisfaction was revealed by Prime Minister Manmohan Singh in May 2009 when he reportedly stated, 'General Musharraf and I had nearly reached an agreement, a non-territorial solution to all problems, but then General Musharraf got into many difficulties with the Chief Justice and other forces and therefore the whole process came to a halt' (Tellis 2017, 60). According to Sanjaya Baru, a former media adviser to the prime minister, Manmohan Singh was quite keen on renewing the process with Musharraf's successors—President Asif Ali Zardari and Prime Minister Syed Yousaf Raza Gilani—even in the aftermath of the terrorist attacks in Mumbai in November 2008 (Baru 2014, Kindle Edition, 3283–3291).

Khurshid Mahmud Kasuri, who, as the then foreign minister, was part of the small group that monitored and guided the progress of the back channel negotiations on the Pakistan side, has revealed that the group comprised top military leaders and diplomats including the vice chief of army staff, director general of the Inter-Services Intelligence, corps commanders, and the foreign secretary (Kasuri 2015, Kindle Edition, 4563–4578). Yet, President Musharraf's successors, both civilian and military, distanced themselves from the framework that had been evolved. Prime Minister Gilani dismissed the framework proposals as 'half-baked things that didn't have the mandate of Parliament' (Tellis 2017, 61). General Ashfaq Parvez Kayani, who as director general of the Inter-Services Intelligence was part of the core group that monitored the back channel negotiations, 'distanced himself from the negotiations' after becoming army chief and even informed US officials that 'Musharraf had operated independently, that he was unaware of the agreement's details, and that it was, at any rate, untenable because it did not enjoy the support of the army's corps commanders' (Tellis 2017, 61). Kayani's term as chief of Pakistan Army coincided with the November 2008 terrorist attacks in Mumbai, which effectively put paid to any immediate prospects of the back-channel process being revived. His successor, General Raheel Sharif, reverted to 'Kashmir is the jugular vein' rhetoric and to Pakistan's long-held position of seeking a solution in line with United Nations Security Council resolutions (Samanta 2014).

Is There a Change in the Indian Position?

Even as India sought to forge a settlement of the Kashmir issue along the territorial status quo, it did sporadically assert sovereign claims over Pakistan-occupied Jammu and Kashmir (PoJK) during the 1990s and noughties (Singh 2016).[7] The most significant assertion in this regard till date is the resolution unanimously adopted by both Houses of Parliament in February 1994 demanding that Pakistan vacate the portions of Jammu and Kashmir territory which it has 'occupied through aggression' (Parliament Resolution, 1994). The Indian Parliament, however, passed the resolution more as an expression of defiant determination in the wake of Pakistan's diplomatic campaign, with Kashmir consequently becoming a global talking point. In his 1993 address to the United Nations General Assembly, US President Bill Clinton referred to the conflict in Kashmir as a serious global threat (US Department of State 1993). A month later, Robin Raphel, Clinton's assistant secretary of state for South Asia, asserted that the United States does not recognise Maharaja Hari Singh's signature on the instrument of accession 'as meaning that Kashmir is forevermore an integral part of India' (Vaidya 2014). Around this time, Pakistan's diplomatic campaign was reaching a crescendo with the introduction of a resolution in the United Nations Human Rights Council condemning India for grave human rights violations, which, if adopted, had the potential to re-introduce the Kashmir issue at the United Nations (Gupta 1994).

Given this backdrop to the Parliament passing the resolution, once the international pressure eased and India managed to regain its equipoise, the issue of PoJK was ignored. Thereafter, once the back-channel negotiations to find a solution to the Kashmir issue began, the issue of territories under Pakistan's occupation became irrelevant. It was revisited only in the aftermath of the intense emotions generated by the 2008 Mumbai terrorist attack, which was carried out by the Lashkar-e-Taiba with the explicit involvement of Pakistani officials. In 2009 and 2010, the Ministry of External Affairs asserted Indian sovereignty over PoJK on two occasions: first in the context of Pakistan holding elections in Gilgit-Baltistan and the second in the wake of statements that the region has become Pakistan's fifth province and henceforth did not have any connection to Kashmir (Ministry of External Affairs 2009).

Since the coming to power of the Modi government in 2014, the tone of Indian assertions of sovereignty over PoJK has become sharper and their frequency has increased. In June 2015, responding to media questions about the proposed elections in Gilgit-Baltistan, the spokesperson of the Ministry of External Affairs not only asserted Indian sovereignty but also dismissed the elections as a camouflage for Pakistan's 'forcible and illegal occupation of the regions' (Ministry of External Affairs 2015). A few months later, exercising its right of reply during the United Nations General Assembly debate, an Indian representative called out Pakistan as a foreign occupier of the territory of Jammu and Kashmir (Ministry of External Affairs 2015). Further, after a gap of some ten years, the ministry appears to have renewed engagement with the diaspora from Gilgit-Baltistan and even explored the possibility of inviting their members for the 2017 edition of the Pravasi Bharatiya Divas (Roy 2016). There is, however, no confirmation as to whether anybody who had origins in the region actually participated in that or subsequent editions of the Divas. When asked in the run-up to the event in 2017, the ministry's secretary in charge of overseas Indian affairs provided an ambiguous answer to the effect that the event is open to all non-resident Indians and persons of Indian origin (Ministry of External Affairs 2017). Nor is it clear whether there was any member of the PoJK diaspora among the 3,121 delegates from 91 countries including four listed under 'Others' who participated in the 2019 edition of the Divas (Unstarred Question No. 521, 2019).

This change in India's approach to the issue of Pakistan-occupied Jammu and Kashmir has evidently come at the express direction of the political leadership. Prime Minister Narendra Modi himself has referred to the region on at least three occasions. His first reference was at the All-Party Meeting he convened in August 2016 to discuss the unrest in Kashmir following the killing of Burhan Wani. Modi not only emphasised the importance of winning the people's confidence while ensuring national security but also highlighted the fact that PoJK is a part of Jammu and Kashmir (*The Indian Express* 2016). Four days later, addressing the nation on Independence Day, he thanked the people of Gilgit and Pakistan-occupied Kashmir (PoK) for honouring the Indian nation by honouring him and showing goodwill towards him (PM India 2016). A third occasion when Modi referred to PoJK was in February 2018, albeit as part of his criticism of the main opposition party. Speaking in the Lok Sabha, he observed that '[h]ad Sardar Vallabhbhai Patel been the first Prime Minister, a part of Kashmir would not have been under control of Pakistan' (*India Today* 2018).

Senior Cabinet ministers of the government have followed Modi's lead. Following the abrogation of Article 370 and the establishment of the Union Territories of Jammu and Kashmir and Ladakh, Home Minister Amit Shah averred in Parliament that all his references to the State of Jammu and Kashmir should be understood as including Pakistan-occupied Kashmir. More significantly, he added that PoJK is worthy of the ultimate sacrifice (Bhardwaj 2019). Here, it is also worth noting the informed speculation about Shah's criticism of Prime Minister Atal Bihari Vajpayee for foreclosing the option of regaining PoJK by precipitately conducting the 1998 nuclear tests and, thus, providing Pakistan an opportunity to demonstrate its own nuclear weapons capability (*National Herald* 2020). Shah's statements in Parliament were followed up by Defence Minister Rajnath Singh and Foreign Minister S. Jaishankar. Speaking at an election rally in Haryana in August 2019, Singh stated that, if talks are held with Pakistan, India will not discuss any issue other than Pakistan-occupied Kashmir (*The Times of India* 2019). A few weeks later, addressing the press on the occasion of 100 days of the second Modi government, Jaishankar affirmed that PoJK is a part of India and expressed the hope that the country will someday obtain 'physical jurisdiction' over the region (Ministry of External Affairs 2019).

These statements from members of the Modi government reflect the long-standing position advocated by the Bharatiya Janata Party (BJP), its predecessor Bharatiya Jana Sangh, and the parent body RSS. While the BJP's election manifestos for the 2014 and 2019 elections did not refer to issue of PoJK, the 2009 manifesto specified that the parliamentary resolution of 1994 'shall remain the cornerstone of future decisions and actions of our Government' when it came to 'dealing with issues related to Jammu and Kashmir' (Bharatiya Janata Party 2009, 44). Likewise, the party's manifestos issued in 1991, 1996, and 1998 referred to the territory under Pakistan's occupation and affirmed Indian sovereignty over the whole of Jammu and Kashmir including PoJK. Given that the 1999 manifesto was issued in the name of the National Democratic Alliance, there was understandably no reference to PoJK. It is not clear why the party did not refer to the region and to the Indian claims in the manifestos issued for the 1984 and 1989 elections (Bharatiya Janata Party 2009).

Notwithstanding these and the more recent lapses in 2014 and 2019, the fact remains that the BJP's predecessor—Bharatiya Jana Sangh—had, since its inception in 1951, highlighted Pakistan's occupation of Jammu and Kashmir territory and advocated efforts to regain it. At its very first annual conclave in December 1952, the Jana Sangh, under the leadership of Syama Prasad Mukherjee, critiqued the Nehru government for pursuing policies that have resulted in Pakistan's continued occupation of one-third of the territory of Jammu and Kashmir. At subsequent conclaves, the party called upon the government to undertake efforts to regain that territory at the earliest. The party also promised in its election manifestos that, if elected, it would make the necessary effort to regain PoJK. It is also important to note here that the Jana Sangh had criticised the Indira Gandhi government for concluding the Simla Agreement of 1972 as well as for not liberating 'the areas of Kashmir occupied by Pakistan since 1947' during the course of the 1971 War (Yadav 2019).

The issue of Pakistan vacating the portion of Jammu and Kashmir territory it occupies has also been repeatedly flagged over the decades by the RSS. As far back as 1963, the Akhil Bharatiya Pratinidhi Sabha of the RSS asserted that the main issue in India–Pakistan talks should be addressing Pakistan's aggression from the portion of Jammu and Kashmir it has been occupying. After Parliament passed the 1994 resolution, the Sabha expressed hope that the Rao government would abandon its ambivalent attitude on the Kashmir issue. Eleven years later, another RSS body, the Akhil Bharatiya Karyakari Mandal, reminded the Manmohan Singh government of the 1994 parliamentary resolution and called upon it to 'stand firmly against any international pressure' to compromise on the issue (Yadav 2019).

There is, thus, reason and evidence to suggest that the Government of India's position on the contours of a settlement of the Kashmir issue has changed during the last several years. What it portends is a prolongation of the stalemate on Kashmir, at a minimum, and, perhaps, even future aggravation of conflict.

Manifestations of Conflict

Given this combination of factors—Pakistani intransigence on Kashmir and the changing Indian position on the contours of a settlement, Pakistan's inveterate hostility towards India and Indian conceptions of national identity that question the rationale of Pakistan, and Pakistan's persistent quest for parity with India—the conflict between India and Pakistan is likely to endure for the foreseeable future. Indeed, it is most likely to last for a few more decades, with India and Pakistan 'shooting for a century' in Stephen Cohen's felicitous phrase (Cohen 2013). What form this 'shooting' has hitherto assumed, and will assume, is a function of both the evolving military balance between the two countries as well as the political aims and military objectives that they have sought or will seek to pursue.

Pakistan's Efforts to Change the Status Quo

Pakistan's lack of conventional superiority and its enduring quest to alter the territorial status quo in Jammu and Kashmir has meant that it has been largely content to limit its political aim and military objectives in war. Indeed, its political aim and military objectives have been more or less coterminous, namely, conquering all or as much of Jammu and Kashmir as possible under the circumstances. However, to offset its matériel disadvantage vis-à-vis India, Pakistan has used the 'militant proxy strategy' (Kapur 2017),[8] which entails deploying Islamist militants as a primary offensive tool. Employing militant proxies has not only proved to be cost effective, but for long, it has also undermined India's ability to respond to Pakistani provocations through denial and punishment campaigns. It has also ensured that the Kashmir issue remained internationally alive, besides exacting blood and treasure from India (Kapur 2017, 112–115).

Thus, Pakistan employed irregulars in the form of tribal *lashkars* (militia) and backstopped them with regular forces in order to wrest Jammu and Kashmir in 1947–1948. In 1965, it went a step further by first seeking to foment a popular rebellion in Jammu and Kashmir and then launching a full-fledged military invasion to conquer the state. Although the 1971 War was principally fought in East Pakistan and for the liberation of the Bangladeshi nation from Pakistani military repression and genocide, Pakistan did make a determined effort to wrest Indian territories abutting West Pakistan, especially in Jammu and Kashmir. In 1999, Pakistan employed a combination of regular and irregular forces to, at a minimum, alter the territorial status quo in the Kargil sector and, at a maximum, catch Indian forces in a pincer between advancing Pakistani forces and an orchestrated insurgent/terrorist uprising in the hinterland of Jammu and Kashmir.

In addition, since the mid-1990s, Pakistan has been supporting and sponsoring the anti-India terrorist campaigns of Pakistani jihadi groups, in particular those of the Jaish-e-Mohammed (JeM) and Lashkar-e-Taiba (LeT). The JeM's objective, as declared by its emir, Masood Azhar, is the liberation and establishment of 'Islamic rule in Kashmir' and ultimately the destruction of India (in addition to America) (Singh 2011, 234; Hussain 2016). Established in the year 2000, the group carried out a flurry of terrorist attacks, including the suicide bombing on the main gate of the Jammu and Kashmir Legislative Assembly in October 2001 and the terrorist attack on Parliament in December 2001. Subsequently, incensed by Pakistan's decision to abandon the Taliban, the group turned its ire on President Musharraf—there were two failed suicide bombings which attempted to assassinate him. While Pakistan's subsequent crackdown as well as Indian intelligence action debilitated the group's strength, the last few years have seen the Jaish regaining the Pakistan establishment's favour and re-emerging as a terrorist actor in India. In January 2016, the Jaish carried out simultaneous attacks on an Army camp in Pathankot and the Indian mission in the Afghanistan city of Mazar-e-Sharif, in the process scuttling Prime Minister Modi's outreach to his Pakistani counterpart Nawaz Sharif (Jaleel 2016a, 2016b). Its most recent activity was the car bomb attack of a convoy of the Central Reserve Police Force in Pulwama in February 2019, which killed 40 personnel. Key evidence that points to the involvement of the group include 'the "forensically matched" voice of JeM Chief Masood Azhar's brother, Rouf Asgar, discussing the attack, and a Pakistan government identity card issued to Azhar's nephew, Mohammed Umer Farooq, the key conspirator' (Tiwary 2020).

For its part, the LeT seeks not just the liberation of Kashmir but also the independence of '200 million Indian Muslims'. According to Hafeez Mohammed Saeed, the group's emir, the jihad against India 'would continue till the independence of Himachal Pradesh, Bihar, Hyderabad, Uttar Pradesh and Junagadh' (Zahab 2002, 122). On other occasions, he has proclaimed that Kashmir is only a 'gateway to capture India', announced 'the break-up of India', and vowed not to rest 'until the whole [of] India is dissolved into Pakistan' (Tellis 2012, 3–4).

That Pakistan's establishment shares these objectives can be deduced from the close control that its army and intelligence agency, the Inter-Services Intelligence (ISI), exercise over the LeT and the extraordinary assistance they render to its terrorist campaign in India. The evidence in this regard is compelling. In his study on the LeT, Stephen Tankel observes that the Pakistan Army and ISI 'essentially built LeT's military apparatus from the mid-1990s onward specifically for use against India' (Tankel 2011, 5). In Tankel's assessment, the training primer used by the LeT in its initial years was most probably written in consultation and collaboration with the Pakistan Army. This is evident from the primer's emphasis upon 'a drawn-out war with India' aimed at depleting its manpower, exhausting its security forces and diminishing their morale, and exploiting logistical weaknesses. Further, Pakistani military personnel 'were present at LeT's training camps, where they helped to develop the training regimen designed to realize these objectives and to train the trainers' (Tankel 2011, 5). To top it all, military representatives actively participated in the planning of terrorist attacks in India and the tactics to be employed. Overall, the Pakistani military's assistance to the group included 'operational funding, specialized weapons, sophisticated communications equipment, combat training, safe havens for the leadership, shelter and operational bases for the cadres, intelligence on targets and threats, campaign guidance, infiltration assistance, and ... fire support when crossing the border into India' (Tellis 2012, 9).

Although Pakistan ostensibly cracked down upon the activities of the LeT and other anti-India jihadi terrorist groups in the wake of India's exercise of coercive diplomacy in 2001–2002, the group was not just 'allowed to maintain its training camps and ... operate relatively openly and unfettered', but the ISI continued to hold regular official meetings with its operatives as well (Tankel 2009, 5–6, 26). This is demonstrated by evidence relating to the LeT's terrorist attacks in Mumbai in November 2008, which resulted in the killing of 166 people. According to court testimony provided by David Headley, who played a critical role in enabling these attacks, 'every major LeT operative had an ISI handler and all of the group's major operations were conducted in coordination with these officers' (Tankel 2011, 20). Headley, an American citizen with Pakistani roots and originally named Daood Sayed Gilani, testified to have met with 'six different Pakistani intelligence officers' during his association with the LeT and 'identified several ISI officers who helped to plot and support the 26/11 attacks'—evidence that the United States used to indict an ISI officer by the name of Major Iqbal for providing 'direction and funding for the Mumbai attacks' (Tankel 2018).

According to Tankel, both Indian and American officials believed that 'a plot of this nature could never have moved forward without approval at the highest levels of the ISI' (Tankel 2018). But he also posits a few other possibilities in this regard: the then director general of ISI 'may have approved the attack without knowing the details' and on the assumption that it would be 'a more limited affair like previous attacks'; or, the LeT's handlers 'were given broad guidance' that planning for terrorist attacks against India 'could move forward' but were never told to stop (Tankel 2018).

Whatever the level of knowledge that senior Pakistani officials had about specific attacks, the essential point to note is that, through its continuing support for the LeT's and a revived JeM's terrorist campaigns against India, Pakistan has been pursuing multiple objectives: ensure the incorporation of all of Jammu and Kashmir into Pakistan; keep India off-balance and destabilised; and endeavour, through a well-orchestrated jihadi terrorist campaign, to bring about India's collapse and dissolution *à la* the Soviet Union (Tellis 2012, 8–9).

Indian Attempts to Maintain the Status Quo

Since the initial years of Independence, India has sought to maintain a measure of conventional superiority over Pakistan—a fact that Sardar Vallabhbhai Patel had noted in his famous November 1950 epistle to

Pandit Jawaharlal Nehru on the issue of revisiting and recalibrating India's China policy (Das 1974, 338). Conventional superiority enabled India to initiate full-scale war for the purpose of denying Pakistan its territorial objective, compelling it to accept the status quo, and even dismembering it in 1971. But with Pakistan's acquisition of nuclear weapons capability, its declared policy of first use of nuclear weapons to neutralise Indian conventional superiority, and its deployment of tactical nuclear weapons, India can no longer contemplate engaging in a full-scale war. It can, at best, wage a limited war to deny Pakistan its territorial objective, an option that it exercised during the Kargil conflict. Further, in the wake of the continuing terrorist campaigns of Pakistani jihadi groups, India has had to consider the idea of a limited war as a means of compelling Pakistan to stop using or supporting these terrorist groups.

Although Indian decision makers have not chosen to exercise the option of a limited war so far, there is no guarantee that they would not initiate one in the future. A limited war may ensue even if India were to launch only calibrated military strikes because Pakistan might feel compelled to even the scores, as happened in the aftermath of the calibrated Indian air strikes on a terrorist target in Balakot in 2019 (Joshi 2016). That such an action-reaction cycle has not escalated to a war until now is no guarantee that it would not ensue in war in the future. War, as Carl von Clausewitz emphasised, 'is not the action of a living force upon a lifeless mass … but always the collision of two living forces' (Clausewitz 1976, 77). It has been confirmed by Lieutenant General D.S. Hooda, the Northern Army commander at the time of the 2016 surgical strikes, that there was a 'fair amount of panic' on the Pakistani side, with even leaves for personnel being cancelled (Chhina 2018). In any event, as has been acknowledged by Prime Minister Narendra Modi himself, it would be 'a big mistake' to conclude that Pakistan would desist from sponsoring jihadi terrorist groups because of a single surgical strike (*The Times of India* 2019). What Modi left unsaid was that something more than surgical strikes would be needed to compel Pakistan into ceasing support for and sponsorship of jihadi terrorist groups targeting India. That something more includes the option of war.

Summary

Three main issues have sustained India–Pakistan conflict and rivalry. First, both countries have defined themselves in ways that aggravate conflict. Whereas Pakistan has chosen to define its national identity in anti-India terms, Indian conceptions tend to question the rationale for Pakistan's existence. Second, fuelled by anti-Indianism, Pakistan has consistently sought parity with India and challenged Indian leadership in the subcontinent, including through the expenditure of a greater share of its economic resources on building up a robust defence apparatus. Third, Pakistan's stubborn refusal to forge a compromise solution to the Kashmir issue has sustained conflict for more than seventy years. Given its relative weakness, Pakistan has consistently depended upon a hybrid strategy of employing a combination of regular and irregular forces to wrest Kashmir. Recent decades have, however, seen Pakistan relying more on its home-grown jihadi terrorists to 'liberate' Kashmir and, perhaps, other 'Muslim' territories in India. With Pakistan's nuclear weapons capability constraining India's conventional military options and given the limited utility of 'surgical' strikes to compel Pakistan to change policy, the Indian politico-military establishment confronts the challenge of crafting a strategy that brings political aims into alignment with the application of force.

Notes

1 Some of these China-specific divisions are also employed in counter-insurgency tasks in Northeast India.

2 In 2006, Pakistan's then army chief and president, Pervez Musharraf, is reported to have stated so.

3 Ambedkar's phrase is cited by Cohen, *The Idea of Pakistan*, p. 121.

4 For a recapitulation of the Pakistani contention in this regard, see Fair and Ganguly (2013, 176–179).

5 For articulations by Prime Minister Nawaz Sharif and Army Chief Raheel Sharif in this regard, see *The Indian Express* (2015); Khan (2014).

6 Musharraf too reportedly called for making the Line of Control 'irrelevant'.

7 PoJK is the new term being used by the Government of India since 2016.

8 For details on Pakistan's Militant Proxy Strategy, see Kapur (2017).

References

Ayoob, Mohammed. 1989/90. 'India in South Asia: The Quest for Regional Predominance'. *World Policy Journal*, 7(1): 107–133.

Baru, Sanjaya. 2014. *The Accidental Prime Minister: The Making and Unmaking of Manmohan Singh*. Penguin Books Kindle Edition.

Bass, Gary J. 2016. 'Bargaining Away Justice: India, Pakistan, and the International Politics of Impunity for the Bangladesh Genocide'. *International Security*, 41(2): 140–187.

Behera, Laxman Kumar and Vinay Kaushal. 2020. 'Defence Pension Reforms: Recommendations of the Past Committees and Commissions'. *IDSA Special Feature*, 28 February. Available at: https://idsa.in/system/files/comments/Defence-lbehera-vinay-280220_com_n.pdf (accessed on 3 March 2020).

Bharatiya Janata Party. 2009. 'Good Governance Development Security: Manifesto Lok Sabha Election 2009'. Available at: http://library.bjp.org/jspui/bitstream/123456789/262/1/bjp_lection_manifesto_english_2009.pdf (accessed on 24 March 2021).

Bhardwaj, Ananya. 2019. 'Amit Shah Tells Lok Sabha J&K Also Means PoK and Aksai Chin, Ready to Die for This'. *The Print*, New Delhi, 6 August.

Chhina, Man Aman Singh. 2018. 'Surgical Strike Overhype Did Not Help, Says General Who Oversaw Operations'. *The Indian Express*, Chandigarh, 8 December.

Clary, Christopher. 2013. 'Deterrence Stability and the Conventional Balance of Forces in South Asia'. In *Deterrence Stability and Escalation Control in South Asia*, edited by Michael Krepon and Julia Thompson. Washington D.C.: Stimson Center.

Clausewitz, Carl von. 1976. *On War*. Translated and edited by Michael Howard and Peter Paret. Princeton, NJ: Princeton University Press.

Cohen, Stephen P. 2003. 'The Jihadist Threat to Pakistan'. *The Washington Quarterly*, 26(3): 5–25.

Cohen, Stephen P. 2005. *The Idea of Pakistan*. New Delhi: Oxford University Press.

Cohen, Stephen P. 2013. *Shooting for a Century: Finding Answers to the India–Pakistan Conundrum*. Noida: HarperCollins Publishers.

Colaresi, Michael P., Karen Rasler, and William R. Thompson. 2007. *Strategic Rivalries in World Politics: Position, Space and Conflict Escalation*. New York: Cambridge University Press.

Cordesman, Anthony. 2002. *The India–Pakistan Military Balance*. Washington D.C.: Center for Strategic and International Studies.

Crawford, Timothy. 2002. 'Kennedy and Kashmir 1962–63: The Perils of Pivotal Peacemaking in South Asia'. *India Review*, 1(3): 1–38.

Das, Durga. ed. 1974. *Sardar Patel's Correspondence 1945–50, Vol. 10.* Ahmedabad: Navajivan Publishing House.

Dhar, P.N. 2000. *Indira Gandhi, the 'Emergency', and Indian Democracy.* New Delhi: Oxford University Press.

Dhulipala, Venkat. 2015. *Creating a New Medina: State Power, Islam, and the Quest for Pakistan in Late Colonial North India.* Delhi: Cambridge University Press.

Elkin, Jerrold F. and W. Andrew Ritezel. 1986. 'The Indo-Pakistani Military Balance'. *Asian Survey*, 26(5): 518–538.

Fair, C. Christine and Sumit Ganguly. 2013. 'Lives on the Line'. *The Washington Quarterly*, 36(3): 173–184.

Fair, C. Christine. 2014. *Fighting to the End: The Pakistan Army's Way of War.* Oxford: Oxford University Press.

Gandhi, Rajmohan. 1991. *Patel: A Life.* Ahmedabad: Navajivan Publishing House.

Ganguly, Sumit. 2016. *Deadly Impasse: Indo-Pakistani Relations at the Dawn of a New Century.* Cambridge: Cambridge University Press.

Ganguly, Sumit. 2020. *Conflict Unending: India–Pakistan Tensions Since 1947.* New Delhi: Oxford University Press.

GlobalSecurity.org. 2016. 'Indian Army Divisions'. Available at: https://www.globalsecurity.org/military/world/india/divisions.htm (accessed on 19 March 2021).

Gupta, Shekhar. 1994. 'On a Short Fuse'. *India Today*, 15 March.

Haider, Mateen. 2015, 'Pakistan's Acquisition of Nuclear Power Smashed India's Dreams: Sartaj Aziz'. *The Dawn*, Islamabad, 31 May.

Haqqani, Husain. 2010. *Pakistan: Between Mosque and Military.* Brookings Institution Press, Kindle Edition.

Haqqani, Husain. 2015. 'Pakistan's Elusive Quest for Parity'. *The Hindu*, 2 February.

Hussain, Zahid. 2016. 'The Demon We Created'. *The Dawn*, 20 January.

India Today. 2018. 'Had Sardar Patel Been First PM, Entire Kashmir Would Have Been Ours: PM Modi in Lok Sabha'. *India Today*, New Delhi, 7 February.

Indian Express. 2015. 'Nawaz Sharif Calls Kashmir as Pakistan's "Jugular Vein"'. *The Indian Express*, Islamabad, 6 February.

Indian Express. 2016. 'PoK is Part of Jammu and Kashmir, Says PM Narendra Modi at All-Party Meeting'. *The Indian Express*, New Delhi, 12 August.

Jaffrelot, Christophe. 2002. 'Nationalism Without a Nation: Pakistan Searching for its Identity'. In *Pakistan: Nationalism without a Nation?*, edited by Christophe Jaffrelot, 7–42. New Delhi: Manohar Publishers.

Jalal, Ayesha. 2014. *The Struggle for Pakistan: A Muslim Homeland and Global Politics*. Harvard University Press, Kindle Edition.

Jaleel, Muzamil. 2016a. 'Afzal Guru and the Jaish's Jihad Project'. *The Indian Express*, 12 January.

Jaleel, Muzamil. 2016b. 'Explaining the History of Masood Azhar's Jaish-e-Mohammad, the Mystery of its Re-emergence'. *The Indian Express*, New Delhi, 5 January.

Joshi, Shashank. 2016. 'Everything that We Know about India's cross-LoC Strikes before Uri'. *Scroll in*, 5 October 2016.

Kapur, S. Paul. 2017. *Jihad as a Grand Strategy, Islamist Militancy, National Security, and the Pakistani State*. New Delhi: Oxford University Press.

Kasuri, Khurshid Mahmud. 2015. *Neither a Hawk Nor a Dove: An Insider's Account of Pakistan's Foreign Policy*. Gurgaon: Penguin Books.

Khan, Iftikhar A. 2014. 'Insurgents Must Accept State's Writ, Says COAS'. *The Dawn*, Islamabad, 1 May.

Khilnani, Sunil. 2003. *The Idea of India*. Penguin Books, Kindle Edition.

Lambah, Satinder Kumar. 2014. 'A Possible Outline of a Solution'. *Outlook India*, 14 May.

Lok Sabha. 2019. 'Unstarred Question No. 521: Pravasi Bharatiya Divas'. Available at: https://mea.gov.in/lok-sabha.htm?dtl/30984/question+no521+pravasi+bharatiya+divas (accessed on 26 March 2021).

Ministry of External Affairs. 2004. *Kashmir The True Story*. Available at: https://mea.gov.in/Uploads/PublicationDocs/19156_Kashmir_The_True_Story_19-01-2004.pdf (accessed on 17 August 2016).

Ministry of External Affairs. 2009. 'GOI Protests to Pakistan against the "Gilgit-Baltistan Empowerment and Self Governance Order—2009"', Available at: http://mea.gov.in/press-releases.htm?dtl/1329/GOI+protests+to+Pakistan+against+the+GilgitBaltistan+Empowerment+and+-Self+Governance+Order+2009 (accessed on 8 February 2016).

Ministry of External Affairs. 2010. 'Official Spokesperson on Remarks by the So-Called CM of Gilgit-Baltistan'. Available at: http://mea.gov.in/media-briefings.htm?dtl/2707/Official+Spokesperson+on+remarks+by+the+so-called+CM+of+GilgitBaltistan (accessed 8 on February 2016).

Ministry of External Affairs. 2015. 'Official Spokesperson's Response to a Media Question on Elections Which Are to be Held in Gilgit-Baltistan on June 8, 2015'. Available at: http://mea.gov.in/media-briefings.htm?dtl/25307/Official+Spokespersons+response+to+a+media+question+on+elections+whi ch+are+to+be+held+in+GilgitBaltistan+on+June+8+2015 (accessed on 8 February 2016).

Ministry of External Affairs. 2015. 'Statement by India Exercising India's Right of Reply during the General Debate of 70th Session of UN General Assembly (September 30, 2015), Available at: http://mea.gov.in/Speeches-Statements.htm?dtl/25873/Statement_by_India_exercising_Indias_Right_of_Reply_during_the_General_Debate_of_70th_session_of_UN_General_Assembly_September_30_2015 (accessed 2 May 2016).

Ministry of External Affairs. 2017. 'Transcript of Pravasi Bharatiya Divas 2017: Curtain Raiser Briefing (January 2, 2017)'. Available at: https://mea.gov.in/media-briefings.htm?dtl/27891 (accessed on 26 March 2021).

Ministry of External Affairs. 2019. 'Transcript of Press Conference by External Affairs Minister on 100 Days of Government (17 September 2019)'. Available at: https://www.mea.gov.in/media-briefings.htm?dtl/31833/Transcript_of_Press_Conference_by_External_Affairs_Minister_on_100_days_of_Government_September_17_2019 (accessed on 18 September 2019).

National Herald. 2020. 'Did Amit Shah Write a Protest Note to PM Vajpayee on Nuclear Tests in 1998?'. *National Herald*, 14 December.

Nehru, Jawaharlal. 1996. *Selected Works of Jawaharlal Nehru*, Second Series, Vol. 19. New Delhi: Jawaharlal Nehru Memorial Fund.

Nehru, Jawaharlal. 2001. *Selected Works of Jawaharlal Nehru*, Second Series, Vol. 28. New Delhi: Jawaharlal Nehru Memorial Fund.

Palit, D.K. 1991. *War in High Himalaya: The Indian Army in Crisis, 1962*. New Delhi: Lancer International.

Paul, T.V. 2006. 'Causes of the India–Pakistan Enduring Rivalry'. In *The India–Pakistan Conflict: An Enduring Rivalry*, edited by T.V. Paul, 1–24. Delhi: Cambridge University Press.

Paul, T.V. ed. 2006. *The India–Pakistan Conflict: An Enduring Rivalry*. Delhi: Cambridge University Press.

Pew Research Center's Religion and Public Life Project. 2010. 'Muslim Population by Country in 2010'. Available at: http://globalreligiousfutures.org/explorer#/?subtopic=15&countries=Worldwide&chartType=map&year=2010&data_type=number&religious_affiliation=23&age_group=all (accessed on 10 October 2014).

PM India. 2016. 'PM's Address to the Nation from the Ramparts of the Red Fort on 70th Independence Day'. Available at: http://www.pmindia.gov.in/en/news_updates/preliminary-text-of-prime-minister-shri-narendra-modis-address-to-the-nation-from-the-ramparts-of-the-red-fort-on-the-70th-independence-day/?comment=disable (accessed on16 August 2016).

PM India. 2019. 'PM's Address at Joint Session of Parliament on 70th Constitution Day'. Available at: https://www.pmindia.gov.in/en/news_updates/pms-address-at-joint-session-of-parliament-on-70th-constitution-day/?comment=disable (accessed on 24 February 2021).

PM India. 2020. 'PM Addresses United Nations General Assembly'. Available at: https://www.pmindia.gov.in/en/news_updates/pm-addresses-united-nations-general-assembly/?comment=disable (accessed on 24 February 2021).

Prasad, S.N. and U.P. Thapliyal. 2011. *The India–Pakistan War of 1965: A History*. New Delhi and Dehradun: Ministry of Defence and Natraj Publishers.

Rashtriya Swayamsevak Sangh. 2020. 'Address by Param Poojaniya Sarsanghchalak Dr. Shri Mohan ji Bhagwat on the Occasion of Sri Vijayadashami Utsav 2020'. Available at: https://www.rss.org/Vijayadashami_Speech_2020_Eng.pdf (accessed on 26 February 2021).

Roy, Shubhajit. 2016. 'Centre Planning to Call Diaspora from Gilgit-Baltistan for Pravasi Divas 2017'. *The Indian Express*, New Delhi, 27 August.

Samanta, Pranab Dhal. 2014. 'Line of No Control'. *India Today*, 22 August.

Savarkar, V.D. 1922. *Essentials of Hindutva*. Available at: http://library.bjp.org/jspui/bitstream/123456789/284/3/essentials_of_hindutva.v001.pdf (accessed on 23 February 2021).

Singh, Manmohan. 2006. 'PM's Speech on Launch of Amritsar–Nankana Sahib Bus Service'. Available at: https://archivepmo.nic.in/drmanmohansingh/speech-details.php?nodeid=293 (accessed on 28 November 2018).

Singh, Manmohan. 2013. 'Statement in the General Debate of the 68th Session of the UNGA'. Available at: http://mea.gov.in/Speeches-Statements.htm?dtl/22267/Prime+Ministers+statement+in+the+General+Debate+of+the+68th+Session+of+the+UNGA (accessed 21 May 2014).

Singh, Priyanka. 2011. 'Jaish-e-Mohammed'. In *Non-State Armed Groups in South Asia: A Preliminary Structured Focused Comparison*, edited by Arpita Anant, 232–244. New Delhi: Pentagon Press.

Singh, Sushant and Shubhajit Roy. 2018. 'Pakistan Elections 2018: Fingers Crossed in Delhi, Mission was in Touch with Team Imran'. *The Indian Express*, New Delhi, 27 July.

Singh, Vijaita. 2016. 'In a First, PoK Becomes PoJK in MHA Document'. *The Hindu*, New Delhi, 25 March.

South Asia Terrorism Portal. 'Parliament Resolution on Jammu and Kashmir'. Available at: http://www.satp.org/satporgtp/countries/india/document/papers/parliament_resolution_on_Jammu_and_Kashmir.htm (accessed on 2 May 2016).

Tankel, Stephen. 2009. 'Lashkar-e-Taiba: From 9/11 to Mumbai'. *Developments in Radicalisation and Political Violence*. London: The International Center for the Study of Radicalisation and Political Violence.

Tankel, Stephen. 2011. 'Lashkar-e-Taiba: Past Operations and Future Prospects'. *National Security Studies Program Policy Paper*. Washington D.C.: New America Foundation.

Tankel, Stephen. 2018. 'Ten Years After Mumbai, the Group Responsible is Deadlier Than Ever'. *War on the Rocks*. Available at: https://warontherocks.com/2018/11/ten-years-after-mumbai-the-group-responsible-is-deadlier-than-ever/ (accessed on 2 December 2018).

Tellis, Ashley J. 1997. *Stability in South Asia*. Santa Monica, CA: RAND.

Tellis, Ashley J. 2012. 'The Menace That Is Lashkar-e-Taiba'. *Policy Outlook*. Washington D.C.: Carnegie Endowment for International Peace.

Tellis, Ashley J. 2017. 'Are India–Pakistan Peace Talks Worth a Damn?'. Washington D.C.: Carnegie Endowment for International Peace.

The Constitution of Jammu and Kashmir. 1956. Available at: http://jklegislativeassembly.nic.in/Costitution_of_J&K.pdf (accessed on 8 July 2015).

Times of India. 2014. 'Text of RSS Chief Mohan Bhagwat's Vijayadashami Speech'. *The Times of India*, 3 October.

Times of India. 2019. 'Any Talks with Pak Now Will Only Be on PoK: Rajnath Singh'. *The Times of India*, Kalka, 19 August.

Times of India. 2019. 'One Surgical Strike Won't Make Pakistan Fall in Line: PM Narendra Modi'. *The Times of India*, New Delhi, 2 January.

Tiwary, Deeptiman. 2020. 'Pulwama Attackers Wanted Strike to Spark India–Pak War: NIA Chargesheet'. *The Indian Express*, New Delhi, 26 August.

United States Department of State. 1993. 'Address by President Bill Clinton to the UN General Assembly'. Available at: https://2009-2017.state.gov/p/io/potusunga/207375.htm (accessed on 26 March 2021).

Vadlapatla, Sribala. 2021. 'Akhand Bharat Possible, Will be Good for Pakistan, Says Bhagwat'. *The Times of India*, Hyderabad, 26 February.

Vaidya, Abhay. 2014. 'The Robin Raphel Saga: What Happened in Washington That Soured Indo-US Ties'. *First Post*, 11 November.

Vaidya, Manmohan. 2019. 'Bharat's Identity is Intrinsically Tied with the Eternal Philosophy of Hindutva'. *The Indian Express*, 8 May.

Yadav, Shyamlal. 2019. 'Explained: How PoK Has Featured in RSS, Jana Sangh Discourse for Nearly 7 Decades'. *The Indian Express*, New Delhi, 12 August.

Zahab, Mariam Abou. 2002. 'The Regional Dimension of Sectarian Conflicts in Pakistan'. In *Pakistan: Nationalism Without a Nation*, edited by Christophe Jaffrelot, 115–130. New Delhi: Manohar.

3

The Half War of 1947–1948

'We were promised peace if we accepted Partition!' observed Deputy Prime Minister Vallabhbhai Patel in the wake of the catastrophic communal violence unleashed by the division of Punjab into Indian and Pakistani portions (Brecher 1998, 376). For his part, Jawaharlal Nehru had asserted two months earlier that '[p]artition is better than [the] murder of innocent citizens' in the communal riots then raging in parts of Bengal, Bihar, and Punjab (Iyengar 2007, 201).[1] At first glance, these statements may appear limited to the communal violence angle. But they did also reflect the larger reasons that impelled Patel and Nehru to accept India's partition in the name of the two-nation theory—something which they did not believe in or subscribe to. As Nehru later observed, '[w]e [the Congress leadership] consented [to Partition] because we thought that thereby we were purchasing peace and goodwill, though at a high price' (Brecher 1998, 374). Embedded in this reasoning was also the fear that an 'artificial and enforced unity' would result in 'a tragic civil war' and derail India's progress and the project of building a strong India (Brecher 1998, 376–377).[2]

The peace and goodwill that the Indian leadership expected to ensue in the wake of Partition and the creation of Pakistan remained a mere hope. Within a few weeks, the two countries became embroiled in a series of disputes over the status of the princely states of Junagadh, Hyderabad, and Jammu and Kashmir. A direct armed conflict between them over Junagadh and Hyderabad was impossible because the former was a coastal state that shared a border only with India, and the latter was completely surrounded by Indian territory (Raghavan 2010, 26–100). However, that was not the case with Jammu and Kashmir, which shared borders with both countries. As a result, an armed conflict over Jammu and Kashmir did ensue in October 1947. This conflict was the formative experience that subsequently determined India's defence policy and strategy towards Pakistan.

The Backdrop

The origins and persistence of the Kashmir issue lay in the decisions and approaches of five actors—Britain, India, Pakistan, Maharaja of Kashmir, and Sheikh Abdullah. The roots of the India–Pakistan conflict over Jammu and Kashmir lie in the British decision to divide India into two states based on communal considerations. Two factors emerged from this decision, which eventually led to the conflict over Jammu and Kashmir. The first is Pakistan's claim that Muslim-majority Jammu and Kashmir should accede to it in accordance with the two-nation theory as well as owing to the geographical contiguity (Fair and Ganguly 2013, 176–179). What made Pakistan's contention possible was the British decision of not transferring the paramountcy enjoyed by the Raj over the princely states to the successor governments. Second, the conflict over Jammu and Kashmir was a consequence of the indeterminate legal status into which India's princely states were thrown when Britain wound up its Raj in India. When it decided to grant independence to India, the British government declared that it 'will not in any circumstances transfer' the paramount power it enjoyed over the princely states to a successor government. Instead, British paramountcy over the princely states would simply lapse, meaning that all the rights that the princely states had surrendered to the Raj—the paramount power—'will return to the states'. Consequently, the extant '[p]olitical arrangements between the States on the one side and the British Crown and British India on the other will thus be brought to an end' (Mansergh 1978, 522–523).[3]

Despite that declaration, the British Cabinet Mission to India in 1946 envisaged at the same time a 'Union of India embracing both British India and the [Princely] States' to deal with foreign affairs, defence, and communications, but guided by the caveat that the princely states 'will retain all subjects and powers other than those ceded to the Union' (Mansergh 1978, 587).[4] Although the Indian National Congress and the Muslim League rejected the Cabinet Mission's proposals on Indian independence, the Mission's stated position on the future disposition of the princely states became the basis for ordering the post-Raj relationship between the princely states and the two successor dominions of India and Pakistan. The British government acknowledged this position in the 3 June 1947 plan on the basis of which India was partitioned and Pakistan created. The 3 June plan specifically declared that the envisaged partition of India does not extend to the princely states and that Britain's 'policy towards Indian States contained in the Cabinet Mission Memorandum of 12th May 1946 remains unchanged' (Moon 1982, 93).[5]

An arrangement of the sort that prevailed during colonial rule was indeed necessary, given that the British Raj had evolved as a single economic unit with common customs, transit and communications, posts and telegraphs, etc., under a system of coordinated administration on all matters of common concern. This was largely a result of the crown representative to the princely states and the viceroy of the British-ruled territories having been one and the same person. With the severance of the British link, an alternative mechanism had to be put in place to avoid chaos, which would affect the princely states first and foremost. Moreover, the territories of practically all princely states, barring Jammu and Kashmir, were encompassed within, or exclusively contiguous to, the envisaged territories of India and Pakistan. Hence, as pointed out by Mountbatten in his July 1947 address to the Chamber of Princes, they would not be able to evade 'certain geographical compulsions' (Carter 2003, 381–385).[6]

Only two among these more than 500 princely states—Junagadh and Hyderabad—sought to evade these geographical compulsions, though unsuccessfully because the former shared a border only with India and the latter was completely surrounded by Indian territory (Guha 2007, 36).[7] Jammu and Kashmir stood in a category of its own, given that it shared borders with both India and Pakistan as well as with Afghanistan and China. In addition, a Hindu maharaja, Hari Singh, ruled over a population that then comprised a little over 77 per cent of Muslims. Moreover, Sheikh Abdullah—the leader of the National Conference, Hari Singh's political nemesis, and the most popular leader in the state—sent out confusing messages. In a rally in Srinagar on 2 October 1947, Abdullah proclaimed the slogan of 'freedom before accession' (Abdullah 1993, 86). At another public meeting, Abdullah referred to his role as the president of the All India States Peoples' Conference and its policy of accession to India, his friendship with Nehru, his respect for Gandhi and the full support extended by the Congress to the Kashmiri movement, but then went on to say that

> the question of accession will be decided in the best interests of the people of Kashmir. Our first priority is to get rid of the Dogra domination. Then if the people decide to accede to Pakistan, I will be the first one to sign my name. (Abdullah 1993, 86)

Yet, he went on to declare that even if Kashmir accedes to Pakistan, Kashmiris 'shall never support the two-nation theory' (Abdullah 1993, 86).

Hari Singh found himself on the horns of a dilemma. Acceding to India was an attractive option, given his religious persuasion and family antecedents. But it meant an inevitable loss of power, given the Congress Party's socio-political inclinations and Nehru's close friendship with Sheikh Abdullah. Similarly, accession to Pakistan was also marked by mixed fortunes. Pakistani leaders had assured Hari Singh that they would respect his internal sovereignty. At the same time, the maharaja had also received pledges of loyalty from both the leaders of the Jammu and Kashmir Muslim Conference and the chieftains of outlying territories such as Chitral, Hunza, etc. But some of these pledges soon turned into threats of military invasion, as happened in the case of the Mehtar of Chitral and the Nawab of Dir (Mahajan 1963, 130; Jha 2003, 55–56). Moreover, the extreme emotions evoked by the prevalent communal polarisation compelled Hari Singh to seriously consider three other unwelcome possibilities: his Hindu subjects becoming targets of violence, communal disturbances bringing his government machinery to a grinding halt and rendering his rule untenable, and Pakistan divesting him of his rule over a Muslim-majority population (Jha 2003, 46, 54–58; Birdwood 2005, 53–54; Mahajan 1963, 130, 144; Hodson 1985, 445).

Under these circumstances, remaining independent appeared to be an attractive option. But an independent Jammu and Kashmir was unacceptable to almost every other actor in this drama—the Congress party, the Muslim League, the British viceroy, and the government in London. Congress leaders had conveyed to Mountbatten that they were against an independent Jammu and Kashmir but that they would neither regard the state's accession to Pakistan as an unfriendly act nor raise objections in that regard (Sarila 2005, 343–344). Conveying this message to the state's leadership, Mountbatten urged the maharaja and his prime minister to ascertain the will of the people with regard to whether the state should accede to India or Pakistan (Moon 1982, 194–195). For their part, Pakistani leaders did not conceive of an independent Jammu and Kashmir because the country's 'very name and concept … included Kashmir as an integral part' (Ali 1967, 283). The British government in London was also against an independent Jammu and Kashmir. While Prime Minister Clement Attlee stated in the House of Commons that all princely states 'will, in due course, find their appropriate place within one or the other of the new Dominions', his secretary of state, Lord Listowel, informed the House of Lords that the British government 'do not, of course, propose to recognise any [Princely] States as separate international entities' (Gupta 1966, 76–77).

Thus, finding himself checkmated at every turn, Hari Singh dithered and sought to maintain the status quo through standstill agreements with both India and Pakistan. While Pakistan conveyed its consent to this arrangement, India invited the maharaja to either visit New Delhi himself or send a representative for the purpose of negotiating a standstill agreement in accordance with its declared policy of 'no standstill agreement without accession' (Menon 1956, 114, 317–336).[8]

Indian Approach to Jammu and Kashmir

As they awaited Hari Singh's final decision, India and Pakistan adopted contrasting approaches towards Jammu and Kashmir. Indian leaders found themselves in an especially delicate situation. They wanted Hari Singh to accede to India, on the one hand, but insisted that he arrive at a *modus vivendi* with Sheikh Abdullah and his National Conference, on the other. Patel, for instance, assured Hari Singh that neither the Congress nor Nehru were his enemy and stressed that the state's interests lay in joining the Indian Union (Das 1970, 33). And he repeatedly advocated the release of Sheikh Abdullah so that the maharaja would gain popular support. Patel advocated this position even on the eve of the tribal raid, when he urged the state's Prime

Minister Mehr Chand Mahajan to make 'a substantial gesture to win Abdullah's support' and, thus, be in a strong position to 'crush the disruptive forces which are being raised and organised' by Pakistan (Das 1970, 32, 62). Nehru, as is well known, also advocated a similar course of action. By late September 1947, he had become aware of the preparations being made in Pakistan to militarily wrest Jammu and Kashmir after the onset of winter severed the state's communication links with India. Expressing his apprehension in this regard to Patel, Nehru noted that Hari Singh had no choice but to release Sheikh Abdullah and other leaders of the National Conference to gain popular support, seek their cooperation, and 'declare adhesion to the Indian Union' (Das 1970, 37–43; Mahajan 1963, 127).

For the Indian leadership, the task at hand was a delicate one given the twin imperatives of supporting the maharaja and his government, on the one hand, and convincing him of the need to accommodate Sheikh Abdullah and the popular National Conference he led, on the other. Patel, responsible for dealing with the princely states in his capacity as minister for home affairs, sought to coax and cajole the maharaja and his Cabinet into adopting a more favourable view of India. For this purpose, in addition to welcoming the various political steps taken by the maharaja, Patel also expedited the provision of practical help sought by the state, especially after violence broke out in the Poonch district and the state authorities began to accuse Pakistan of providing assistance to 'evilly-disposed persons' (Korbel 1966, 67).[9] Thus, work on the establishment and improvement of road, air, and telecommunications between Jammu and Kashmir and India began to be expedited. In addition, India loaned a sitting high court judge to serve as the state's prime minister as well as a serving lieutenant colonel to command the state forces (Das 1970, 37–43; Mahajan 1963, 127). But on the crucial issue of military supplies, Patel's efforts were thwarted by British military officers then serving at the helm of India's armed forces as well as by the Supreme Headquarters, which was then in the process of overseeing the division of the armed forces and the movement of respective national units between the two dominions (Jha 2003, 197–205).[10]

What the Indian leadership thereby sought was to strengthen the maharaja's hands by providing practical assistance even as it sought to impress upon him the imperative of politically accommodating Sheikh Abdullah, which would boost the ability to deal with the emerging threat from Pakistan. Further, they also reckoned that the growing evidence of Pakistani support for the violence in Poonch combined with Abdullah's favourable inclinations towards India would enable Hari Singh to shed his diffidence and decide upon acceding to the Indian Union.

The Poonch Rebellion

Pakistani leaders were utterly convinced that Jammu and Kashmir had to accede to their dominion. Given, however, Hari Singh's indecision and concerned about his inclination to opt for accession to India, Pakistan decided to force the maharaja's hand. An opportunity for exerting pressure presented itself when popular disaffection rose in Jammu and Kashmir's Poonch province.

Poonch was a poor region, and, consequently, military service was one of the principal avenues of employment for its residents. During the Second World War, some 70,000 out of a total population of 400,000 served in the British Indian Army. At the end of the war, nearly 60,000 of these soldiers were rapidly demobilised. Upon returning home, they discovered that several new taxes had been imposed, which resulted in economic hardship. There are two contrasting views on these new taxes. Richard Symonds, a refugee worker who travelled to Poonch via Rawalpindi in November 1947 under Nehru's express permission, was informed by the rebels that 'some' of these taxes 'applied to Muslims only' (Symonds 2001, 74–79). Pointing out that there is neither any mention of Muslim-specific taxes in the reports of British officials nor any contemporary references to them, Prem Shankar Jha posits that the rebels must have misrepresented the issue to Symonds (Jha 2003, 19).

Even as resentment began to simmer, Sardar Ibrahim Khan, a member of the Muslim Conference that advocated accession to Pakistan, travelled to Pakistan sometime in August 1947. In the next few weeks, he established contact with Pakistani leaders, including Prime Minister Liaquat Ali Khan, and sought military assistance for initiating an armed struggle (Korbel 1966, 67; Lamb 2000, 124; Khan 2002, 11).

At the time Ibrahim Khan was doing the rounds in Pakistan, a party of about 30 Pakistani nationals infiltrated Poonch towards the end of August 1947 and began to incite the people to agitate against the maharaja and in favour of accession to Pakistan. Major General Scott, the then commander of the Jammu and Kashmir State Forces, recorded that this resulted in a march undertaken by about 10,000 locals towards Poonch town in early September. The protestors aired their grievances, particularly with regard to high food prices, and also raised slogans demanding the state's accession to Pakistan. While dispersing the protest, Scott's troops killed 20 protestors. Thereupon, Sardar Abdul Qayyum Khan, a principal organiser of the protest, and three others fled to the mountains and set about organising a resistance movement there. Scott recorded that there was no further trouble in Poonch until the end of his tenure on 29 September 1947 (Dasgupta 2002, 39–40; Jha 2003, 18–20; Symonds 2001, 79).

Pakistan's Coercion of Jammu and Kashmir

In the meantime, Ibrahim Khan's plea for help had led to two key meetings in Lahore on 12 September 1947. The first was in the office of Sardar Shaukat Hayat Khan, a minister in Punjab's provincial government; and the second at the residence of Prime Minister Liaquat Ali Khan. The aim of these meetings was to chart a course of military action in Jammu and Kashmir in order to—in the words of a prominent Muslim League leader Mian Iftikharuddin—'prevent the State's accession to India' (Raghavan 2010, 105). What Iftikharuddin left unsaid was that Jammu and Kashmir was to be prevented from acceding to India by overthrowing Hari Singh's government and engineering the state's forcible accession to Pakistan.

Two different plans were discussed at these meetings. Akbar Khan, who was then director of weapons and equipment at General Headquarters in Rawalpindi, had prepared one of these, titled *Armed Revolt in Kashmir*, at the express request of Mian Iftikharuddin. Assuming that it would be undesirable for Pakistan to overtly and militarily interfere in Jammu and Kashmir, Akbar Khan proposed that Kashmiris be strengthened internally and, at the same time, efforts be made to block the routes through which India could provide military assistance to Hari Singh's government. In the event, Akbar Khan's plan was not approved, and he was assigned the limited task of making available rifles and ammunition from the military stock for the proposed action. Instead, the choice fell on the second plan presented that day by Sardar Shaukat Hayat Khan of the Punjab provincial government. Hayat Khan envisaged the employment of two groups under his overall command. One group, composed of former Indian National Army (INA) personnel, was to operate across the Punjab border. And the other, composed of tribal *lashkars* from the North-West Frontier Province, was to operate north of Rawalpindi (Khan 2002, 10–20; Lamb 2000, 125; Jha 2003, 25–31).[11]

Pakistani irregulars had resumed raiding Kashmir since early September, and by the start of October, they were better equipped with light machine guns (LMGs) and wireless sets, besides being assisted by batches of the Pakistani Army (Prasad and Pal 2005, 13–14). Pakistan also began to impose an economic blockade on Jammu and Kashmir at the same time, holding up supplies of rice, wheat, salt, cloth, and petrol. When Kashmir authorities complained, Pakistan accused them of carrying out atrocities against Muslims. On 15 October, the Kashmir state also wrote to Prime Minister Attlee detailing these happenings and requesting him to advise Pakistan to treat Kashmir with fairness and justice (Prasad and Pal 2005, 15). Even as letters were exchanged between Pakistan and Kashmir, Pakistan continued invading Jammu and Kashmir.

This Pakistani invasion, wrongly termed the tribal raid, began on the night of 21–22 October 1947. The invasion, code-named 'Operation Gulmarg', was meticulously planned by the Pakistan Army Headquarters and authorised by the commander-in-chief of the Pakistan Army (Prasad and Pal 2005, 17). The operation entailed every Pathan tribe to enlist at least one *lashkar* of 1,000 men and concentrate at Bannu, Wana, Peshawar, Kohat, Thal, and Nowshera by the first week of September 1947, where they were provided with a major, a captain, and 10 Junior Commissioned Officers (JCOs), with the major serving as adviser to the tribal Malik, the captain as staff officer, and the JCOs leading groups of the *lashkars*, besides being responsible for arms, ammunition, and clothing. The whole tribal force was led by Major General Akbar Khan, operating under the code name Tariq, with the assistance of Brigadier Sher Khan (Prasad and Pal 2005, 18).[12] Since there was no pro-Pakistan sentiment in the valley, Pakistan decided to launch an open invasion 'along the main highway linking Rawalpindi to Srinagar via the towns of Domel and Muzaffarabad' (Dasgupta 2002, 40). The broad outline of 'Operation Gulmarg' was (Prasad and Pal 2005, 18–19):

1. Six of the *lashkar*s to advance along the main road from Muzaffarabad to Srinagar via Domel, Uri, and Baramulla, capture the aerodrome, and then advance to the Banihal Pass.
2. Two *lashkar*s to advance from Haji Pir Pass to Gulmarg, thus securing the right flank of the main force moving towards Srinagar.
3. Two *lashkar*s to advance from Tithwal through Nastachhun Pass to capture Sopore, Handwara, and Bandipur, thus covering the left flank of the main force advancing to Srinagar; and
4. Ten *lashkar*s to operate in the Poonch, Bhimbar, and Rawalkot area, capture Poonch and Rajouri and advance to Jammu.

All the tribal *lashkar*s, totalling 5,000, concentrated in Abbottabad by 18 October. Alongside, the 7th Infantry Division of the Pakistan Army moved into the Murree–Abbottabad area by last light on 21 October to move in and back up the *lashkar*s and consolidate their hold on the valley. An infantry brigade was, in addition, held ready at Sialkot to move into Jammu (Prasad and Pal 2005, 19). Finally, the D-Day arrived. The raiders quickly took Muzaffarabad and then the town of Uri. With Baramulla falling on the fourth day, the road to Srinagar was open.

India's Incompatible Political Aims: Rescue Jammu and Kashmir but Avoid Open War with Pakistan

In response to a plea for help from Hari Singh and after obtaining his formal accession to the Union, India despatched a military rescue mission to Jammu and Kashmir (Jha 2003, 64–85). The Indian Army, with the vital support provided by the Indian Air Force, succeeded in thwarting the irregulars' bid to capture Srinagar and even pushed them back to a limited extent. But it was unable to quickly establish full control over the state's territory both in the Kashmir sector, where it had initially concentrated its efforts, as well as in Jammu province and Gilgit Agency, the other two sectors of the state where Pakistani irregulars were active.

Frustrated by the lack of progress and even some inevitable reverses suffered in December 1947, Prime Minister Nehru began to contemplate military strikes against the bases and lines of communication of the irregulars in Pakistani territory. At one point, he even asked the chiefs of staff to consider Kashmir and the Pakistani province of West Punjab as a single theatre (Dasgupta 2002, 98–99). But such an expansion of the conflict was resisted by both the then Governor-General Lord Mountbatten and the British officers then serving at the helm of the armed services. Along with the British government in London, they wished to prevent open war between two members of the Commonwealth, which would have an inevitable adverse impact on Britain's geopolitical interests. Indeed, Mountbatten was keen to bring to an early stop even the fighting between the Indian Army and the Pakistani irregulars. For that purpose, he advocated that India and Pakistan jointly approach the United Nations (UN) and, under its auspices, forge an agreement on holding the plebiscite that Nehru had promised for ascertaining the will of the people on the maharaja's accession to the Union. When that tack failed to gain purchase, he suggested that India make a unilateral appeal to the UN Security Council with a request that Pakistan be directed to stop supporting the irregulars (Dasgupta 2002, 45, 51, 70–85, 92, 97–99, 174).

Mountbatten's insistent appeals did have an impact on Nehru's 'strong sense of moral efficacy' (Kennedy 2012, 199)[13] and on his determination to 'do our utmost to avoid' a war in which, even though Pakistan would be defeated, India would also 'suffer very great injury' (Raghavan 2010, 121). Consequently, he decided to take the issue to the United Nations in the form of a complaint against Pakistan's support for the irregulars. This, Nehru did in the belief that the UN would take an impartial view of the matter and accept the essential correctness of the Indian position. He further believed that the UN's direction would provide Pakistani leaders the necessary excuse for winding down their support to the irregulars. In essence, Nehru sought to enlist the UN Security Council's 'cooperation in pressuring Pakistan to terminate its support' for the irregulars (Kennedy 2012, 179–186).

Mahatma Gandhi, Sardar Patel, and G.S. Bajpai were opposed to such a course of action. In fact, Patel was against the proposal from the outset as he was convinced that India would not 'accomplish much at the United Nations'. He, instead, advocated for 'timely action' on the ground to swiftly bring the matter in India's favour (Kennedy 2012, 183; Gandhi 2013, 448). Patel did not attend the 28 December 1947 meeting of the Cabinet, which approved the text of the letter to the UN Security Council. Later in a note to the British parliamentarian Arthur Henderson in July 1948, Patel said,

> I myself felt that we should never have gone to the UNO, and if we had taken timely action when we went to the UNO, we could have settled the whole case much more quickly and satisfactorily from our point of view, whereas at the UNO not only has the dispute been prolonged, but the merits of our case have been completely lost in the interaction of power politics. (Kennedy 2012, 183)

Jayaprakash Narayan would later say that many leaders believed Patel would have never internationalised the Kashmir issue. Mahatma Gandhi reluctantly consented to Nehru's proposal but not before removing reference to an independent Kashmir as a possible option to accession to either India or Pakistan in India's complaint to the United Nations (Gandhi 2013, 449). Bajpai also argued against reference to the United Nations, citing unsatisfactory results of previous such appeals (Kennedy 2012, 184).

Although, at the same time, Nehru had asked the military leadership to prepare contingency plans for evicting the irregulars from their bases in Pakistan, his contemplation of the idea of taking the war into Pakistani territory was borne out of a mixture of frustration at the lack of progress being made by the army and the anxiety caused by certain setbacks it suffered. Consequently, when the military situation stabilised soon thereafter, he shrank back from expanding the conflict (Raghavan 2010, 123–124). The UN Security Council's subsequent statements and resolutions, which called upon both India and Pakistan to refrain from actions that would aggravate the situation and to take a series of steps for restoring peace and order to enable the holding of a plebiscite,[14] only served to reinforce Nehru's as well as Patel's 'limited sense of martial efficacy' in terms of adopting a cautious approach that did not involve what Patel characterised as an 'unwise' attack upon Pakistan (Kennedy 2012, 191–200).[15]

Nehru was 'anxious to avoid war with Pakistan'. In a letter to the premiers of the provinces on 2 November 1947, he wrote 'War is a dangerous thing and must be avoided'. While Pakistan would be defeated, India would also 'suffer very great injury'. He insisted that '[w]e must do our utmost to avoid war, and this is our definite policy' (Raghavan 2010, 121).

Nehru also wrongly assessed India's ability to win a quick and decisive victory in Kashmir. Therefore, despite India's military superiority over Pakistan, Nehru agreed with Archibald Nye, British high commissioner, that India had extremely 'limited military opportunity in the fall of 1948'. Patel also agreed with Roy Bucher, commander-in-chief of the Indian Army, that war with Pakistan carried an 'unacceptable risk of escalation', and India faced a 'stalemate' (Kennedy 2012, 197–198; Raghavan 2010, 142).

A further cause of Indian caution was Pakistan's induction of its regular troops into parts of Jammu and Kashmir in Spring 1948 to backstop the activities of the irregulars. Pakistan had deployed forces in Kashmir by April 1948. In July 1948, Nehru came to realise that 'very large forces of Pakistan regular army' was operating in Kashmir, and, by August, he estimated that two divisions of the Pakistani Army were operating in Kashmir, which was roughly equal to the Indian strength in the state (Gopal 1988, 284).

Muddle of a Strategy

India's pursuit of such an incompatible set of political aims—evicting Pakistani guerrillas but avoiding open war with Pakistan and even direct military engagements with Pakistani troops in the territory of Jammu and Kashmir, on the one hand, and consolidating Jammu and Kashmir's accession to the Indian Union but subject the accession to a plebiscite, on the other—had an inevitable impact upon the strategy it attempted to craft for dealing with what was a half war.

The consequence of all this was India's inability to craft a clear strategy for prosecuting the conflict. And in the absence of a strategy to wage either a full-scale war or even a limited war against Pakistan, Indian military operations simply attempted to push the irregulars as far back as possible, prevent them from occupying new areas, and relieve besieged towns. For these purposes, the army, ably supported by the air force, undertook offensive thrusts in all three sectors—Jammu, Kashmir, and Ladakh—of the state. The first phase of these thrusts occurred in the immediate aftermath of saving Srinagar from the irregulars in the form of a successful advance to Baramulla and Uri. Partly because of the setting in of winter, which prevented major operations in Kashmir, and partly because of the political leadership's insistence, the army subsequently shifted its focus to the relief of besieged towns in Jammu province. Six of these towns were relieved, but Mirpur fell to the irregulars, who also foiled the bid to relieve Poonch. Jhangar was also captured by the irregulars in December 1947, but this town as well as Rajauri were subsequently secured by the Indian Army in March of the following year. The first phase of operations also saw Leh being secured, although the attempt to relieve Skardu was foiled by the irregulars. While Skardu finally fell in August 1948, the rest of the Gilgit Agency had already come under the control of Pakistan long before that.

The next phase of operations during the course of 1948 also saw a similar effort to push the Pakistani irregulars further back, prevent them from occupying new areas, and relieve the remaining besieged towns. In the Kashmir sector, an advance was undertaken towards Gurais and Domel. While the former was secured and thereby the developing threat to Srinagar neutralised, the advance to Domel encountered fierce resistance, including one from a regular Pakistani division. Although the Indian government called off this offensive because of the impending arrival of the United Nations Commission for India and Pakistan (UNCIP) team to the subcontinent, it permitted the initiation of two localised operations: the capture of Kargil and the subsequent link-up with Leh; and the relief of Poonch (Sinha 1977, passim; Prasad and Pal 2005, passim). When the ceasefire took effect on 1 January 1949, India had gained control over only about two-thirds of Jammu and Kashmir's territory.

Attrition as the Indian Army's Doctrine

The doctrine employed by the army in these operations was that of attrition. Hence the methodical advance from the outskirts of Srinagar to Baramulla, then on to Uri in November–December 1947, and the subsequent push towards Domel in the summer of 1948. Even more tellingly, the link-up with Poonch envisaged six distinct phases—'capture of Pir Badesar, concentration of troops at Rajauri, capture of Pir Kalewa, capture of Sangiot, break-out from Sangiot and the link-up with Punch, [and] reorganisation including construction of a jeep track to Punch' (Sinha 1977, 97). Mountainous terrain, which made manoeuvre impossible, reinforced the army's preference for attrition by necessitating frontal assaults against dominating positions, as witnessed during the forcing of the Zoji La Pass with the help of tanks (Prasad and Pal 2005, 353–358).

Role of the Indian Air Force

For its part, the fledgling air force, consisting of a mere eight squadrons and not directly confronting its Pakistani counterpart, did not employ any specific doctrine. But it did play a vital role in ably supporting the army and providing relief to besieged towns. In the process, the air force carried out a series of critical missions, including ground interdiction of the Pakistani irregulars, armed reconnaissance, close air support for the army's operations, and transportation (Singh 2013, 54–65).

Summary

The half war of 1947–1948 saw an experience of an incompatible set of political aims that led to India's inability to strategise a full-scale war. Consequently, the military operations simply attempted to push back the irregulars and prevent them from occupying new territory. The operations successfully employed the doctrine of attrition, and it proved to be the army's preference in the mountainous terrain. The fledgling air force provided vital air support for the army operations. With the arrival of the United Nations, a ceasefire took effect and only two-thirds of Jammu and Kashmir could be taken under the control of the Indian government. From the Indian point of view, Kashmir is an integral part of the national territory. Since 1948, the efforts of Indian leadership to settle the issue on the basis of the extant status quo, with minor readjustments to establish a rational border, have been unacceptable to Pakistan. The experience of the half war and the persistence of the conflict present a clear sense of the road travelled, thereby providing a strong basis for determining India's defence policy and strategy towards Pakistan.

Notes

1 Nehru's speech at the All India Congress Committee meeting on 15 June 1947 on the Congress Working Committee resolution accepting the 3 June Partition statement. Reprinted as 'The Unavoidability of Partition,' in *The Oxford India Nehru*, ed., Uma Iyengar (New Delhi: Oxford University Press, 2007), p. 201.

2 Brecher, *Nehru*, pp. 376–377. For a discussion on the various reasons that Nehru later cited for accepting Partition, see *idem*., pp. 374–380.

3 'Memorandum on States' Treaties and Paramountcy Presented by the Cabinet Mission to the Nawab of Bhopal on 12 May 1946,' reprinted in *Constitutional Relations Between Britain and India, The Transfer of Power 1942-7. Vol. VII: The Cabinet Mission 23 March–29 June 1946*, ed., Nicholas Mansergh (London: Her Majesty's Stationery Office, 1978), pp. 522–523.

4 'Statement by the Cabinet Delegation and His Excellency the Viceroy (as issued in New Delhi on 16 May 1946),' reprinted in *The Transfer of Power 1942–7. Vol. VII*, p. 587.

5 'Statement of 3 June 1947 (as published),' reprinted in *Constitutional Relations Between Britain and India, The Transfer of Power 1942–7. Vol. XI: The Mountbatten Viceroyalty: Announcement and Reception of*

the 3rd June Plan 31 May–7 July 1947, ed. Penderel Moon (London: Her Majesty's Stationery Office, 1982), p. 93.

6 The text of Mountbatten's 25 July 1947 'Address to a Special Full Meeting of the Chamber of Princes' can be found as Appendix X in *Mountbatten's Report on the Last Viceroyalty: 22 March–15 August 1947*, ed., Lionel Carter (New Delhi: Manohar, 2003), pp. 381–385.

7 Historians disagree as to the actual number of princely states, with some putting the figure at 521 and others at 565. Ramachandra Guha (2007, 36).

8 The only exception that India made in this regard was with respect to Hyderabad, although this particular standstill agreement was signed on 29 November 1947 after protracted negotiations. V.P. Menon (1956, 114, 317–336).

9 The quoted phrase is from a statement on the unrest in Poonch issued under the Maharaja's name on 12 September 1947. Cited in Josef Korbel (1966, 67).

10 This emerges clearly in the Minutes of the Eighth Meeting of the Indian Defence Committee of the Cabinet held on 25 October 1947. The minutes are reprinted as Appendix in Prem Shankar Jha, *The Origins of a Dispute: Kashmir 1947*, pp. 197–205; the reference to military supplies can be found on p. 199.

11 This narrative is drawn from Akbar Khan, *Raiders in Kashmir,* op. cit., pp. 10–20. Akbar Khan does not give dates in his book. The date mentioned here is drawn from Alastair Lamb, *Incomplete Partition*, op. cit., p. 125. Lamb, however, draws the rather limited conclusion that this meeting only served to shape the contacts that subsequently evolved between certain influential official and unofficial Pakistanis and the Poonch rebels. Also see, Prem Shankar Jha, *The Origins of a Dispute: Kashmir 1947*, pp. 25–31.

12 Akbar Khan's HQ was in the same building from which the C-in-C of Pakistan Army functioned. S.N. Prasad and Dharam Pal, *History of Operations in Jammu and Kashmir (1947–48)*, p. 18.

13 Andrew Bingham Kennedy (2012, 199). Kennedy defines moral efficacy as 'the ability to elicit cooperation from other states through diplomacy'. See, *idem.*, p. 4.

14 On the UN Security Council's initiatives and on the British UN representative Philip Noel-Baker's manoeuvres in New York, see Dasgupta (2002, 110–132).

15 Kennedy, *International Ambitions of Mao and Nehru*, pp. 191–200; the quoted phrase and word can be respectively found on pp. 198 and 200.

Kennedy defines martial efficacy as 'the ability to overcome material disadvantages on the battlefield'. See, *idem.*, p. 4.

References

Abdullah, Sheikh Mohammad. 1993. *Flames of the Chinar: An Autobiography*, 86. New Delhi: Viking.

Ali, Chaudhri Muhammad. 1967. *The Emergence of Pakistan*. New York: Columbia University Press.

Birdwood, Lord. 2005. *Two Nations and Kashmir*. Srinagar: Gulshan Books.

Brecher, Michael. 1998. *Nehru: A Political Biography*. New Delhi: Oxford University Press.

Carter, Lionel. ed. 2003. *Mountbatten's Report on the Last Viceroyalty: 22 March—15 August 1947*. New Delhi: Manohar.

Das, Durga. ed. 1970. *Sardar Patel's Correspondence 1945–1950: Vol. 1—New Light on Kashmir*. Ahmedabad: Navjivan Publishing House.

Dasgupta, C. 2002. *War and Diplomacy in Kashmir 1947–48*. New Delhi: Sage.

Fair, C. Christine and Sumit Ganguly. 2013. 'Lives on the Line'. *The Washington Quarterly*, 36(3): 173–184.

Gandhi, Rajmohan. 2013. *Patel: A Life*. Ahmedabad: Navajivan Publishing House.

Gopal, S. 1988. *Selected Works of Jawaharlal Nehru*, Second Series, Vol. 7. New Delhi: Jawaharlal Nehru Memorial Fund.

Guha, Ramachandra. 2007. *India After Gandhi: The History of the World's Largest Democracy*. New Delhi: Picador.

Gupta, Sisir. 1966. *Kashmir: A Study in India–Pakistan Relations*. Bombay: Asia Publishers.

Hodson, H.V. 1985. *The Great Divide: Britain–India–Pakistan*. Karachi: Oxford University Press.

Iyengar, Uma. ed. 2007. *The Oxford India Nehru*. New Delhi: Oxford University Press.

Jha, Prem Shankar. 2003. *The Origins of a Dispute: Kashmir 1947*. New Delhi: Oxford University Press.

Kennedy, Andrew Bingham. 2012. *The International Ambitions of Mao and Nehru: National Efficacy Beliefs and the Making of Foreign Policy*. Cambridge: Cambridge University Press

Khan, Akbar. 2002. *Raiders in Kashmir, revised edition*. Delhi: Army Publishers.

Korbel, Josef. 1966. *Danger in Kashmir*. Princeton, NJ: Princeton University Press.

Lamb, Alastair. 2000. *Incomplete Partition: The Genesis of the Kashmir Dispute 1947–48*. Oxford: Oxford University Press.

Mahajan, Mehr Chand. 1963. *Looking Back*. New Delhi: Asia Publishing House.

Mansergh, Nicholas. ed. 1978. *Constitutional Relations Between Britain and India, The Transfer of Power 1942–7. Vol. VII: The Cabinet Mission 23 March–29 June 1946*. London: Her Majesty's Stationery Office.

Menon, V.P. 1956. *Integration of the Indian States*. Chennai: Orient Longman.

Moon, Penderel. ed. 1982. *Constitutional Relations Between Britain and India, The Transfer of Power 1942–7. Vol. XI: The Mountbatten Viceroyalty: Announcement and Reception of the 3rd June Plan 31 May–7 July 1947*. London: Her Majesty's Stationery Office.

Prasad, S.N. and Dharam Pal. 2005. *History of Operations in Jammu and Kashmir (1947–48)*. Dehradun: History Division, Ministry of Defence, and Natraj Publishers.

Raghavan, Srinath. 2010. *War and Peace in Modern India: A Strategic History of the Nehru Years*. Ranikhet: Permanent Black.

Sarila, Narendra Singh. 2005. *The Shadow of the Great Game: The Untold Story of India's Partition*. New Delhi: HarperCollins Publishers India.

Singh, Jasjit. 2013. *Defence from the Skies: 80 Years of the Indian Air Force*. New Delhi: Knowledge World and Centre for Air Power Studies.

Sinha, S.K. 1977. *Operation Rescue: Military Operations in Jammu and Kashmir 1947–49*. New Delhi: Vision Books.

Symonds, Richard. 2001. *In the Margins of Independence: A Relief Worker in India and Pakistan, 1942–1949*. Oxford: Oxford University Press.

4

Strategy and Force Structure in the 1950s

In early 1950, India's Defence Committee of the Cabinet instructed the chiefs of the three armed services to plan for a military establishment that would be 'large enough to deal with whatever Armed Forces Pakistan was likely to have' and 'not to take into account the Communist menace [read China] nor any possibility of using Indian Armed Forces outside India or to defend India against powers other than Pakistan' (Wainwright 1994, 148).[1] These instructions came in the wake of an assessment about the threat posed by Pakistan carried out the previous year by Indian military planners. The military assessment had stated that it was 'extremely unlikely' that Pakistan would attack India across the borders of Punjab, Rajasthan, or East Pakistan (Kavic 1967, 36–38). While the assessment considered border incidents as inevitable, it contended that the only probable military contingency that India was likely to face was an invasion of Jammu and Kashmir by Kashmiri as well as Pakistani irregulars. Such an invasion would, however, be more elaborate in scale and conception than what had occurred in October 1947, and it would be built around a sizeable core of regular Pakistani troops.

The War Plan of 1950

Indian military planners were clearly aware that in any such conflict Pakistan would enjoy a distinct geographical advantage, given the existence of good communication facilities between Pakistan and Jammu and Kashmir. These would enable Pakistan to make available adequate arms and supplies to the irregulars, thereby tying down large numbers of troops and neutralising the Indian Army's superior numbers in other sectors of the border. This logic would operate even more forcefully if the Pakistan Army were to attempt an overt military campaign to conquer Kashmir. Under either circumstance, India would be forced to deploy a considerable portion of its forces in Kashmir without the guarantee of a decisive victory because both regular Pakistani troops as well as irregulars would enjoy sanctuary in the territory of Pakistan proper.

Under these circumstances, the only practical alternative before India was not to distinguish between irregulars and Pakistani troops or even 'to concede the possibility of another limited war in Kashmir at a time and on a scale determined by Karachi' (Kavic 1967, 36). In other words, within the broader conception of a defensive policy, India would wage a full-scale war against Pakistan if the latter were to encourage another tribal invasion of Kashmir with or without the participation of Pakistan Army personnel. In such a war, India would enjoy a marked superiority in terms of military and material resources as well as considerable geographical advantages. India surrounded East Pakistan, which, moreover, was separated from West Pakistan by nearly 1,000 miles of intervening Indian territory. Further, even West Pakistan had its vulnerabilities. Not only did it lack geographical depth, but its internal transportation and communication facilities were minimal. Nor did it have domestic sources of arms and military stores. Consequently, a blockade of the only Pakistani port of Karachi would severely restrict Pakistan's ability to prosecute a war.

When this assessment was accepted by the Defence Committee of the Cabinet, contingency planning commenced for the 'possible operations in Kashmir, Punjab, and Rajasthan' and the adoption of 'precautionary measures' along the border with East Pakistan (Kavic 1967, 37). The concentration of military operations on Pakistan's western wing was inevitable. From a military point of view, Pakistan had to be forced into taking its eyes off Jammu and Kashmir to direct most of its military energies to protect vital centres of population, commerce, and communications. And this could be achieved only by posing a threat to Pakistan's political and military centres of gravity, which lay in the western wing.

The contingency plan had both offensive and defensive elements. The defensive element was to be implemented in Jammu and Kashmir, where existing troops were to contain the Pakistani offensive. At the same time, the main offensive was to be carried out across the Punjab border in the form of a rapid advance towards Lahore and Sialkot. In order to prevent the concentration of Pakistani forces in this main operational theatre, diversionary thrusts would be made towards Rawalpindi or Karachi.

While the role of the army in this plan would be decisive, the air force in particular as well as the navy were to support the army's efforts. But there are no details as to what actually was envisaged in terms of air and naval operations. All that the publicly available information reveals is the nugget that Pakistan's population centres would not be bombed from the air because of the fear of Pakistani retaliation against Indian cities (Kavic 1967, 42). In other words, the doctrine of strategic bombing would not be adopted. The predominant role assigned to the army in this plan was inevitable because of the limited capabilities possessed by the other two services at that point in time. When these contingency plans were being drawn up in 1950, the Indian Air Force had about 150 odd fighters in its inventory and a couple of bomber squadrons composed of salvaged B-24J aircraft abandoned in India after the Second World War. As for the Indian Navy, its main ships at that time were three destroyers, one light cruiser, four sloops, two frigates, and one corvette (Kavic 1967, 102, 118, 241).

The aim of this war plan was to 'inflict a decisive defeat' on the Pakistan Army and occupy important centres such as Lahore (Kavic 1967, 37). It was believed that such an outcome would compel the Pakistan government to seek peace. However, India's endgame would not be the acquisition of territory but merely the use of captured territory as a bargaining chip during peace negotiations. In essence, India sought to pursue a decisive victory over Pakistan as part of a strategy of exhaustion.

The Crisis of 1951

That this war plan and the strategy it was embedded in was indeed acceptable to the political leadership is evident from the events of June–July 1951 (Raghavan 2010, 188–209). During the summer of 1951, calls for a jihad to liberate Kashmir began to grow in intensity in Pakistan after India announced elections for a constituent assembly in Jammu and Kashmir. It was expected that this popular assembly would formalise the state's accession to India. At first, the Indian government tended to view these Pakistani calls for jihad as a political stunt and consequently ignored the concerns expressed in this regard by the military leadership (Thorat 1986, 116). But events in subsequent weeks compelled it to take the possibility of a Pakistani military intervention in Jammu and Kashmir seriously. First, Pakistani forces began a series of small raids against Indian troops across the ceasefire line in Jammu and Kashmir. Second, in late June, Pakistan began moving a brigade opposite Poonch, which India interpreted as part of the preparations for an impending offensive. Finally, Indian intelligence reported a Pakistani plan to launch a sudden attack on Jammu and Kashmir and commit extensive sabotage in the state (Raghavan 2010, 193, 195).

The Indian government concluded that under such circumstances it would be prudent to 'take full precautions to meet any possible attack by Pakistan' (Gopal 1994, 323).[2] Consequently, the army was mobilised in early July, although, at the same time, it was instructed not to deploy forces too close to the border lest a local incident flare up into a full-scale war (Thorat 1986, 118). The armoured division and an infantry division were moved to Punjab, an additional infantry brigade was deployed along the border with East Pakistan to shore up the defences there, and some readjustments of troops were effected in Jammu and Kashmir (Raghavan 2010, 198, 217). These measures were intended to ensure both the defence of Jammu and Kashmir as well as the ability to take the counter offensive into Pakistani territory as part of a full-scale war. In order to ensure that the Indian intent in this regard went across clearly, Prime Minister Nehru sent a cable to his Pakistani counterpart Liaquat Ali Khan that India would not take 'the slightest step of an aggressive character … so long as no aggression takes place on Indian territory'. And he significantly added, 'I wish to make it clear that this includes Kashmir' (Gopal 1994, 333–334).

Although Pakistan responded to these Indian moves by concentrating its forces along the Punjab border, the crisis did not escalate. This was partly because Pakistan was deterred by India's military deployments from initiating an attack and partly because India was determined not to start a war or even to cause an accidental outbreak of hostilities by deploying its forces too close to the border. With neither side willing to withdraw their forces, the situation remained in stalemate for the next few months and dissipated only in the wake of Pakistan's domestic political uncertainties caused by the assassination of its prime minister in mid-October 1951.

Factors That Shaped the Force Structure

When India adopted the strategy of exhaustion for a full-scale war and drew up an operational plan to achieve a decisive victory, it enjoyed a comfortable military superiority vis-à-vis Pakistan. The Indian Army was more than double the size of the Pakistan Army, and it also enjoyed a more than 3-to-1 superiority in the main teeth arms of armour and artillery. The Indian Air Force was also nearly three times larger than the Pakistan Air Force. And even the rather small Indian Navy enjoyed a 2-to-1 advantage over its Pakistani counterpart (Table 4.1).

Given these advantages, it was but natural that India espied an opportunity to achieve a decisive victory over Pakistan by undertaking an offensive across the Punjab border. As Field Marshal Claude Auchinleck had pointed out in an April 1947 military appreciation, West Pakistan is 'difficult to defend' because it is not only 'all length

TABLE 4.1: India–Pakistan Military Balance 1949

Category	India	Pakistan	Ratio
Personnel in Army	469,000	220,000	2.1 to 1
Armour	850	270	3.1 to 1
Artillery	826	232	3.6 to 1
Main Warships	8	4	2 to 1
War Planes	347	120	2.9 to 1

Source: Adapted from A. Martin Wainwright, *Inheritance of Empire: Britain, India, and the Balance of Power in Asia, 1938–55* (Westport, Connecticut: Praeger, 1994), Charts 10.2 and 10.3, pp. 127–128. Wainwright's data, in turn, is based on Intelligence Staff Study No. 4924, 'Maximum Forces Which Can Be Generated in the Indian Ocean in the Event of War,' 6 June 1949, NAR, P&O 371.01 FW 23/4, pp. 2–3, 5–8.

without breadth' and 'depth', but its land communications 'all converge into a bottle-neck on the lower Indus about Sukkur and Hyderabad (Sind) before running into Karachi'. Consequently, 'if the main North and South communications are severed about Hyderabad or Sukkur, the northern part of the region will be entirely cut off from all direct overseas sources of supply.' West Pakistan is also 'particularly vulnerable to attack from the air ... and the lack of depth ... would make a really efficient defence against such attack almost impossible under modern conditions'. In his view, even the four big rivers that ran from north to south were 'really more of a disadvantage ... owing to the handicap it would place on the free movement of troops and stores within the region'. Further, the very few bridges that span these rivers were 'vulnerable to air attack or sabotage'. Because of these disadvantages, an Indian offensive on 'the general front' between Jalandhar and Bathinda 'would present no serious difficulty' since it 'would be well served by rail and road communications ... and could be well supported from the air'. Moreover, India could also undertake an additional, smaller offensive by employing 'hard hitting and mobile motorized' forces from between Bathinda and Jodhpur to capture Multan 'and the main line of railway connecting Lahore with Karachi' (Menezes 1993, 554–557).[3]

In the light of these advantages, the Indian government felt confident enough to reduce the size of the army by about 52,000 in 1950 and to contemplate a further reduction of another 100,000 the following year. The latter reduction was, however, not implemented because of the outbreak of the India–Pakistan crisis of 1951 (discussed earlier) (Gopal 1994, 320, 324).[4] The idea behind these reductions, effected and contemplated, appears to have been the maintenance of only a modest degree of military superiority over Pakistan (Thomas 1986, 22).[5] Within this overarching principle of maintaining a military edge over Pakistan, three main factors played a critical role in shaping India's force levels during the 1950s. The first was the Indian political leadership's affirmation that defence capability was a function of overall economic and industrial development and its corollary that 'excessive defence spending would retard economic development' (Thomas 1978, 127). The second factor that shaped India's force levels was the report prepared by the British physicist and Nobel laureate P.M.S. Blackett on defence science and the armed forces. And the third was India's concern and anxiety over the erosion of its military edge in the wake of US military aid to Pakistan.

Defence as a Component of Development

Through the 1950s, the dominant perspective in India was that defence and development were distinctly 'alternative objectives' that competed for 'scarce resources' (Subrahmanyam 1973, 1). In this view, defence expenditure consumed resources that would otherwise be available for economic development, and it was, therefore, imperative to maintain the defence outlay at as low a level as possible, especially given India's abysmal levels of poverty, malnutrition, illiteracy, etc. Nehru, in particular, played a critical role in shaping this view.

For Nehru, the biggest struggle before independent India was providing for 'the economic well-being of the masses' (Iyengar 2007, 316).[6] But this did not mean that he completely neglected the defence of the country. On the contrary, his conception of defence was one of building 'an economically strong and well-balanced India with a strong enough defence apparatus' (Nehru 1996, 96).[7] The defence apparatus, in his view, should not be simply reduced to the mere possession of an army, navy, and air force but must necessarily include 'industry and production' as well. Nehru was cognizant of the fact that only industrial strength enables a country to build up its armed forces at short notice, not dependence on imported arms and equipment, whose sources may either simply dry up or spare parts for which may not be available when needed. In this regard, he singled out 'the amazing capacity of American industry and scientific research' for the critical role they played in enabling the United States to win the Second World War (Nehru 1996, 96–97).

Consequently, in Nehru's conception, the equation of defence included not only the armed forces but also the foundational strengths upon which these 'spear points' rested—a broad industrial and technological base that enables the domestic production of weapons and equipment, a sound economy, and the spirit of the people. Hence his contention that 'the five year plan is the defence plan of the country'. Integral to this conception was the view that a rush to establish specialised facilities for the production of tanks or aircraft is unlikely to bear fruit in the absence of a broad background of industrial development and adequately trained technical personnel. It would be far more sensible, therefore, 'both from the point of view of economic development and that of defence, to build up industry, and to build up heavy industry, which produces machines'. Since, however, the development of economic, industrial, and technological capabilities was likely to take time and defence against external challenges had to be provided for in the interim, Nehru emphasised upon evolving a balanced approach between catering for the immediate needs on the one hand and pursuing the long-term objectives on the other (Sharada Prasad and Damodaran 2003, 283–288).[8]

These views ensured that India's defence spending during the decade of the 1950s was maintained at a rather modest average of less than 2 per cent of the gross national product (Subrahmanyam 1973, 3). And they also ensured that no concerted effort was made in the first part of that decade to establish weapons-production plants. Thus, while Bharat Electronics was established in 1954, the Tata Group's initiative for producing armoured vehicles in collaboration with Daimler-Benz was not encouraged. But these views on defence as a component of development began to undergo a slight shift in emphasis in the wake of the provision of US military aid to Pakistan (see below). Consequently, even as India embarked upon the import of tanks, aircraft, and naval vessels, it also took steps to develop a domestic aircraft design and development programme (Gnat and HF-24) as well as a programme for producing the semi-automatic Ishapore rifle (Thomas 1978, 103, 105).

P.M.S. Blackett's Influence

The second factor that determined India's defence modernisation programme between Independence and the 1962 War with China was the influence of Professor P.M.S. Blackett. Blackett served as an advisor to Nehru on military and scientific affairs, and, in that capacity, he was tasked to prepare a report on how to advance India's military and defence science establishments (Anderson 2010). Although Blackett at first intended to offer his counsel only on defence science as it related to the needs of the armed forces, he felt compelled to widen his scope to the larger question of India's defence. In his view, such an expansion became inevitable because the adoption of a practical policy for defence research and development was contingent upon three inter-related factors: the choice of weapons and platforms needed by the armed services, the strategic plan according to which these military instruments would be employed, and, more broadly, the country's industrial development programme as well as foreign policy (Blackett Report 1948, 1).[9]

The Blackett Report

Blackett's starting point was India's economic weakness and the consequent need to 'cut her defence coat according to her scientific, financial and industrial cloth' (Blackett Report 1948, 1). Keeping this in view and being mindful of India's articulated foreign policy of non-alignment, including non-association with the Commonwealth for military purposes, Blackett largely followed the earlier recommendations made in 1946 by Owen Haddon Wansbrough-Jones (Abraham 1998, 56; Blackett Report 1948, 1).[10]

Following Wansbrough-Jones, Blackett endorsed the goal of self-sufficiency in defence that was favoured by the Indian political leadership and noted that the best way to attain that would be to carefully select the weapons systems that the armed forces planned to use. In this regard, India could attain immediate self-sufficiency in the manufacture of simpler weapons, whereas it would have to continue to depend on imports for high-technology platforms until such time that the domestic industrial and technological capabilities matured. To induct more of the simpler, domestically manufactured, weapons, India, in Blackett's view, needed to craft a suitable military strategy and adapt the doctrines and tactics of the three services. If, however, security imperatives were to necessitate the immediate import of even simpler weapons, then it must resort to buying war surplus stock available at a low price, especially given the limited foreign exchange reserves available. In order to make the task of decision makers easier with regard to defence imports, Blackett differentiated between what he called competitive and non-competitive weapons. This differentiation was based on whether superior performance vis-à-vis similar weapons possessed by an adversary was absolutely necessary, as must be the case with fighters, heavy tanks, and aircraft carriers, or inferior performance could be compensated for with larger numbers, as in the case of rifles, guns, light tanks, escort vessels, submarines, and aircraft for coastal defence and anti-submarine operations (Blackett Report 1948, 3–5, 8).

Apart from these economic and self-reliance considerations, the choice of weapons was also necessarily a function of the overall strategic framework developed for the types of war to be waged. India, in Blackett's view, would easily win a war against a very weak adversary and definitely lose a war against a very strong opponent. Hence, it must not plan for such wars and especially not for a world war. Instead, the ideal scenario for India to take into consideration would be a 'marginal war' against a neighbouring country, such as Pakistan, with 'comparable military strength', which, moreover, may be supported by a great power not fully but 'to a moderate degree' (Blackett Report 1948, 7; Anderson 2001, 3710).

This recommendation led to an exchange between Blackett and Admiral William Parry, the then chief of the Indian Navy. Parry considered Blackett's recommendation that India 'only prepare for a local war' against an immediate neighbour 'of comparable strength' as 'unrealistic' and that 'the real danger … is another world war … [and which] will persist for a long time to come' (Blackett Papers). Delivering a lecture at the United Service Institution of India in early 1949, Parry observed that 'to become a real sea power', India 'must be capable of protecting her own trade and her own shipping with a real modern Navy, containing all ships and aircraft, on the sea, over the sea and under the sea'. Therefore, the navy's leadership planned a force structure 'containing all classes of ships necessary for modern naval war, and capable of expansion when the necessity arises' (Parry 1949, 27). Accordingly, he first proposed a 69-ship navy in September 1948, and, when this was rejected because of budgetary constraints, he presented a revised plan for a 47-ship navy in December that year. Similar to the outline plan proposed by the navy's leadership in 1947,

Parry's 47-ship navy plan envisaged two carriers and two squadrons of aircraft, three cruisers, eight escort and four fleet destroyers, four submarines, four anti-aircraft and two anti-submarine frigates, six minesweepers, a landing ship, etc. In the event, the political leadership 'approved only those proposals of the 10-year naval plan which related to the recruitment and training of personnel' (Hiranandani 2000, 5–6).

Blackett was overly critical of the underlying assumptions and the 'extravagant' force levels consequently proposed for the navy and air force respectively by Admiral Parry and Air Chief Marshal Thomas Elmhirst. Years later, he recalled that Parry wanted the navy to be so expanded as to enable it to participate in a future world war with the latest platforms and 'protect India's sea links in all directions'. And this, in his view, involved 'four fleet aircraft carriers … [requiring] 16 new destroyers to protect' them (Anderson 2001, 3709). For his part, Elmhirst, according to Blackett, 'tried to make India buy long range bombers', which would be useless in local wars, open up the country to retaliatory aerial bombardment, and also 'ruin' it economically (Anderson 2001, 3710).

Blackett contended that if India were to plan for a small-scale war with a neighbour of comparable strength, then it needed to structure its armed services for meeting four primary and two secondary challenges. The primary challenges were as follows:

1. a land attack across the frontier;
2. a 'combined land and sea attack along the coast';
3. a small-scale amphibious landing; and,
4. an 'attack on coastal shipping by aircraft, submarines, or surface vessels'.

And the secondary challenges of less 'decisive importance' were an attack on shipping on the high seas, say, more than 1,000 miles from the coast and a 'small-scale' air attacks on 'cities and installations far behind the front line' (Blackett Report 1948, 7–8). It is from this assessment that Blackett's recommendations on structuring the three services flowed.

However, because of his self-acknowledged lack of knowledge about land warfare, Blackett's recommendations about the role of the army and the weapons it must be equipped with were quite general in nature. Thus, he recommended that efforts be made to produce motor transport within the country at the earliest, emphasised upon the 'transportability' by road and rail, as well as the 'manoeuvrability' in varied terrain, of tracked vehicles, and highlighted the greater utility of anti-aircraft guns for protecting key installations rather than entire cities (Blackett Report 1948, 15–16). But in the case of the air force and navy, Blackett's recommendations were far more detailed in nature.

With respect to the air force, Blackett advised against a long-range bombing role, given the cost of these platforms, their need for fighter escorts during day bombings, their lack of accuracy during night bombings, and the risk of Indian population centres being subject to retaliatory bombardment. Nor did he favour jet fighters because they were too fast for Close Air Support missions. Instead, he made two other recommendations: expanding the 'striking power' of the air force by both augmenting the fighter-bomber fleet and acquiring 'low performance night flying bombers for tactical use'; and, acquiring a squadron of night fighters to protect advanced airfields and pursue adversary aircraft in a theatre of land operations (Blackett Report 1948, 13).

Blackett assigned three sets of central missions for the Indian Navy and also identified the most appropriate weapons and platforms needed for each mission. For the mission of protecting their own coastal shipping and at the same targeting the adversary's, he recommended light escort vessels as opposed to high-performance destroyers or cruisers, minesweepers, a few shore-based, long-range reconnaissance aircraft, and shore-based anti-shipping aircraft. The second mission of escorting a small number of ocean convoys up to Aden or Singapore and attacking the adversary's ocean convoys would also require light escort vessels and additionally a light carrier equipped with moderate or low-performance aircraft. And for the third mission of preventing or alternately undertaking small-scale amphibious operations, the navy would require a number of small ships, destroyers, sloops, landing craft and shore-based aircraft. In this regard, Blackett warned against the acquisition of large carriers and cruisers, which were vulnerable to mines and submarines. Finally, as for submarines, he did not consider that the few that India could afford to acquire would in any way achieve 'decisive results' against adversary shipping (Blackett Report 1948, 9–11).

Blackett's Recommendations and Indian Defence Acquisitions

Blackett's recommendations did have an influence on the political leadership's thinking on how the Indian Air Force and the Indian Navy needed to be equipped. For instance, while recommending the Gnat fighter, Prime Minister Nehru pointed out that a light aircraft is preferable to a heavier one for three reasons. First, it would be cheaper. Second, although the Gnat possessed lesser firepower, having more numbers of it would lead to a 'relative increase in firepower', given the formula that '[t]wo aircraft have at least four times the firing power of one of the same type'. Finally, it would be feasible to manufacture these light aircraft in India, thereby strengthening the industrial base for domestic defence (Kumar and Sharada Prasad 1999, 527–528).[11]

Further, in tune with Blackett's recommendation, Nehru also repeatedly stated that the air force did not require long-range bombers (Kumar and Sharada Prasad 1999, 296). Consequently, when the air force indicated the requirement for a bomber in the wake of US plans to equip the Pakistan Air Force, the option favoured by the political leadership was for a light, short-range bomber. Even as preliminary negotiations proceeded with Britain for the Canberra light bomber, the Soviet Union offered the Ilyushin IL-28 at a much cheaper rate along with quicker delivery. However, India opted for the Canberra because of concerns that opting for the Soviet bomber may affect relations with the countries of Western Europe and Britain in particular, which were then the principal sources of India's military imports (Sharada Prasad and Damodaran 2002, 351).[12]

Similarly, Nehru's views on the Indian Navy reflected the influence of Blackett's ideas. Nehru asserted that, given the defensive conception of India's employment of its armed forces, the navy would not be assigned the task of protecting sea routes. Instead, its role would be limited to the protection of ports and the coasts. The navy, therefore, did not 'require big ships (except for training and like purposes)', including long-range submarines and expensive aircraft carriers, but only a number of small, fast, and well-armed ships. For good measure, Nehru added that the same approach should be applied while equipping the other two services as well. The logic that underlay this prescription was Blackettian in inspiration. The short ranges of the platforms to be acquired 'is not only a question of broader policy but a policy suited to our capacity'. If India were to opt for very expensive weapons, then 'to that extent we cannot have a number of cheaper ones which really might be more useful to us for the type of defence that we envisage' (Kumar and Sharada Prasad 1999, 307).[13]

Although Nehru had initially expressed himself against aircraft carriers, he reconsidered this approach after Mountbatten broached the idea of Britain loaning an old carrier to India. In this respect, his dilemma between the advantages of a carrier and its huge expense reflected Blackett's own predicament in this regard. During the course of his conversation with Mountbatten, Nehru in fact referred to Blackett's recommendation that India opt for destroyers and not deep-draught vessels like cruisers. But Mountbatten sought to convince him of the merits of a carrier by listing the many useful tasks that it could perform, including 'protection of the coast', heli-borne anti-submarine operations, evacuation and provision of relief (Kumar and Sharada Prasad 2000, 495–496).[14]

Nehru's reconsideration of the usefulness of a carrier and his critical assessment of what it could and could not do was reflected in a subsequent assessment he made of the needs of the navy. Here, he argued that fast and highly manoeuvrable destroyers/frigates, rather than cruisers or big ships, must be the main platforms of the navy. In addition, one, and only one, aircraft carrier would also be desirable not because it could protect 'all our coast line' but because it could be sent to 'any part of the coast line or a little beyond'. Further, a carrier 'is the link between the Air arm and the naval ship and it makes the Air arm effective at greater distances'. Thus, acquiring a carrier would give India 'certain command over the area where it can reach' and enable the country to emerge as 'an important sea power in the Indian Ocean, both from the actual defence and even more so from the point of defence potential'. However, all this must be considered against the huge expense involved. The questions, therefore, were 'whether we can afford it and what priority we should give to it' (Sharada Prasad and Damodaran 2002, 347–348).[15]

Concerns about Erosion of the Favourable Military Balance

The second factor that shaped Indian defence procurement during the 1950s was US military aid to Pakistan (formalised in February 1954) and the consequent apprehension about the strengthening of Pakistan's military capability, especially in terms of aircraft and armour. At first, however, when the idea of Pakistan receiving US military aid was considered in February 1954, Nehru was not too concerned about the Indian Air Force becoming inferior to its Pakistani counterpart. He reasoned that Pakistan may not be able to easily build up enough trained personnel for a large increase in its air force, particularly to operate the newer types of aircraft. Nevertheless, he understood that a certain degree of 'danger' may arise if the Pakistan Air Force were to acquire even a few of the latest types of aircraft, which would be better than what the Indian Air Force had.

Under these circumstances, the choice before India was between the 'temporary expedient' of new purchases and the long-term approach of developing the domestic ability to manufacture less sophisticated aircraft. While the latter option would strengthen India in the long run, 'the possibility of immediate danger or danger in the near future cannot be provided for by some long distance programme of production.' In resolving this dilemma, a reasonable estimate of the degree of danger had to be made and the danger at that moment was 'not perhaps as great as one might be led to expect'. Consequently, Nehru suggested a three-pronged approach to the issue. First, the defence establishment must keep itself 'fully informed' of developments in Pakistan, particularly with regard to its air force. Second, it should pursue the programme of domestic manufacture of aircraft in India. And third, it must 'investigate possibilities of purchasing better types of aircraft'. In the case of new purchases, interceptors would be 'more necessary than other types'. As for bombers, it would be preferable to think in terms of short-range aircraft (Kumar and Sharada Prasad 1999, 295–96).[16]

But as US military aid to Pakistan began to flow in the next few years, this relatively guarded early assessment gave way to alarm that the Pakistan Air Force was rapidly becoming as large as the Indian Air Force and that too with aircraft of superior quality. Further, in the wake of Pakistan's induction of the latest type of US tanks, even its armoured force had become 'in many ways much better and stronger than ours'. But the bigger concern still remained the modernisation of the Pakistan Air Force. The Indian prime minister contended that 'we cannot keep pace with the flow of bombers and fighters from the US to Pakistan'. In his view, US military aid 'has completely changed the position of India vis-à-vis Pakistan, so far as defence is concerned' (Hasan 2006, 391).[17]

This alarm was caused by the receipt of 'full details' about US military supplies to Pakistan, the correctness of which was indirectly confirmed by Secretary of State John Foster Dulles when he told Nehru that all this aid 'might not be much because America thought in terms of millions and billions' (Sharada Prasad and Damodaran 2003, 380).[18] But from the Indian perspective, it was simply too much. Between 1954 and 1965, US military supplies to Pakistan and financial assistance for establishing logistics facilities, communication systems, training facilities, etc. totalled between 1.5 and 2 billion US dollars. At the then prevalent exchange rate of 4.78 Indian rupees to the dollar, this translated into between 7 and 7.5 billion rupees. By way of comparison, India's total defence expenditure between the fiscal years 1954–1955 and 1959–1960 amounted to only 15.12 billion rupees (Kavic 1967, 223–225).[19] Thus, US military assistance to Pakistan represented roughly between 47 and 63 per cent of India's defence spending in these years. The military equipment supplied to Pakistan by the United States and the facilities established with its assistance are as follows: for the Army, 640 tanks, the latest artillery, and modern equipment for five divisions; for the Navy, a submarine, a fleet tanker, other ships, as well as the Karachi naval dockyard and the base at Chittagong; and, for the Air Force, two squadrons of B-57 bombers, nine squadrons of F-86 Sabre jet fighters, one squadron of interceptors, 30 armed helicopters, a squadron of C-130 transports, and three modern air bases (Bass 2013, 4; Nawaz 2008, 183–184; Thomas 1978, 37–38).

Especially given the fact that the aircraft supplied by the United States to Pakistan were superior to the older British and French aircraft that

India had earlier acquired or was likely to acquire, Nehru concluded in April 1957 that the Pakistan Air Force had become 'stronger than the Indian Air Force'.[20] As a result, the Indian government rushed to make fresh aircraft purchases in the latter half of the 1950s. The aircraft acquired during this period included the Canberra light bomber and several fighters—Vampire, Ouragan, Mystere, and Hawker Hunter (Smith 1994, 68–69).

The alarm and even panic that impelled these acquisitions was clearly evident from the discussion that occurred in the Defence Committee of the Cabinet on the question of purchasing the Hawker Hunter. In their briefing, the chiefs of the army and air force highlighted the 'relative weakness of the present Indian aircraft and some other arms in view of the new aircraft, etc., that Pakistan had obtained'. Given the importance of being well-prepared against Pakistan, it was imperative that the Hawker Hunter be purchased immediately. This request for additional aircraft of a new type came only a few months after approval had been granted for the purchase of the Ouragan. When asked by the political leaders for the reason behind this sudden demand, the air chief referred to fresh information about US military supplies to Pakistan. Although the committee and the government as a whole was extremely concerned about the prevalent financial situation and, in particular, the shortage of foreign exchange, it nevertheless was unwilling to overlook the 'risk and danger … of not being fully prepared in case a war emergency arose' and authorised the Hunter purchase (Hasan 2006, 440–442).[21]

The 1964 Rearmament Programme

The moderate modernisation programme that India had pursued through the 1950s was catered only for a possible threat from Pakistan and proved insufficient during the limited war with China in 1962. In the wake of its shocking defeat in the unexpected war imposed by China, India initiated a major rearmament programme in 1964. This programme envisaged equipping the army with more modern weapons and transports and increasing its size from 550,000 to 825,000, including through the creation of 10 mountain divisions to be deployed on the China front. In the case of the air force, the programme provided for expanding its size to 45 squadrons, replacing its old aircraft with modern ones, strengthening its air defence capability, and enhancing its transport capacity. In contrast to the expansion of the army's and air force's capabilities, the navy was to be maintained at its existing strength, although provision was made for the replacement of old vessels, the construction of the Leander-class frigates in India with British help, and the initiation of a submarine arm through the acquisition of a submarine for training purposes (Kavic 1967, 192–203, 242–243, Smith 1994, 80–82).

Summary

An assessment made in 1949 by the Indian military planners, which pointed to the threat posed by Pakistan, led India's Defence Committee to instruct the chiefs of the armed services to deal with the armed forces of Pakistan and not against powers other than Pakistan. This policy shaped India's force levels during the 1950s. The other factors that played a critical role were the affirmation of the Indian leadership that defence spending would retard economic growth, P.M.S. Blackett's report, and India's anxiety over the US military aid to Pakistan. Nehru's notion of the equation of defence resting on domestic production of weapons and equipment, a sound economy based on industrial and technological development, and the spirit of the people played a part in shaping the force structure. The policy for defence research and development rested on the interrelated factors of the choice of weapons, the strategic plan for employing these military instruments, industrial development of India, and foreign policy. In the 1950s, the defence policy was 'a policy suited to our capacity'. In the subsequent decade, after its shocking defeat in the 1962 War with China, the Indian politico-military establishment crafted a strategy that brought the political aims into alignment with the application of force by initiating a major rearmament programme in 1964.

Notes

1 These instructions were reported by senior British officers then serving in the Indian military to Frank K. Roberts, the United Kingdom's acting high commissioner in India.

2 Nehru to Krishna Menon, 22 July 1951, *Selected Works of Jawaharlal Nehru*-Second Series (hereafter *SWJN-SS*), Vol. 16, Part II.

3 Auchinleck to Mountbatten, 'The Military Implications of Pakistan,' 24 April 1947. All quotations in this paragraph are from this source.

4 Nehru to Mountbatten, 'To Lord Mountbatten,' 19 July 1951, in *SWJN-SS*, Vol. 16, Part II. Nehru to Krishna Menon, 'To V.K. Krishna Menon,' 22 July 1951.

5 Other scholars have, however, asserted that India's defence build-up was driven by the principle of maintaining 'matching capabilities' vis-à-vis Pakistan. See, for instance, Thomas (1986, 22).

6 Nehru's address at the Associated Chambers of Commerce, Calcutta, 15 December 1947.

7 Nehru's speech at the Industries Conference, New Delhi, 18 December 1947.

8 Nehru's intervention in Lok Sabha debate, 21 March 1956. The quoted phrases can be found, respectively, on pp. 283, 285, and 286.

9 P.M.S. Blackett (1948).

10 Dr Sir Owen Wansbrough-Jones was a defence scientist and soldier then serving as the scientific advisor to the British Army Council. He was asked to prepare a report on the 'Scientific Organisation for the Defence Services' by the interim government that took office under Nehru's leadership in September 1946.

11 Note to Defence Minister, 'Selecting a Fighter for the Air Force,' 11 April 1955, *SWJN SS*, Vol. 28. The quoted phrases can be found on p. 527.

12 Note to secretary-general, Ministry of External Affairs, 'Purchase of Light Bombers,' 10 November 1955, *SWJN-SS*, Vol. 30. All quotations in this paragraph are from this source.

13 Note to defence secretary, 'Naval Policy,' 12 May 1954, *SWJN-SS*, Vol. 25.

14 Note to the Defence Ministry, Minister of Defence Organisation, and the defence secretary, 'Usefulness of Aircraft Carrier,' 30 January 1955, *SWJN-SS*, Vol. 27. The quoted phrase can be found on p. 496.

15 Nehru to Defence Minister Kailas Nath Katju, 22 September 1955, *SWJN-SS*, Vol. 30. All quotations in this paragraph are from this source.

16 Note to the Ministry of Defence Organisation, 'Manufacture and Purchase of Aircrafts [sic],' 21 February 1954, *SWJN-SS*, Vol. 25. All quotations in this paragraph are from this source.

17 Nehru to Ghanshyamdas Birla, 2 April 1957, *SWJN-SS*, Vol. 37. All quotations in this paragraph are from this source.

18 Note recording conversation with J.F. Dulles, 10 March 1956, *SWJN-SS*, Vol. 32.

19 Author's calculation based on data in Kavic, *India's Quest for Security*, pp. 223–225. Kavic also notes that the official exchange rate between 1947 and 1966 (when the rupee was devalued) stood at 4.78 rupees to the dollar. See his note on the Indian currency on p. 220.

20 Note to Foreign Secretary, 'Impact of US Aid to Pakistan,' *SWJN-SS*, Vol. 37.

21 'Appraisal of Defence Policy,' *SWJN-SS*, Vol. 38, ed., Mushirul Hasan (New Delhi: Jawaharlal Nehru Memorial Trust, 2006), pp. 440–442. All quotations in this paragraph are drawn from this source.

References

Abraham, Itty. 1998. *The Making of the Indian Atomic Bomb: Science, Secrecy and the Postcolonial State*. New Delhi: Orient Longman.

Anderson, Robert S. 2001. 'Empire's Setting Sun? Patrick Blackett and Military and Scientific Development of India'. *Economic and Political Weekly*, 36(3): 3703–3720.

Anderson, Robert S. 2010. *Nucleus and Nation: Scientists, International Networks, and Power in India*. Chicago and London: The University of Chicago Press.

Bass, Gary J. 2013. *The Blood Telegram: India's Secret War in East Pakistan*. Noida: Random House India.

Blackett, P.M.S. 1948. *Scientific Problem of Defence in Relation to the Indian Armed Forces: A Report to the Hon'ble Defence Minister* (Blackett Report). New Delhi, 10 September.

Gopal, S. ed. 1994. *Selected Works of Jawaharlal Nehru*, Second Series, Vol. 16, Part II. New Delhi: Jawaharlal Nehru Memorial Fund.

Hasan, Mushirul. ed. 2006. *Selected Works of Jawaharlal Nehru*, Second Series, Vol. 37. New Delhi: Jawaharlal Nehru Memorial Fund.

Hasan, Mushirul. ed. 2006. *Selected Works of Jawaharlal Nehru,* Second Series, Vol. 38. New Delhi: Jawaharlal Nehru Memorial Fund.

Hiranandani, G.M. 2000. *Transition to Triumph: History of the Indian Navy 1965–1975.* New Delhi: Naval Headquarters and Lancer.

Iyengar, Uma. ed. 2007. *The Oxford India Nehru.* New Delhi: Oxford University Press.

Kavic, Lorne J. 1967. *India's Quest for Security: Defence Policies, 1947–1965.* Dehradun: EBG Publishing and Distributing Co.

Kumar, Ravinder and H.Y. Sharada Prasad. eds. 1999. *Selected Works of Jawaharlal Nehru,* Second Series, Vol. 25. New Delhi: Jawaharlal Nehru Memorial Fund.

Kumar, Ravinder and H.Y. Sharada Prasad. eds. 2000. *Selected Works of Jawaharlal Nehru,* Second Series, Vol. 27. New Delhi: Jawaharlal Nehru Memorial Fund.

Kumar, Ravinder and H.Y. Sharada Prasad. eds. 2001. *Selected Works of Jawaharlal Nehru,* Second Series, Vol. 28. New Delhi: Jawaharlal Nehru Memorial Fund.

Menezes, S.L. 1993. *Fidelity and Honour: The Indian Army from the Seventeenth to the Twenty-First Century.* New Delhi: Viking.

Nawaz, Shuja. 2008. *Crossed Swords: Pakistan, Its Army, and the Wars Within.* Karachi: Oxford University Press.

Nehru, Jawaharlal. 1996. *Jawaharlal Nehru: Selected Speeches Vol. 1: 1946–1949,* 6th edn. New Delhi: Publications Division, Ministry of Information and Broadcasting.

Parry, William E. 1949. 'India and Sea Power'. *Journal of the United Service Institution of India,* 79: 334–335.

Raghavan, Srinath. 2010. *War and Peace in Modern India: A Strategic History of the Nehru Years.* Ranikhet: Permanent Black.

Sharada Prasad, H.Y. and A.K. Damodaran. eds. 2002. *Selected Works of Jawaharlal Nehru,* Second Series, Vol. 30. New Delhi: Jawaharlal Nehru Memorial Fund.

Sharada Prasad, H.Y. and A.K. Damodaran. eds. 2003. *Selected Works of Jawaharlal Nehru,* Second Series, Vol. 32. New Delhi: Jawaharlal Nehru Memorial Fund.

Smith, Chris. 1994. *India's Ad Hoc Arsenal: Direction or Drift in Defence Policy?* Oxford: Oxford University Press.

Subrahmanyam, K. 1973. *Defence and Development.* Calcutta: Minerva Associates.

Thomas, Raju G.C. 1978. *The Defence of India: A Budgetary Perspective of Strategy and Politics.* Delhi: Macmillan.

Thomas, Raju G.C. 1986. *India's Security Policy*. Princeton, NJ: Princeton University Press.

Thorat, S.P.P. 1986. *From Reveille to Retreat*. New Delhi: Allied Publishers.

Wainwright, Martin. 1994. *Inheritance of Empire: Britain, India, and the Balance of Power in Asia, 1938–55*. Westport, Connecticut: Praeger.

5

The 1965 War

Before the envisaged expansion in the capabilities of its army and air force could take effect, India became embroiled in a war with Pakistan in September 1965. But this war was preceded by a military confrontation in the Rann of Kutch in January 1965. Because this confrontation occurred a few months before the 1965 War, it has been correctly described as Pakistan's 'low-cost test of Indian will and capabilities' (Brines 1968, 288) and as having been intended to take 'a measure of the Indian Army's capabilities' as well as to test its own 'new Army, equipped and trained with most modern weapons' (Mankekar 1967, 52) That it was not an accidental flare-up, as has been characterised by the official Indian historian of the 1965 War, is evident from his own admission that Pakistan began its military build-up in the Rann of Kutch 'from about the third week of January 1965' as well as from the course of events (Chakravorty 1992, 20, 38).[1]

Confrontation in the Rann of Kutch

Spread over 23,310 square kilometres, the Rann of Kutch separates the Kutch district of Gujarat state from Pakistan's Sindh province. But it lies submerged during the monsoon months and becomes a barren desert once the sea water recedes. Consequently, demarcating the border in this area was never easy, although, before India's Partition, an attempt had been made in this regard by planting border pillars. After Partition and Independence, Pakistan began to insist that the boundary in this area was disputed and claimed half the area according to the principles of international law. But India maintained that there was no dispute and that the entire Rann belonged to it. To assert their respective claims, India and Pakistan initiated armed patrols in this area, and this did lead to an odd local incident (Chakravorty 1992, 15–19).

The confrontation began in February 1965 in the form of a local jockeying for position between the two border guarding forces in the Kanjarkot area. The Pakistani side built a vehicle track running through the Indian territory. And the Indian side responded by increasing its night patrols. The Pakistani side then established a standing patrol, to which the Indian side responded by establishing both the Sardar Post to block the Pakistani track and a few other posts to protect the Sardar Post. Subsequently, the Pakistani side established a platoon post to the northeast of Sardar Post. And the Indian side responded with another post to the north of the Sardar Post. The Pakistani side then upped the ante by launching a poorly coordinated attack by their regular army units against these Indian posts. Although the attack was beaten back, subsequent Pakistani artillery attacks compelled the Indian side to vacate Sardar Post. Given the increase in the intensity of the conflict, the Indian Army reorganised and expanded its forces in the area. And Pakistan, too, brought in reinforcements. Subsequently, in the third week of April, Pakistan expanded the area of conflict beyond Kanjarkot to other nearby areas in the Rann and began employing artillery and even armour in these attacks. These blows forced the Indian Army to vacate Sera Bet and Biar Bet (Chakravorty 1992, 20–24).

In response to these setbacks and concerned about the increasing intensity of the conflict, the Indian government ordered general mobilisation and resorted to the exertion of military pressure on Pakistan along the Punjab border. First announced by Defence Minister Y.B. Chavan in Parliament, the rationale behind this move was soon articulated by Prime Minister Shastri. After highlighting the difficult terrain in which the Indian troops were operating, Shastri declared that '[i]f Pakistan continues to discard reason and persists in its aggressive activities, our Army ... will decide its own strategy and the employment of its manpower and equipment in a manner which it deems best' (Shastri 1974, 294).[2] Shastri's decision in this regard was made after consultations with the Chief of the Army Staff, General J.N. Chaudhuri (Srivastava 1996, 197).

To reflect the prime minister's intent and following his formal approval on 29 April, the Indian Army initiated Operation Ablaze in early May by putting on alert formations that were earmarked for the Punjab front. Accordingly, defensive minefields were laid and three infantry divisions were concentrated in Punjab. If given the final political go-ahead, the plan was for each of these three divisions to secure one particular stretch of the Ichhogil Canal or the Bambanwalla–Ravi–Bedian (BRB) link canal as it is known in Pakistan (Chakravorty 1992, 96). The objective was to exert pressure on Lahore and Pakistan's heartland and, thus, deter that country from further escalating the conflict. For its part, Pakistan responded by ordering its own army formations to move into battle positions at 12 hours' notice, lay mines, and prepare to demolish bridges over the Ichhogil Canal. In addition, it also placed its air force and navy on alert (Nawaz 2008, 223; Chakravorty 1992, 35).

Even as these military moves and countermoves were being set in motion, the British prime minister had initiated a diplomatic effort to bring about a ceasefire, followed by a return to the status quo and negotiations. But no progress was made in this regard until the Indian prime minister and Pakistan's president met in June 1965 during the Commonwealth Conference held in London. On that occasion, the two sides reached a preliminary understanding to sign a ceasefire agreement and submit the dispute to international arbitration (Chakravorty 1992, 35–37). In the wake of the agreement that was eventually signed on 30 June, the two armies stood down. While most Indian formations moved back to their peace locations, the 1 Armoured Division was prudently relocated 'to an interim location in the Jullundur-Kapurthala-Kartarpur complex' because Pakistan continued to exhibit 'aggressive activities across the Cease Fire Line' in Jammu and Kashmir (Singh 1991, 8).

The Pursuit of a More Limited Military Objective

One important point to note about the later stages of the confrontation in the Rann of Kutch is the difference between the military objectives of Operation Ablaze and the earlier war plan designed in 1950. While the war plan of 1950 aimed at inflicting a decisive defeat on the Pakistan Army and occupying Lahore, the plan evolved for Operation Ablaze did not seek a decisive victory but only envisaged a limited advance and the occupation of a portion of Pakistani territory. This scaling down of the Indian Army's war objectives was a function of the change in the India–Pakistan military balance during the latter half of the 1950s. At the same time, the political leadership's conception of an India–Pakistan war was affected by changes in the diplomatic context, which was marked by Pakistan's military pact with the United States and its anti-communist allies in Asia as well as by its evolving entente cordiale with China.

Changes in the Military Balance

As noted in the previous chapter, in the early 1950s, India enjoyed a comfortable military superiority vis-à-vis Pakistan. But this opportune circumstance changed during the latter half of the 1950s and early 1960s. By signing a mutual defence agreement with the United States and enrolling into US-led anti-communist military pacts in Asia (South East Asia Treaty Organisation [SEATO] and Central Treaty Organisation [CENTO]), Pakistan received a substantial amount of qualitatively superior weapons systems for its armed forces. As noted earlier, American military aid to Pakistan between 1954 and 1965 totalled between 1.5 and 2 billion US dollars. This was over and above Pakistan's own defence expenditure, which had steadily expanded from 136.5 million US dollars in 1950–1951 to 265.2 million US dollars in 1964–1965 (Gupta and Radhakrishna 1971, 112; Nawaz 2008, 186).[3] Consequently, by the eve of the confrontation in the Rann of Kutch, the Pakistan military had considerably closed the gap between itself and the Indian military.

By this time, India's numerical superiority lay only in the numbers of infantry units, artillery pieces, and frontline aircraft squadrons. Here, it is important to note that the expansion envisaged by India's rearmament programme in 1964 had not yet come into effect. It is, therefore, necessary to consider the military balance as it existed at that time. As of November 1964, the Indian Army's total strength, including that of the Territorial Army, was 700,000, while the Pakistan Army's total strength, inclusive of lightly armed militia and 'Azad Kashmir' troops, stood at 510,000 (The International Institute for Strategic Studies 1963, 25, 29). Another area in which the Indian Army had a slight advantage was in the total number of artillery pieces. Whereas the Indian Army possessed 628 artillery pieces of various types, the Pakistan Army had 552 of these (Singh 1991, 7). But in the other main teeth arm of armour, the Pakistan Army held a marginal advantage with 765 tanks vis-à-vis the Indian Army's 720 (Rao 1973, 4).[4] As for the two air forces, India again had a larger overall advantage, with the Indian Air Force fielding about 700 aircraft comprising 30 combat squadrons, including the still forming MiG-21 squadron of seven aircraft, and the Pakistan Air Force possessing 11 squadrons and a total of 260 aircraft (Chakravorty 1992, 10,12).

But these figures do not reflect either the actual force levels that India could bring to bear during the war or the qualitative differences between India's older weapons systems and Pakistan's new US-supplied armoury. Thus, although India enjoyed a numerical superiority in terms of the total number of troops, it had to necessarily maintain deployments along the China front. Both countries, of course, also maintained a minimum level of troops on either side of the India–East Pakistan border. Similarly, in the case of the Indian Air Force, only 15 of its squadrons were deployed along the western front (the remainder being deployed in the central and eastern sectors) as against the Pakistan Air Force's 10 squadrons (one squadron was based in East Pakistan) (Singh 2013, 114). These deployments of troops and aircraft in other theatres automatically reduced the force levels that India was able to employ against Pakistan in the war.

Another equally significant factor impacting the military balance between the two countries was the definite advantage that Pakistan enjoyed in terms of the quality of its latest US-supplied tanks, artillery, and combat aircraft. In contrast, the weapons systems in the Indian arsenal were of an older vintage, such as the nine squadrons of Vampire and Ouragan aircraft, several regiments of Stuart and Centurion tanks, and Second World War-era artillery pieces (Chakravorty 1992, 12–13, 246). Consequently, the Indian Army, in particular, was indeed concerned about the qualitative advantage enjoyed by its Pakistani counterpart. An indication in this regard is the conclusion of the official Indian historian of the 1965 War that the Indian Army chief, General J.N. Chaudhuri, was 'perhaps initially … afraid of the much touted, ultra modern Patton tanks' (Chakravorty 1992, 334).

Even if we are to set aside both the qualitative aspects of the weaponry in the arsenals of the two countries and India's commitments on the China front, a comparison of the military balances as they existed in 1949 and 1964 clearly establishes the significant change that had occurred in the meantime (Table 5.1). In almost every category, barring the number of frontline warplanes, the advantage that India enjoyed earlier had considerably whittled down. And Pakistan had even established a quantitative superiority in armour.

TABLE 5.1: Comparison of India–Pakistan Military Balance in 1949 and 1964

Category	Ratio in 1949 (India:Pakistan)	Ratio in 1964 (India:Pakistan)
Army	2.1 to 1	1.4 to 1
Armour	3.1 to 1	1.1 to 1
Artillery	3.6 to 1	1 to 1.1
War Planes	2.9 to 1	2.7 to 1

Changes in the Diplomatic Context

In addition to this dramatic change in the overall military balance, India was also equally concerned that Pakistan's mutual defence pact with the United States as well as its membership in SEATO and CENTO might mean that these countries may diplomatically and even militarily back Pakistan in a future conflict. Indian concerns in this regard mounted when the SEATO Council issued a communique at the end of its March 1956 meeting in Karachi affirming 'the need for an early settlement of the Kashmir question through the UN or direct negotiations' (Sharada Prasad and Damodaran 2003, 337). It was left to the Indian imagination as to what might happen if an early settlement were not arrived at. Although American leaders expressly sought to reassure Nehru that no diplomatic or military support was being contemplated or would be forthcoming or even that the US military aid to Pakistan was in any way directed against India, the Indian prime minister noted that '[i]t is not a question of motives, but rather of certain results which inevitably follow certain actions, and it has seemed to us in regard to this matter of military aid to Pakistan, that the results were bound to be unfortunate' (Kumar and Sharada Prasad 1999, 336–339; Sharada Prasad and Damodaran 2003, 379–380).[5]

A further source of Indian concern at this time was the emerging entente cordiale between Pakistan and China and what it might mean in the context of a war between India and Pakistan. In March 1963, China and Pakistan concluded an agreement to demarcate their boundaries, which involved Pakistan recognising China's sovereignty over portions of Jammu and Kashmir. A subsequent statement by Pakistan's Foreign Minister Zulfiqar Ali Bhutto in July 1963 and a joint communique that China and Pakistan issued in 1964 added to Indian concerns. Speaking in Pakistan's National Assembly, Bhutto stated that 'Pakistan would not be alone' if India were to wage a war and that '[a]n attack by India on Pakistan involves the territorial integrity and security of the largest state in Asia', that is, China. What Bhutto seems to have meant thereby was that the China–Pakistan border agreement had given Beijing a rationale and justification to militarily protect the territories it possessed in Jammu and Kashmir (Brines 1968, 211–212). Although China never made a 'definite commitment' in this regard, the joint communique it issued with Pakistan during Premier Zhou Enlai's visit expressing 'hope that the Kashmir dispute would be resolved in accordance with the wishes of the people' did indicate the prospect of close collaboration between the two countries in the event of a future conflict (Brines 1968, 212).

The War Plan of 1964

Given these changes in the larger diplomatic context as well as in the military balance, India's political and army leaderships recalibrated their strategy and war plan to make these accord with the new correlation of forces that had emerged. Indeed, the change in the military balance resulted in a debate within the Indian Army on how best to defend Punjab against a better-equipped Pakistan.

Two schools of thought were evident in this regard. The first school favoured the adoption of a defence line along the Beas River, while the second insisted on the defence of Amritsar and other important areas lying close to the border. The Beas River school was especially concerned about the Pakistan Army's superiority in armour and artillery. In its view, the Pakistan Army's superiority in these teeth arms would enable it to easily defeat the Indian forces deployed west of the Beas, that is, in the area between that river and the international border. Such a defeat would lay the road to Delhi open for a Pakistani armoured offensive, especially given the Indian Army's lack of reserves to successfully wage a second major battle. Wisdom, therefore, lay in first exploiting the defence potential of the Beas to hold the Pakistan Army's offensive and then concentrating a substantial force for crossing the river and defeating Pakistani forces.

But the defence of Amritsar school pointed out that a withdrawal behind the Beas had several disadvantages. First, the surrender of populated and fertile areas without a fight would adversely affect the morale of both the troops and the people living in these areas. Second, it would enable Pakistan to completely secure the entire area west of the Beas. Thirdly, Pakistan would be able thereafter to capture Pathankot at leisure and, thus, isolate Indian forces in Jammu and Kashmir. And fourthly, Pakistan's control over this area would provide it with a powerful negotiating leverage to acquire territory in Jammu and Kashmir, which was precisely its motive in starting a war in the first place. Although the then Chief of the Army Staff, General J.N. Chaudhuri, was inclined towards the Beas River school, he eventually reconciled the two positions by deciding to 'defend the Punjab at the Ichhogil Canal' (Lehl 2005, 284–285; Pradhan 2013, 277).

This reconciliation occurred during the Rann of Kutch confrontation. According to General Chaudhuri, the plan for Operation Ablaze was drawn up in consultation with Prime Minister Lal Bahadur Shastri and Defence Minister Y.B. Chavan. One of the plan's key assumptions was that Indian troops would be authorised to carry the war into Pakistan 'the moment Pakistani troops came across the international border' (Narayan 1978, 188). In such an event, the Indian Army planners had to choose from among 'three alternatives':

1. 'the occupation of some unguarded [Pakistani] territory';
2. 'the occupation of and probably substantial destruction to a big city', such as Lahore; and,
3. 'the destruction of [Pakistani] equipment ...'

Of these, they considered the third alternative as the 'correct choice' because of very practical reasons. On the one hand, the occupation of unguarded territory would be 'unproductive and non-permanent' and, hence, inconsequential. On the other hand, the occupation of a major city would be highly intensive in terms of destruction and very expensive in terms of manpower requirements because such an attempt would invariably encounter determined resistance. In his autobiography, Chaudhuri points out how it took two corps to secure 'beleaguered Berlin' in 1945, that too after the Nazi regime had collapsed. But 'any substantial destruction of a major population and historical centre' of Pakistan was viewed with disfavour by the Indian political leadership because that would 'leave a raw wound' and unduly delay the restoration of 'amity'. For its part, the Indian Army simply did not have the luxury of being able to divert a substantial number of troops to occupy a major city, especially given that the effective number of troops available to it on the West Pakistan front was 'roughly equivalent' to what the Pakistan Army held in that theatre. In light of all this, Indian Army planners concluded that the best course of action was to concentrate on the destruction of Pakistan's war machine, which that country would find quite expensive to replace (Narayan 1978, 189, 194).

During the course of the next two months, the finer contours of the war plan evolved under Operation Ablaze became a subject of disagreement between the army chief and the commander of Western Command. The broad outline of the plan that the Army Headquarters had evolved for Operation Ablaze was as follows:

1. to adopt the defensive in Jammu and Kashmir, ensure the security of lines of communication, and inflict as much attrition as possible on Pakistani forces in this theatre;

2. to ensure the security of Indian territory in the Punjab and Rajasthan theatres and destroy Pakistani forces that might undertake an offensive;
3. to undertake a limited offensive across the Punjab border with a view to gaining territory and securing the lines of communication between Jammu and Kashmir and the rest of India.

In accordance with this outline, the Western Command under Harbakhsh Singh evolved its own plan of campaign. In Jammu and Kashmir, the XV Corps would ensure the security of the Kashmir Valley, protect the lines of communication, and defend Ladakh against Chinese aggression. In Punjab and Rajasthan, it would 'hold ground as close as possible to the International Border with a view to destroying' Pakistani forces that might undertake an offensive in these theatres. At the same time, the XI Corps would launch an offensive across the Punjab border in two phases. Apart from eliminating the Pakistani bridgehead at Dera Baba Nanak, it would secure Pakistani territory up to the Ichhogil Canal in the first phase and transform that water obstacle into a strong Indian defensive line. In Harbakhsh Singh's conception, the Indian Army's hold over the Ichhogil Canal would 'automatically pose a threat to the politically sensitive city of Lahore and thus compel Pak[istan] to retain a large proportion of her reserves in that sector'. That, in turn, would minimise the Pakistan Army's ability to oppose the second phase of the XI Corps' offensive towards the Marala–Ravi Link Canal. Not only would this plan of operation gain an expanse of Pakistani territory for India, but it would also, at the same time, help to considerably whittle down the Pakistan Army's war machinery. Further, it would enable Indian forces to establish themselves 'on a contiguous massive water obstacle' and be poised 'to pose a threat either towards Lahore or the strategically vital road link, Lahore–Wazirabad', if a decision were to be taken for further continuing the offensive (Singh 1991, 13–15).

While Chaudhuri was agreeable to the overall contours of the Western Command's plan of campaign, he was chary of starting an operation 'with the crossing of an opposed water obstacle' and, therefore, 'ruled out Lahore or a crossing at Dera Baba Nanak' (Chakravorty 1992, 97).[6]

Consequently, he suggested that the Western Command 'examine the possibility of employing 1 Armoured Division and 6 Mountain Division on a limited offensive into the Shakargarh Salient from the general area of Samba' (Singh 1991, 15). In his view, such an offensive had three other advantages. First, the terrain was suitable for the employment of armour. Second, it 'would have a direct and close influence on' Pakistan's operations in the Akhnoor and Naushera sectors and indeed compel the Pakistan Army to pull troops out of Jammu and Kashmir to defend Sialkot. And third, an offensive from Samba would 'automatically give added depth and security' to the line of communication that linked Pathankot with Jammu and Srinagar (Lehl 2005, 241).

Harbakhsh Singh did not consider such a thrust line to be tactically or logistically sound because of four main reasons. First, since India's lines of communication ran parallel to the border, preparations for an offensive thrust from Samba would be easily detected, leading to the loss of surprise and the consequent reinforcement of this front by Pakistan. Second, neither did the Samba area have 'sufficient space to deploy the full complement' of India's strike force nor was the terrain there 'suitable for the employment of armour'. Third, the communication network in the Shakargarh–Sialkot sector was relatively poor, and the Pathankot–Samba road, which was the army's 'main logistical line', was moreover vulnerable to Pakistani interdiction. And finally, launching an offensive 'in a series of parallel lines' would tantamount to a 'dispersion of effort' and result in 'inconclusive results'. In contrast, Harbakhsh Singh pointed out that a pincer movement, 'consisting of a thrust across the River Ravi in conjunction with an offensive from the general direction of Jammu, would crush the enemy in a "hammer and anvil" action'. He, therefore, suggested a slightly altered three-phase plan: the capture of the Ichhogil Canal in the Lahore–Kasur sector in the first phase; undertaking an offensive into Shakargarh by crossing the Ravi River in Nainakot and Narot during the second phase; and reinforcing the Shakargarh offensive during the third phase by regrouping and concentrating the 1st Armoured Division and an infantry division (Singh 1991, 15–16).

Chaudhuri remained unconvinced about the wisdom of launching an offensive by crossing a water obstacle, the Ravi River. And Harbakhsh Singh continued to insist that crossing a water obstacle within Indian territory would not pose an insurmountable problem. To break the deadlock, Chaudhuri delegated the responsibility for launching the Sialkot offensive to the newly raised I Corps in early July 1965 and reassigned several formations to it for performing this task (Singh 1991, 17–18, 130). In the wake of this decision by the army chief, the Western Command redrew its plan as follows:

1. The XI Corps would counter the Pakistan Army's offensives in Punjab and Rajasthan, eliminate the Pakistani bridgehead in Dera Baba Nanak, and undertake a three-pronged advance up to the Ichhogil Canal and, if ordered, thereafter advance to Lahore.
2. The XV Corps would defend Ladakh, ensure the security of the Kashmir Valley, protect lines of communication in Jammu and Kashmir, attrite Pakistani infiltrators into the state, capture suitable ground across the Ceasefire Line and advance towards Bhimber or Mirpur or Kotli or the Haji Pir Pass, and undertake a limited advance towards Sialkot.
3. The I Corps would establish a bridgehead in the Phillora area and advance up to the Marala–Ravi Link Canal.
4. The Delhi and Rajasthan Area would undertake limited raids across the Rajasthan border to disrupt Pakistani communications (this area was subsequently placed under a separate Southern Command prior to the 1965 War).
5. And finally, the Punjab and Himachal Pradesh Area would protect and maintain lines of communication to Jammu and Kashmir as well as defend all airfields in the Western Command with the exception of Pathankot and Amritsar (Singh 1991, 18–19).

It was this plan of campaign that was eventually implemented during the 1965 War.

The India–Pakistan War of 1965

The origins of the war lay in three related structural developments. As noted earlier, in the wake of its defeat in the 1962 War with China, India had initiated a major rearmament programme. This threatened to completely overturn the military balance and render Pakistan's ability to wrest Jammu and Kashmir highly improbable. Even more disconcerting for Pakistan was America's military assistance to India in the wake of the Chinese aggression, even though this assistance was deliberately designed keeping Pakistan's sensitivities in mind[7] and consequently limited to a total of 80 million US dollars' worth of equipment for the new mountain divisions being raised (Subrahmanyam 1972, 13). Finally, attempts by the United States and the United Kingdom to push through a diplomatic resolution of the Kashmir issue in the wake of the 1962 India–China War had failed, and it appeared that the issue would disappear from the international agenda.[8]

Pakistan's Strategy and Military Initiatives

Against this backdrop, when popular protests erupted in Jammu and Kashmir in May 1965 over the arrest of the state's pre-eminent leader Sheikh Abdullah, Pakistan began to plan the organisation of a full-fledged uprising. Codenamed Operation Gibraltar, the plan was implemented in early August 1965 with the despatch in batches of approximately 7,000 trained and armed infiltrators into Jammu and Kashmir. Their short-term objectives were the 'sabotage of military targets [and] disruption of communications', and their long-term objectives were the 'distribution of arms to the people … and initiation of a guerrilla movement' (Musa 1983, 35–36). Pakistan's calculation was that India would not be able to militarily suppress the rebellion in the short-term because of international pressure, and, in the long run, it would find 'continued "occupation" of Kashmir too expensive in men and material' (Paul 1994, 111). But neither did the expected rebellion break out, nor did Kashmiris provide support for the infiltrators.

But what Operation Gibraltar did result in was the initiation by both the Indian and Pakistani armies of a series of small-scale military actions across the ceasefire line in Jammu and Kashmir in order to bring pressure to bear upon the other. Thus, a Pakistani force, estimated to have numbered about 1,000 men, entered the Jammu sector on 14 August 1965 and captured nine Indian positions. In response, the Indian Army occupied several posts and hill features in the Kargil sector. When the Pakistan Army subsequently shelled villages and troop positions in Tithwal, Poonch, and Uri, the Indian Army responded by capturing other positions across the Ceasefire Line, including the Pir Saheba peak and the Haji Pir Pass (Brines 1968, 318–319). In turn, on 1 September, the Pakistan Army executed Operation Grand Slam—an armoured thrust aimed at the town of Akhnoor.

Operation Grand Slam was slated to unfold in three phases. In the first phase, Indian positions in Chhamb up to the Manawar Tawi River were to be destroyed. The second phase involved the capture of Akhnoor, which would have severed all land communications between Jammu and Kashmir and the rest of India. And in the third phase, a brigade was to be despatched to capture Rajauri (Nawaz 2008, 211). Although the Pakistan Army eventually captured Jaurian four days later and the Indian troops withdrew to Akhnoor, the momentum of its offensive was stalled on the very first day (1 September) by India's employment of air power (Srivastava 1996, 224–225; Pradhan 2013, 236–239). At first glance, it might appear that this Pakistani plan was a response to the escalating conflict in Jammu and Kashmir proper. But the fact is that the idea of targeting Akhnoor was raised by President Ayub Khan when Operation Gibraltar was being discussed (Musa 1983, 36). In implementing Grand Slam, Pakistani leaders assumed that India would not have a casus belli to initiate a full-scale war because Akhnoor was located in 'disputed' Jammu and Kashmir, and, hence, Pakistan's crossing of the border in this sector would not tantamount to the violation of the international border (Nawaz 2008, 207).

Nevertheless, the Pakistan Army had earlier prepared a plan based on an 'offensive defence' posture to counter a possible Indian attack against West Pakistan. Its assessments of a possible Indian offensive were as follows: (1) the main Indian offensive would occur across the Punjab border to capture or contain Lahore; (2) this effort would be preceded and accompanied by diversionary attacks against Sialkot, Kasur, and Sind to prevent the concentration of Pakistani forces in the main theatre; (3) at the same time, an attempt would be made to capture 'Azad Kashmir' by occupying Muzaffarabad and advancing in the direction of Rawalkot or Pallandri; and (4) the overall aim of the Indian offensive would be to 'destroy the fighting power of our forces and capture as much of our territory as she could'. Based on this assessment, the Pakistan Army deployed the bulk of its forces in the Punjab theatre to prevent an Indian breakthrough as well as destroy 'the fighting power' of Indian forces. More specifically, its plan consisted of two elements: (1) holding Indian forces 'opposite Lahore and Kasur along the BRB canal' as well as in Sialkot and 'Azad Kashmir'; and (2) launching an armour-led counter-offensive to capture Amritsar (Musa 1983, 14–23).[9]

For its part, the Pakistan Air Force apparently had pre-existing plans to launch an air interdiction campaign against Indian air bases to attain command of the air. But there is a doubt about this claim of Asghar Khan—who had demitted office as chief of the Pakistan Air Force a few weeks earlier—given that the Air Headquarters witnessed a debate on 6 September about the merits of adopting a defensive approach. In this view, the Pakistan Air Force would be better off waiting for an Indian air offensive and fighting the air war over Pakistani territory. This debate was resolved, and a decision to initiate an air interdiction campaign was taken only at about 3 p.m. that afternoon (Khan 1979, 4, 15–16, 19–20).

Indian Strategy

In the face of the concerted threat to India's territorial integrity posed by Operation Grand Slam, the Indian government resolved to wage a full-scale war against Pakistan. Shastri explained his rationale for adopting such a course to the Emergency Committee of the Cabinet (ECC) thus: 'to defend Kashmir it was essential to make a diversionary attack on West Pakistan which would force the Pakistanis to give up their Kashmir venture in order to defend their own territories' (Srivastava 1996, 227). Upon gaining the ECC's formal approval, the prime minister conveyed the decision to embark upon a full-scale war to the armed forces on 3 September. The framework adopted by the Indian political leadership for waging the war was the strategy of exhaustion, and the aim was to attain strategic success. This is reflected in the three broad war objectives that the political leadership evolved in consultation with the chiefs of the army and air force:

1. To defeat the Pakistani attempts to seize Kashmir by force and to make it abundantly clear that Pakistan would never be allowed to wrest Kashmir from India.
2. To destroy the effective power of Pakistan's armed forces.
3. To occupy only the minimum Pakistan territory necessary to achieve these purposes, [and] which would be vacated after the satisfactory conclusion of the war. (Srivastava 1996, 228)

According to R.D. Pradhan, the then private secretary to India's defence minister, these war objectives constituted the government's 'Higher Direction of War' and were meant to 'enable the army and the air force to plan their offensive operations within the framework of the government's aims and objectives' (Pradhan 2013, 241).

A significant absence in this strategic framework was a role for the navy. With several of its vessels, including the sole carrier, undergoing repair and refit and the lone refueller not in a condition to be able to 'steam reliably', the navy was directed by the political leadership to play a defensive role and 'not to operate beyond the latitude of Porbandar' (Chakravorty 1992, 281–283, 286–288).[10] In essence, its role was limited to the protection of ports on the western seaboard.

Another deliberate omission in the government's 'Higher Direction of War' was military measures on the East Pakistan front. As noted earlier, the contingency plan that evolved in 1950 had only envisaged precautionary military measures on this front. This approach was maintained during the 1965 War even when Pakistani warplanes based in East Pakistan bombarded Indian Air Force facilities across that border. And when the Indian Air Force, of its own accord, launched a retaliatory raid against the Pakistan Air Force targets on that front, it was instructed by the political leadership to desist from any further offensive action. Recording this instruction to the chief of the air staff in his diary, Defence Minister Y.B. Chavan noted not only the practical need to avoid 'any wasteful escalation' on the East Pakistan front but also the political imperative of not doing 'anything which might provoke China at this moment' (Pradhan 2013, 255). As a result, the air force limited itself to air defence and combat air patrol missions on this front during the remainder of the war (Chakravorty 1992, 257–258).

The Indian government's decision not to embark upon any military action against East Pakistan was motivated by the concern that China might use an expansion of the war to this front as a pretext to militarily intervene in the conflict. A two-front situation would considerably complicate India's efforts against West Pakistan and prevent the achievement of the war objectives that had been defined. Motivated by the consideration of ensuring that China did not intervene in the conflict and, thus, acquire a larger role in Asian affairs, the US government had also come to a similar conclusion and conveyed its views to New Delhi in this regard. In a cable to Ambassador Chester Bowles, Secretary of State Dean Rusk noted that an expansion of the war to the East Pakistan front 'would substantially increase risks of Chinese involvement' and 'Indian authorities' would, therefore, be better off 'conserving their resources in the East to meet a possible Chinese move' (Srivastava 1996, 255).[11]

Operation Riddle of the Indian Army

In accordance with the war objectives determined by the political leadership, the Indian Army executed the modified plan that it had evolved in the aftermath of the Rann of Kutch confrontation. Now named Operation Riddle (Pradhan 2013, 245; Lehl 2005, 180), the plan consisted of two thrusts—one in the Lahore sector and the other in the Sialkot sector. The first, initiated by the XI Corps on 6 September, aimed at securing the east bank of the Ichhogil Canal. If successful in stabilising the front there, its subsequent task was to threaten Lahore, not occupy it,[12] as well as damage or destroy the bridge over the Ravi River. The original war plan had called for a simultaneous second thrust by the I Corps towards Sialkot—a key 'nodal point of communications' (Lehl 2005, 242) as well as the Pakistan Army's 'nerve-centre', housing its IV Corps, 6 Armoured Division, and two infantry divisions (Mankekar 1967, 121). But many elements of the I Corps, with the exception of the 1 Armoured Division and the 26 Infantry Division, were dispersed in Central India and moved forward to the concentration area over a period of four days only after the government's decision to wage a full-scale war. As a result, the I Corps became operationally ready only by the late afternoon of 7 September and initiated its offensive early the next morning (Singh 1991, 129–130, 134–136). The objectives of this thrust were to advance to the general line of the Marala–Ravi Link Canal and cut Sialkot off from Lahore (Rao 1991, 128). In addition to these main offensives, the XV Corps attempted to capture suitable ground across the ceasefire line in Jammu and Kashmir, and the 11 Infantry Division, under the Southern Command, launched a diversionary attack across the Rajasthan border to tie down Pakistani forces in Sind (Chakravorty 1992, 228–244).

The two offensive thrusts in the Lahore and Sialkot sectors relieved Pakistan's military pressure on Jammu and Kashmir by compelling the Pakistan Army to withdraw the offensive elements (two armoured regiments, one artillery brigade, and an infantry brigade) of its forces from the Chhamb sector and concentrate them for the defence of its heartland (Musa 1983, 42; Lehl 2005, 253). In the Lahore sector, the swift forward movement of Indian forces along three axes generated surprise and helped gain some initial successes. Within its sub-sector, the 15 Infantry Division secured the east bank of the Ichhogil Canal, the bridge on the Grand Trunk axis, and the bridge at Bhaini Dhilwal. Similarly, in its sub-sector, the 4 Mountain Division captured Pakistani positions across the border except for Ballan Wala. And in the 7 Infantry Division sub-sector, the Hudiara Drain position and Noorpur village were captured, but not the Bedian village; the capture of Bedian became impossible when Pakistani forces breached the Upper Bari Doab Canal and flooded the area.

But soon thereafter, fierce Pakistani counterattacks forced Indian troops to either abandon some of the captured territories or altogether fall back into Indian territory on two of the three axes. In the 15 Infantry Division sub-sector, the 3 Jat fell back from its position on the east bank of the Ichhogil Canal to Gosal Dial, while the 1 Jat retreated to the Indian side of the border first to Ranian and thereafter to Lopoke. The situation was much worse in the 4 Mountain Division sub-sector, where Indian troops were compelled to withdraw to Asal Uttar and establish a defensive position there. Only the 7 Infantry Division sub-sector saw a positive result when advancing Indian troops captured the well-defended village of Barki after a battle that lasted five days (Singh 1991, 89–100).

With the momentum of war turning in its favour, Pakistan embarked upon the only counter-offensive it was capable of mounting—an armoured offensive to capture Amritsar, sever the Grand Trunk Road, and isolate the Indian Army's 7 Infantry Division (Musa 1983, 21). But this offensive was literally stopped in its tracks on 10 September by forces under India's 4 Mountain Division at the Battle of Asal Uttar, where Pakistan's 1 Armoured Division lost 97 tanks including 72 Pattons (Chakravorty 1992, 174).

Thereafter, the war in the Lahore sector settled down to a series of minor actions that could not fundamentally change the battle lines. The 7 Infantry Division improved its position slightly but could not fully mop up Pakistani pockets in either area or destroy the bridges across the Ichhogil. The 15 Infantry Division did a little better by capturing Dograi on the east bank of the Ichhogil. In contrast to these minor successes, the 4 Mountain Division failed to recapture Khem Karan (Singh 1991, 112–121).

In the meantime, the armour-led offensive by the Indian Army's I Corps got off to an unspectacular start on 8 September in spite of achieving a tactical surprise that enabled the swift establishment of a bridgehead in Pakistani territory by the 6 Mountain Division and 26 Infantry Division. The 1 Armoured Division's commanders separated the lorried brigade from the 1 Armoured Brigade and launched them on two separate axes of advance towards Chawinda. As a result of such a separation of these two integral elements of a whole, this two-pronged offensive managed only a shallow penetration of four miles, and the objective of capturing Phillora and Pagowal by the evening of 8 September was not realised (Singh 1991, 141–143).

Further, unaware that Pakistan's defences in the sector were temporarily disorganised due to the hasty redeployment of the 6 Armoured Division to Wazirabad for countering a reported Indian paradrop there, the commanders of the 1 Armoured Brigade concluded on the basis of the opposition faced and the 15 tanks lost that Pakistan possessed considerable tank strength in the area (Lehl 2005, 253, 256, 264). This led to a temporary stalling of the Indian offensive for the next two days, with the 1st Armoured Division, in the reported words of the then Adjutant-General P.P. Kumaramangalam, behaving like 'a buffalo in the summer in a pond: It does not go forward. It does not come back. It just sits' (Lehl 2005, 266).

After sitting thus for two days, a reunited 1st Armoured Division, beefed up with the additional strength provided by the 35 Infantry Brigade and a battalion of the 11 Infantry Brigade, launched a frontal attack and captured Phillora on 11 September. But two subsequent attempts to capture Chawinda and move forward towards Sialkot and the Marala–Ravi Link Canal proved unsuccessful (Singh 1991, 151–157). With the flagging of the army's offensive and the mounting of international pressure for an early conclusion of the war, the Indian political leadership chose to accept a ceasefire.

Army's Doctrine of Attrition

The doctrine that guided the Indian Army's operations was attrition—a fact that was acknowledged by the then army chief, General J.N. Chaudhuri (Chakravorty 1992, 334). That it was so is also borne out by the manner in which the Indian offensive unfolded. As noted in the previous chapter, attrition was preferred by the Indian Army during this period, and it involved set-piece battles, phased programmes to secure positions, and undertaking a methodical advance from one position to another only after regrouping and reinforcement.

Thus, for instance, in the area of operations of the XI Corps, the 15 Infantry Division, tasked to secure Pakistani territory up to the east bank of the Ichhogil Canal as well as capture and hold the bridges over that obstacle, planned a two-phased offensive. The first phase involved securing the canal and three bridges over it; and the second, the capture of Bhasin and Dogaich. Significantly, there was a clear direction from the top that the second phase 'was to be launched NOT before six hours after H hour', H hour being the time when the offensive first commences [capitalised in the original] (Singh 1991, 89).

The 54 Brigade, a part of this division, planned its own move in three distinct phases: capture Gosal Dial and secure the Upper Bari Doab Canal, including the bridges over it that lay immediately across the border; thereafter seize the Grand Trunk bridge over the Ichhogil

Canal in Dograi; and then attempt a build-up on the Ichhogil near Jallo. The 54 Brigade's offensive began on a successful note largely because of the surprise it achieved. One of its units, the 3 Jat, captured Gosal Dial and thereafter rushed forward to capture the east bank of the Ichhogil Canal. But the absence of both close air support and logistical back-up as well as Pakistani counter-attacks from the air and ground compelled it to fall back to Gosal Dial (Singh 1991, 89–91).

Even individual battles were characterised by a similar pattern. In the Battle of Barki, for instance, the 65 Infantry Brigade launched 'a series of preliminary operations' at the outer line of defence with the intent of 'exposing the main defence … to a direct assault' (Singh 1991, 96). First, Barka Kalan was captured. The next day, Barka Khurd was attacked. And two days later, Brahmanabad was captured. Thereupon, when the main battle for Barki commenced, both sides employed tanks in an essentially attritional role. In addition, Pakistan unleashed an artillery barrage that saw 2,500 shells being fired on Indian positions in just 45 minutes (Singh 1991, 96).

While the doctrine of attrition is more than likely to be adopted when infantry formations are involved, it is significant that even armour was employed in an attritional mode by both sides in the 1965 War. The Battle of Asal Uttar and the 15-day tank battle in the Sialkot sector stand out in this regard. It is true that Pakistan had sought to employ its armoured forces in blitzkrieg mode in the Khem Karan sector to advance to the Beas and isolate Indian forces west of that river—the one and only counter-offensive that it could undertake and which was envisaged in its war plan, as noted earlier. But the Battle of Asal Uttar, which lasted two days, saw India employing its armour to essentially attrite Pakistan's 1st Armoured Division. And again, in the 15-day tank battle around Phillora, which involved a total of 400 tanks, both sides essentially employed their armour for attritional purposes (Mankekar 1967, 112–125). In the first phase of that battle, Pakistan exploited the exposed flank of the advancing Indian column, which moreover got separated from its complement of Lorried Brigades. The second phase, which saw India's capture of Phillora, actually began with an Indian artillery bombardment. Only thereafter did the armoured forces venture forward, that too to engage in an attritional battle, albeit a successful one. Significantly, this battle was followed by a period of 'consolidation and regrouping' during which the infantry 'firmed in at Phillora' (Singh 1991, 147). And in the third phase, Indian armour was again employed to destroy Pakistani armour during the failed bid to capture Chawinda. (Singh 1991, 151–152).

Role and Doctrine of the Air Force

Although the strategy and contingency plan evolved in the early 1950s envisaged the air force playing a supporting role in a future war with Pakistan, no joint plan was ever crafted (Chakravorty 1992, 267). Indeed, the Indian Army launched its offensive across the Punjab border without even informing the Indian Air Force (Lehl 2005, 106). To extrapolate from the experience of the Western Army Command, all that was done was to delegate the task of providing close air support to the Advance Headquarters of each Air Command, which, in turn, handed over control of the 'sub allotted air effort to the Tactical Air Centres' either on 'a day-to-day basis or for the duration of a phase of operation'. But even this was not 'strictly followed' because of 'uncertainty as to the proportion of the fighter bomber force ... required for obtaining a reasonable air situation and for interdiction in the initial stages of the conflict'. Further, because only 'a vague allocation of force was made' to the Advance Headquarters of each Air Command, the latter 'could rarely make sub allocation of force to Tactical Air Centres'. As a result, the Joint Operations Centres at the corps level 'could not plan with certainty'. Even if Tactical Air Centres were able to place demands, 'there was no guarantee' that these would be met (Singh 1991, 172).[13]

Let alone a joint plan, there is no indication about the existence of even an air force plan for the conduct of operations during the war. Nevertheless, it is possible to glean the overall framework of the air force's campaign as well as its doctrinal orientation from the number and types of sorties generated. All in all, the Indian Air Force generated 3,937 sorties during the war. Of these, 2,369 sorties, constituting a little over 60 per cent of the total, were devoted to aerial combat and combat air patrol missions by fighter aircraft. A majority of these were, moreover, flown over Indian territory, thereby reflecting a defensive mindset. Another 839 sorties, making up 21.3 per cent of the total, were air interdiction (or counter-air strike) missions by bombers and fighter-bombers.[14] And 729 sorties, 18.5 per cent of the total, were close air support missions by both bombers and fighter bombers (Chakravorty 1992, 269). From these figures, it is quite evident that aerial combat was the main doctrine that drove the air force's operations, with the indirect doctrine of air interdiction constituting a significant add-on. Needless to add, the provision of close air support is only a critical mission of the air force and not a doctrine.

Through these missions, the air force made a vital contribution to the Indian war effort. In fact, its very first mission on 1 September was to provide close air support for Indian troops facing the Pakistani onslaught at Chhamb in the Jammu sector. During this 45-minute mission towards the end of the day, air force planes destroyed 10 out of 30 or 40 Pakistani tanks, two anti-aircraft guns and 30 to 40 vehicles (Chakravorty 1992, 247). This, as indirectly admitted by Pakistani officers involved in Operation Grand Slam, disrupted 'command and control' and 'arrested the speed and momentum of the [Pakistani] operation' to capture Akhnoor (Singh 2013, 127–128; Khan Chaudhry 1977, 51, 55).

Overall, the air force's various close air support missions succeeded in causing significant attrition among Pakistani ground forces. Depending upon whether one goes by the army count or the air force count, 70 (army claim) or 123 (air force claim) tanks were destroyed, and 7 or 20 others were damaged; 19 or 56 guns were destroyed, and 4 or 3 others were damaged; and 145 or 281 vehicles were destroyed, and 19 or 27 others were damaged (Singh 1991, 171).[15] As Jasjit Singh has noted, even if one were to accept the lower figures of the army in this regard, it still amounts to the 'destruction of an equivalent of one-third of an armoured division' (Singh 2013, 108).

In terms of air interdiction or counter-air strikes, the air force initiated its campaign with six consecutive attacks on 6 September on Pakistan's main air base, Sargodha, as well as on its satellite airfields. These attacks resulted in the Pakistan Air Force losing five aircraft on the ground and one in the air; it also incurred some damage to installations and facilities (Singh 2007, 135–137). This was followed by several other similar raids on Pakistani air bases at Peshawar, Quetta, Chaklala, Multan, and Mauripur. During the course of the war, this air interdiction campaign resulted in the destruction of an estimated 25 Pakistani warplanes on the ground. Pakistan, which initiated the air war with its own air interdiction campaign, destroyed 35 Indian warplanes on the ground on both the western and eastern fronts (Chakravorty 1992, 270–271).

In aerial combat as well, the Pakistan Air Force's losses were lower at 18 as compared to the Indian Air Force's 24 (Chakravorty 1992, 270–271). Thus, while Pakistan lost a total of 43 aircraft to air and ground action, India's figure in this regard stood at 59. A high proportion, nearly 60 per cent, of the destruction of Indian aircraft occurred on the ground as a result of Pakistan's successful employment of air interdiction, especially in the initial days. The Indian Air Force contributed to this loss by not adequately dispersing or camouflaging its aircraft. Despite these comparatively higher losses, the Indian Air Force's operations were not unduly hampered. Indeed, it was able to generate and maintain a higher sortie rate through the course of the conflict (Singh 2013, 117, 121–122).

The Balance Sheet

At the end of the war, India can be said to have attained a strategic advantage instead of the strategic success that it had aimed for. It had prevented Pakistan from militarily wresting Jammu and Kashmir. Although it had lost some territory in the Jammu sector, this was compensated for by the capture of posts in the Kargil sector as well as Haji Pir Pass across the ceasefire line. In the other sectors, too, India's territorial gains were larger than Pakistan's. Overall, the Indian Army had gained approximately 740 square kilometres, while the Pakistan Army wrested about 210 square kilometres (Singh 1991, 205; Mankekar 1967, 159). But the fact remains that the objective of establishing continuous control over Pakistani territory up to the general line of the Marala–Ravi Link Canal and the Ichhogil Canal was not attained.

India's third objective—destroying the offensive power of the Pakistani military—was also only partially realised. Although Pakistan's 1st Armoured Division was crippled at Asal Uttar and 'the striking power' of its armoured formations, in general, blunted, India's overall advantage was not too large (Brines 1968, 344). Pakistan is estimated to have lost between 165 (Pakistan's claim) and 200 (Indian estimate) tanks, and India 128 (Chakravorty 1992, 333, 339). Only in the aerial domain were India's total losses more than Pakistan's. While 59 of the Indian Air Force's aircraft were destroyed, including many on the ground during Pakistan's air interdiction campaign, the Pakistan Air Force fared relatively better, with only 43 of its aircraft destroyed (Chakravorty 1992, 271). But even in this regard, it has been argued that the Indian Air Force fared much better than the Pakistan Air Force if judged according to the international norm of calculating the attrition rate not as a percentage of the total inventory but 'as a proportion of the air effort undertaken' (Singh 2013, 116). Accordingly, the Indian Air Force's attrition rate was only 1.5 per cent per 100 sorties generated (59 aircraft lost in 3,937 sorties), whereas the Pakistan Air Force's attrition rate stood at 1.8 per cent per 100 sorties generated (43 aircraft lost in 2,364 sorties).

Why Only a Strategic Advantage?

Several reasons have been identified for India's failure to achieve strategic success in the war. At the top of this list stands the lack of strategic planning by the army chief in terms of crafting a coordinated war plan with the other two services, evolving a suitable doctrine for the land campaign and managing logistics in a professional manner. According to the then vice chief of the air staff, the more senior and experienced General J.N. Chaudhuri 'treated the whole business [of the war] as his personal affair, or at any rate that of the Army's alone, with the Air Force as a passive spectator and the Navy out of it altogether' (Lal 2008, 163). The absence of coordination between the two services was reflected in the fact that, as noted earlier, the army launched its first offensive across the Punjab border without informing the air force. In this regard, it has been stated that the commander of the XI Corps did not seek air support for the offensive because of either a lack of conviction about the utility of air support or the assumption that the air force would be engaged in attaining air superiority and, therefore, could not be expected to accede to the army's request for air support (Chakravorty 1992, 146–147, 188). Whatever be the actual reason, this episode demonstrated the lack of coordination between the two services in the run-up to the war. Nor had army–air force cooperation improved during the course of the war. When the 1st Armoured Division planned the capture of Chawinda in the Sialkot sector, it failed to integrate air support into its plan (Lehl 2005, 324).

For its part, the air force failed to undertake 'pre-emptive' air interdiction missions at the very outset of the war 'to destroy the bulk of the PAF [Pakistan Air Force] on the ground' or carry out 'strategic air bombardment missions' (Chakravorty 1992, 329–330). What has been left unsaid is that the air force does not appear to have conceived of air interdiction as a doctrine or even as a mission before the war. And when it did embark upon such a campaign, it was more of a response to the Pakistan Air Force's successful air interdiction missions against Indian air bases and facilities.

Indeed, Nirad Chaudhuri observed at that time that the entire Indian military effort was marked by impulsive responses to what Pakistan did rather than being the result of 'coordinated and deep thinking on the problems of an all-out war with Pakistan' and of 'detailed planning in respect of strategy, and exercises in respect of tactics'. Consequently, the principle of concentration—the very essence of a successful strategy in both offensive and defensive modes—was ignored. Instead, dispersed and scattered offensives were undertaken. The improvised nature of these Indian offensives meant that they were not 'deliberate' parts of a strategy 'but angry ripostes to provocations, a set of acts of retaliation, undertaken without political or military calculation'. In other words, what was witnessed was not war but 'a private quarrel accompanied by blows and counterblows from two angry men'.[16]

A final failure at the top level of the military hierarchy was the lack of professional management of logistics, leading to 'non-intensive sectors' becoming 'choked with relays of ammunition trains … whereas sectors in the thick of the fighting were running short and clamouring for resupply' (Palit 1991, 426). This, in turn, led the army chief to come to the unsubstantiated and unverified conclusion that 'most of India's frontline ammunition had been used up', whereas in reality 'only about 14% of India's frontline ammunition had been fired' (Chakravorty 1992, 333–334).

A major consequence of the lack of strategic clarity at the top military level was the inadequate understanding among military commanders about the type of war they were engaged in (full-scale or limited) as well as the objectives they were expected to pursue (capture of Pakistani territory or attrition of its forces). This was compounded by the lack of 'good generalship' at both the corps and division levels as well as by deficient command and control at all levels. In the judgement of the official Indian historian of the war, 'proper planning, preparation, strategic and tactical execution of the war' would have enabled the Indian military to cripple the Pakistani military machine instead of merely 'mauling' it (Chakravorty 1992, 328–329, 334, 338).

The doctrine of attrition employed by the Indian Army has especially been singled out in several post-mortems as the principal reason for the lack of success. The official historian states that the war of attrition that the Indian Army embarked upon involved the delivery of 'a large number of inconsequential jabs' instead of 'a few selected, powerful thrusts' as well as 'fighting … against well-defended enemy positions' instead of bypassing, encircling, and finishing them off later. In his view, the result of this 'faulty' doctrinal concept was 'stalemate' and 'no strategic decisions' (Chakravorty 1992, 334–335). Writing this history as he did immediately after completing a similar history of the 1971 War, the official historian was overly critical of the army's employment of the doctrine of attrition while fetishising the doctrine of manoeuvre that it employed in 1971 (Chakravorty 1992, v). And his judgement in this regard has been echoed by senior military officers such as Harbakhsh Singh and D.K. Palit who participated in the 1965 War.

Harbakhsh Singh notes that while the Indian Army did whittle down Pakistan's war potential, especially its armour, and occupied portions of its territory, most of its 'offensive actions … fizzled out into a series of stalemates without achieving decisive results'. This, in his view, was because of 'a faulty strategic concept of the campaign' involving 'a number of ineffective jabs instead of a few selected thrusts in force'. These jabs, in turn, led to 'slugging matches spread over a vast area' without producing 'strategic decisions' (Singh 1991, 193). Given his initial opposition to the thrust line of the offensive in the Sialkot sector, he is particularly critical of this 'strategic venture fraught with catastrophic possibilities from which we escaped by a series of lucky coincidences'. In addition to its 'faulty … strategic conception', this offensive was also implemented in an unimaginative manner by the I Corps' divisional and brigade level leaderships. Instead of leveraging the flexibility and manoeuvrability of the armoured forces for delivering a coup de grâce, a lack of 'competent direction' ensured that the offensive ground to a halt after an initial surprise-enabled flourish (Singh 1991, 160–161).

For his part, Palit scathingly observes that '[i]nstead of pursuing his objective through a war of movement, Chaudhuri chose to play safe and decided on a war of attrition'. Elaborating upon this indictment, Palit states that Chaudhuri's 'strategic plan was to make a number of limited advances into Pakistani territory on a wide front and then dig in, in the hope that the enemy would wear himself down in a series of counter-attacks' (Palit 1991, 428). Palit's indictment of Chaudhuri's war plan overlooks the fact that capturing the Ichhogil Canal and transforming it into an Indian defensive position was an idea that Harbakhsh Singh and other senior generals also subscribed to. If everyone at the top level of the army's leadership was responsible for the overall contours of the war plan evolved, the military objectives sought, and the doctrine of attrition adopted, then there is no merit in assigning blame to any particular individual.

Limitations of Attrition in a Short War

While most of the above reasons did contribute to the middling advantages that India attained, two other inter-related factors played a more fundamental role in the final outcome of the war. The first of these was the Indian Army's marginal superiority over the Pakistan Army. And the second was the limited time available for the doctrine of attrition to produce the desired result.

The essence of the doctrine of attrition lies in destroying that proportion of adversary forces which breaks their cohesion and causes retreat or defeat. It is a slugfest in which the side that can absorb greater losses and outlast the other emerges as the victor. A prerequisite for absorbing greater losses and outlasting the adversary is the possession and generation of greater resources. At the same time, such superiority needs time to take effect. Although, as Michael Howard has observed, the attritional approach to war privileges the logistical dimension over operational aspects, it does have a distinct advantage in the course of a long, grinding war such as the American Civil War or the two World Wars. In these multi-year conflicts, the side that depended on attrition was able to absorb even significant battle defeats and yet ultimately prevail in the war by mobilising, equipping, and maintaining larger forces in the field and grinding down the opposition through greater logistical capabilities (Howard 1979, 975–977). In a short war, however, and especially one in which neither side enjoys an overwhelming military superiority, the possession of even a relatively larger margin of material capabilities by one side is unlikely to prove decisive.

This limitation was clearly demonstrated in the 1965 War, during which India possessed only a marginal degree of military superiority vis-à-vis Pakistan. As pointed out earlier, this marginal superiority lay in India's larger numbers of troops and artillery pieces, whereas in the other teeth arm of armour, Pakistan had a numerical advantage. But an even more significant measure to consider is whether the Indian Army was able to generate a 3-to-1 superiority at those points where it undertook the offensive, given that such a rule of the thumb is considered necessary for success in breaking through the frontline (Mearsheimer 1989, 54–89). In this regard, it is pertinent to consider the force levels in the Sialkot and Lahore sectors, where the Indian Army undertook its main offensives.

In the Sialkot sector, the Pakistan Army's IV Corps Headquarters had one armoured division, two infantry divisions, and an artillery component, while the Indian Army's I Corps Headquarters consisted of one armoured division, three infantry divisions minus one brigade, and an artillery component (Singh 1991, 9, 18). From this array of forces on either side, it is evident that the only major difference between them was in terms of the number of infantry divisions each possessed. Given that one of India's divisions (6 Mountain) had one brigade less, there is consequently a need to establish the ratio between the two forces based on a similar criterion. Since a standard infantry division in both India and Pakistan consists of three infantry brigades, the total number of brigades on each side is an appropriate criterion for the purposes of comparison. Accordingly, in the Sialkot sector, the Pakistan Army had six infantry brigades (two divisions made up of three brigades each), and the Indian Army had eight brigades (three divisions minus one brigade). The differential between the Indian and Pakistani forces in this sector was thus only 1.33-to-1.

In the Lahore sector, Pakistan's I Corps Headquarters was composed of one armoured division, one infantry division, and one infantry brigade—making for a total of four infantry brigades—and an artillery component (Singh 1991, 9). And India's XI Corps possessed one independent armoured brigade, a total of nine infantry brigades, and an integral artillery component (Chakravorty 1992, 142). In this sector, the Indian Army was actually at a disadvantage in armour, given that its armoured brigade faced a Pakistani armoured division. But it did enjoy a 2.3-to-1 advantage in terms of infantry brigades. Given the limited numerical superiority that the Indian Army enjoyed in both these sectors, it was but natural that its offensives attained only limited success during the course of 15 days between 6 September, when the Indian offensive began, and 20 September, when the Indian government agreed to order an unconditional ceasefire.

Another aspect of Indian superiority lay in its possession of a greater amount of ammunition and other reserves. Consequently, when the war ended, the Indian Army had, as mentioned earlier, used up only 14 per cent of its frontline ammunition. The official Indian history of the war also notes that at the end of the war, the Indian Army possessed 'twice the number' of tanks as the Pakistan Army did. In support of this claim, it cites the deposition made by the then Home Secretary L.P. Singh as well as a letter sent by K. Subrahmanyam (Chakravorty 1992, 334, 339). But this appears to be an inaccurate claim, given the official history's own acknowledgement that Pakistan possessed 765 tanks vis-à-vis India's 720 before the war and that Pakistan had lost between 165 (Pakistan's claim) and 200 (Indian estimate) tanks during the war whereas India lost 128 tanks (Chakravorty 1992, 10, 333, 339). If we take these figures into account, then, at the end of the war, Pakistan possessed between 565 and 600 tanks, and India 592. That is, India either had 27 tanks more or eight tanks less, depending upon whether Pakistan lost 165 or

200 tanks. In light of this, the only logical conclusions that can be arrived at are that either the official history's figures are wrong or the data set used by L.P. Singh and K. Subrahmanyam was faulty.

Government of India's Cussed Attitude to Declassification

One surprising fact that needs to be highlighted here is the reliance of the official history of the 1965 War on a secondary source—data generated by the International Institute for Strategic Studies, London—for the number of tanks possessed by the Indian Army. Was this because the Ministry of Defence and the Indian Army at that time were incompetent enough not to have maintained such basic data? Or was the official historian denied the available data, thus defeating the very purpose of writing an official history? Neither reflects well on the government apparatus and its extreme disinclination to declassify information. Nothing much has changed in the 27 years since the official history of the 1965 War was completed in 1992. The team recently commissioned to write the official history of the Kargil War was denied access to the 'war diaries of all divisions and brigades which participated in the war' as well as to the war diary of the Directorate General of Military Operations (DGMO) because the 'material contained in these documents have current operational value'. According to a former director-general of military operations, Lieutenant General Vinod Bhatia (retd), many of the army's 'current deployments in the area are based on what happened in 1999, and the DGMO can't possibly share them. Also, the tactics we used, our launch pads for operations, we can't let that information out even now. Our operational and logistics build-up, location of reserves etc., are not a matter of detail, but one of military capability and hence, need not be in the public domain'. In contrast, not only the Navy, which is far removed from the scene of action, but even the Air Force, which played a critical role in the war, have transferred 'everything related to the Kargil War to the history division' of the Ministry of Defence.

Source: Sushant Singh, 'Kargil War history will not have details of Army operation,' *The Indian Express*, 26 July 2016, available at: http://indianexpress.com/article/india/india-news-india/kargil-war-vijay-diwas-kargil-defence-ministry-srinath-raghavan-kargil-history-2935728/ (accessed on 26 July 2016).

Be that as it may, in contrast to India's otherwise comfortable materiel situation, by the closing stages of the war 'the Pakistanis "were hurting" ... and senior officers were frightened [because] ... the army was short of supplies ... running out of ammunition and had lost heavily in equipment and trained men and officers, particularly junior officers' (Brines 1968, 346). And in the aerial dimension, the Indian Air Force 'started prevailing' over the 'smaller but more modern' Pakistan Air Force. 'Had the war continued', the Pakistan Air Force 'would have felt the pinch of its losses more than the larger' Indian Air Force (Chakravorty 1992, 330). This latter judgement of the official Indian historian of the war is reinforced by the ruminations of the chief of the Pakistan Air Force, Nur Khan, who is said to have observed that '[a] prolongation of the war would inevitably result in attrition, and unless losses were replaced a stage would be reached when the air force would perforce be grounded. The Indian Air Force could, he felt, outlast the Pakistan Air Force, by sheer weight of numbers' (Khan 1979, 98).

Why Was the War Short?

Instead of utilising these greater reserves in a longer war 'lasting several months', which indeed was its military planning parameter (Singh 2007, 147),[17] India agreed to a ceasefire after a mere three weeks. Why? It has been contended that these reserves were probably not employed because the army chief, who also served as the chairman of the Chiefs of Staff Committee at that time, was fearfully cautious of Pakistan's military capabilities (Chakravorty 1992, 333–334). Basing his critique of Chaudhuri's management of military logistics on this episode, Palit, as noted earlier, has castigated the army chief's lack of professionalism in terms of not knowing and not bothering to check the exact situation as far as the availability of war reserves is concerned (Raghavan 2010). These judgements are, however, based on a dramatically brief anecdote recalled by the then Home Secretary L.P. Singh: when Prime Minister Lal Bahadur Shastri asked whether 'India could win *a spectacular victory* if the war was prolonged *for some days*' [emphases added], the army chief answered that 'most of India's frontline ammunition had been used up and there had been considerable tank losses also' (Chakravorty

1992, 333–334). The conclusion, therefore, is that since the army chief wrongly believed that his service had run out of ammunition, there was no scope for 'a spectacular victory', and India would be better off agreeing to an early ceasefire.

But a more nuanced picture and the broader context in which the Indian government decided to consent to a ceasefire emerges from other accounts. But before that, one possible explanation for the tone and tenor of this exchange between Shastri and Chaudhuri may be explored. And that explanation may lie in the army chief's forceful plea against a premature cessation of hostilities during the course of the 13 September Cabinet discussion on the pros and cons of agreeing to a ceasefire. On that occasion, Chaudhuri had asserted that the army 'was on the verge of a *decisive victory* in the Punjab and should be allowed to inflict the maximum damage on Pakistani power' [emphasis added] (Brines 1968, 367).[18] What the army chief was likely to have had in mind then was the I Corps' ongoing offensive in the Sialkot sector, which, after capturing Phillora and inflicting considerable losses on Pakistani armoured forces in the process, was poised against Chawinda (Chakravorty 1992, 207).[19] But Shastri preferred to accept a ceasefire, albeit with certain conditions, in accordance with the UN Security Council's 6 September resolution and the UN Secretary-General U Thant's written appeal in this regard (Srivastava 1996, 259). The prime minister had to convince Chaudhuri to accept his position by advancing the argument that Pakistan was likely to reject the UN Security Council's and secretary-general's ceasefire calls, and India's acceptance of the same would give it an opportunity 'to stigmatise' Pakistan 'in world opinion for continuing the war' (Brines 1968, 367).

In light of this earlier episode, it is possible that during the 20 September Cabinet discussion on the government agreeing to an unconditional ceasefire, the prime minister may have asked the army chief, tongue firmly in cheek, whether his forces would be able to attain a 'spectacular victory' if the war were prolonged for a few more days. By this time, the offensive in the Sialkot sector had ground to a halt after the failure of two successive attempts to capture Chawinda (Lehl 2005, 315–347). Nor was any substantial progress being made in the Lahore sector, with the attempts to capture and destroy the Jahman bridge on the Ichhogil and retake Khem Karan failing to succeed (Singh 1991, 115–116). Consequently, a sheepish army chief appears to have responded to the prime minister's question with the lame excuse that such an outcome was no longer possible because the army had used up most of its frontline ammunition and had also suffered considerable tank losses.

Whether the above explanation has any validity or not, the fact remains that the Indian government's decision to agree to a ceasefire did not simply hinge on the army chief's off-the-cuff remark with regard to the service's matériel position but was indeed a function of other broader diplomatic and military factors. That the military leadership was not unaware of these factors is also evident from an assessment of the pros and cons of a ceasefire that the army chief himself had prepared. On the morning of 20 September—the day India finally accepted the UN call for a ceasefire without conditions—when Defence Minister Chavan asked the service chiefs about their view on the ceasefire, the army chief mentioned the existence of a military assessment on the issue and subsequently shared it with the minister.

As briefly recorded in the defence minister's diary, the 'thesis' of the army chief's assessment was that the two objectives of the war—defeating Pakistan's attempt to wrest Jammu and Kashmir and inflicting damage on the 'war potential and military machine of Pakistan'—had been achieved. Since India was 'on top of the situation', the army would support the government's decision to agree to a ceasefire. The resulting 'respite ... will be good to put things right as far as supplies were concerned'. More significantly, Chaudhuri's assessment also stated that India stood 'completely isolated' in the diplomatic arena. Further, to reject a ceasefire would also be 'unwise' from the military point of view because of China's interest in ensuring the continuation of the India–Pakistan war so that it can 'fish in the troubled waters'. After recording this gist of the army chief's assessment of the ceasefire, Chavan noted in his diary that 'it is good that the military and political thinking was moving in the same direction' (Pradhan 2013, 285–286).

In this assessment, the army chief does mention the depletion of war supplies, although it is not clear whether he believed that these had been exhausted. But, more importantly, he highlighted two specific issues—

the prospect of China initiating hostilities and international diplomatic pressure—that had a much greater bearing on the calculations of both the political and military leaderships.

The Threat of Chinese Military Intervention

The prospect of China initiating hostilities became evident as early as 7 September when Beijing issued a statement accusing New Delhi of 'naked aggression' against Pakistan and violating 'all principles guiding international relations'. In the Chinese view, India's expansion of the 'local conflict … in Kashmir into a general conflict' constituted 'a grave threat to peace in this part of Asia'. And in an apparent attempt to lay the ground for its own military intervention, China concluded by asserting that 'India's aggression against any one of its neighbours concerns all of its neighbours … [and that India] cannot evade responsibility for the chain of consequences arising therefrom' (White Papers 1966, 134–135).[20]

The very next day, Beijing sent a formal note to New Delhi in which it accused India of several border violations along the Sikkim–China boundary and constructing military structures on Chinese territory. Establishing a connection between these Indian 'provocations' and its 'armed aggression against Pakistan', the note stated that 'China cannot but pay attention to the Indian Government's expansionist actions against its neighbours and strengthen China's defences and heighten her alertness along her borders'. Finally, demanding that India 'dismantle all the aggressive military structures … withdraw its aggressive armed forces and stop all its acts of aggression and provocation against China', the note warned that New Delhi must otherwise 'bear responsibility for all the consequences arising therefrom' (White Papers 1966, 38–39).[21] To reinforce this warning, Zhou Enlai stated at a North Korean embassy reception on 9 September that India was the 'aggressor' in the ongoing war with Pakistan. After thus condemning India, the Chinese premier noted that 'India's acts of aggression pose a threat to peace in this part of Asia, and China cannot but closely follow the development of the situation' (Srivastava 1996, 274–275).

After remaining quiet for the next eight days, China once again attempted to establish a basis for its military intervention through a note delivered to the Indian Embassy in Beijing on 16 September. The note asserted that India continued to illegally occupy Chinese territory and drew an explicit linkage between India's 'armed attack' against China in 1962 and the ongoing 'armed attack' against Pakistan with the aim of 'grabbing' those territories of its neighbours that it covets. To fully reinforce the Chinese interest in the affairs of the subcontinent, the note went on to assert that China's 'non-involvement' in the India–Pakistan dispute 'absolutely does not mean that China can approve of depriving the Kashmiri people of their right of self-determination or that she can approve of Indian aggression against Pakistan on the pretext of the Kashmir issue'. These Indian actions, according to the note, 'cannot but arouse the grave concern of the Chinese Government'. It then averred China's support for the Kashmiri people's right to self-determination as well as for Pakistan's 'just struggle' against Indian aggression. After establishing the connection between its own interests and the unfolding situation in the subcontinent, the Chinese note issued an ultimatum demanding that within three days India 'dismantle' the 56 'military works' it had established along the Sikkim–China border, 'immediately stop all its intrusions' into Chinese territory, 'return the kidnapped' Tibetans as well as the 'seized livestock', and 'pledge to refrain from any more harassing raids across the boundary'. The ultimatum ended by stating that if the Indian government were to fail to do all this, then it 'must bear full responsibility for all the grave consequences arising therefrom' (White Papers 1966, 42–44).[22]

The day after delivering its ultimatum, China began to move troops closer to the border both in Sikkim as well as in the Demchok area of Ladakh (Srivastava 1996, 279). Three days later, on 20 September, Chinese troops directed fire against Indian positions at several places along the border, including Nathu La in Sikkim (Pradhan 2013, 290).[23]

Although a large-scale Chinese attack was discounted, political and military leaders in India did think that China might initiate limited military action in order to divert Indian attention from the Pakistani front. The prime minister, for instance, concluded that a Chinese attack on the scale of 1962 was unlikely because China 'had no important and immediate objective' of its own 'to achieve', although the possibility of 'a limited attack' intended to 'bruise India's morale' could not be ruled out (Srivastava 1996, 275–76). In order to ensure that no pretext was even unwittingly made available for China to initiate such a limited aggression, Shastri decided to adopt a conciliatory, yet firm, posture towards China.

Accordingly, in its response to China's 8 September note demanding that India dismantle its military structures on and withdraw its troops from Chinese territory, the Indian government expressed its willingness 'to allow an independent and neutral observer' to investigate the issue—a modification of an earlier Chinese proposal for joint Sino-Indian investigation—while at the same time reiterating India's claims to areas that had been occupied by China. Further, the Indian response also sought to undercut China's attempt to establish a linkage between the India–China boundary dispute and India–Pakistan affairs. Explicitly referring to this 'mischievous' Chinese attempt, the Indian note pointed out that the 'involvement of external forces in the current unfortunate conflict ... will only impede a peaceful solution ... [and] the restoration of peace' between India and Pakistan. Finally, the note concluded by reaffirming India's 'hope' that India and China would be able to arrive at 'a peaceful settlement of the border question' (White Papers 1966, 40–41).[24]

The point in all this is that China's entry into the war, however limited its military intervention might have been, would have made it impossible for India to fully focus on the ongoing war with Pakistan. Not agreeing to a ceasefire would only add to that possibility.

International Diplomatic Pressure on India

Second, India stood alone in the international arena. The Soviet Union adopted a position of studied neutrality from the very beginning of the conflict. In late August, it urged India to avoid taking any action that would lead to a major conflict. Once the war officially began, it repeatedly urged both India and Pakistan to stop the conflict and even offered its own good offices for mediation. And for the first time since the United Nations was formed, the Soviet Union voted along with the United States in favour of resolutions calling for an immediate ceasefire. The main driver of the Soviet Union's studied neutrality was its concern about China exploiting the conflict to make further inroads into Pakistan.

Preventing China from entering the conflict was also an important motive for the United States. Its main effort in this regard went towards working with the Soviet Union at the United Nations to pass resolutions that explicitly sought to dissuade China from entering the war. But, at the same time, it also secretly warned China that a Chinese entry into the India–Pakistan conflict would mean the United States and other United Nations members retaliating against China. Even as it sought to thus dissuade China, the United States also worked with Britain to exert pressure on both India and Pakistan to end the conflict. This pressure assumed the form of a suspension of economic as well as military assistance to both countries.

In addition to the diplomatic pressure exerted by the major powers, the UN secretary-general made persistent efforts to bring about a ceasefire at the earliest and even visited India and Pakistan during the course of the conflict. Even India's non-aligned friends, such as Egypt and Yugoslavia, adopted a neutral position and called on both India and Pakistan to agree to an early ceasefire. In effect, India stood quite isolated diplomatically (Brines 1968, 353–381). These developments in the larger diplomatic context had a major impact on the calculations of India's political leadership when it came to agreeing to the ceasefire.

The point to note in all this is the mismatch between the doctrine of attrition employed by the army and the time that was available for it to attain the objectives set. The shortage of time was a function of unavoidable international diplomatic intervention and the unignorable possibility of a Chinese military intervention. Together, these factors shrank the time available for India to attain strategic success through the doctrine of attrition, which seeks to grind down the adversary through the application of superior material and logistical capabilities over an extended period of time.

Impact of the 1965 War on Service Doctrines and Plans

There was no noticeable change in India's overall strategic framework for dealing with Pakistan. However, each armed service did effect some changes either in its war plans or doctrines. In the case of the Indian Army, the most important and visible change was in its approach to the East Pakistan front. As noted earlier, the war plan developed in 1950 had only envisaged 'precautionary measures' on the East Pakistan front. And during the 1965 War, the political leadership directed the armed services not to initiate any military action on this front, even in retaliation. This approach was changed in the aftermath of the 1965 War because of the possibility of China initiating hostilities during a future India–Pakistan war. In such an eventuality, it was conceivable that Pakistani forces based in East Pakistan may attempt a link-up with Chinese forces coming down through Sikkim. The consequent reconsideration resulted in the Indian Army developing a new contingency plan for this front in the late 1960s.

Although the army's new plan continued to be based on the assumption that a future India–Pakistan war would be principally fought on the western front, given the concentration of Pakistan's military machine in West Pakistan, it, at the same time, envisaged military action on the East Pakistan front. There, the Pakistan Army had deployed one infantry division composed of four brigades, one armoured regiment of about 50 tanks, and a few artillery units. In addition, the Pakistan Air Force fielded a squadron of fighter aircraft, some helicopters, and a few light transport aircraft in East Pakistan (Palit 1972, 47). To cater for the contingency of a joint China–Pakistan military initiative on this front, the Indian Army's new contingency plan for the East Pakistan front envisaged two armour-supported thrusts. One would take place due east from Calcutta with the aim of disrupting a potential Pakistani offensive towards that city as well as capturing territory. And the second would move south from the Siliguri Corridor.[25] Its objectives would be to disrupt a possible Pakistani plan to employ armour for effecting a link-up with Chinese forces coming down through Sikkim and to capture territory that would enable the widening of the narrow Siliguri Corridor 'at least for the duration of the operations if not permanently' (Chopra 1973, 103, 120). In the absence of any indications to the contrary, it appears that the army's doctrinal orientation continued to be that of attrition.

The changes effected in the Indian Air Force's approach to a future war with Pakistan reinforced its doctrinal orientation of aerial combat and air interdiction. Because of the several successful bombing raids carried out by the Pakistan Air Force during the 1965 War, it was decided in early 1969 that air defence of the homeland and of air bases would be the service's first priority. This necessarily involved aerial combat or pursuit. At the same time, given the many complaints from the army about the lack of air support during the 1965 War, close air support for the army was assigned the second priority. Further, to the extent possible, the navy would also be provided similar support. Bombing aimed at neutralising the Pakistan Air Force as well as targeting Pakistan's energy and transportation infrastructure—air interdiction—came third in the air force's list of priorities. And the last priority was given to missions involving paradropping, transport, etc. (Lal 2008, 174).

As for the Indian Navy, the latter half of the 1960s saw heightened government, parliamentary, and public interest in building up the hitherto neglected service (Thomas 1978, 201–219). And the navy itself engaged in fresh thinking about its role and strategic approach. The then naval chief repeatedly articulated a broader strategic perspective, which was not immediately related, and, in fact, omitted references to the specific naval threats posed by Pakistan or China. One such statement sought to explain that the concept of sea power needs to be seen in a broader framework, which includes 'a flourishing mercantile marine fleet, a sea-faring community, a commerce minded people, and a Navy capable of defending our shipping at sea' (Thomas 1978, 203–204). Another emphasised that a strong navy would enable India to exert influence and provide friendly help to countries in the Indian Ocean region during times of crisis. And a third envisaged the Indian Navy assuming charge of the Indian Ocean after the British withdrawal from the East of Suez. This line of thinking was reinforced by the recommendations of a study group comprising high-ranking naval officers. Established in 1969 with the task of defining India's 'strategic situation from the naval perspective', the study group 'envisaged the Indian Navy taking over the functions of the Royal Navy as the British withdrew their forces east of Suez' (Thomas 1978, 204). Criticism of such Royal Navy-inspired 'grandiose, world-power outlook', which neglected India's immediate defence requirements, does not seem to have affected either the navy's or the government's efforts to build up the service during this period (Thomas 1978, 205).[26]

Summary

India enjoyed a comfortable military superiority vis-à-vis Pakistan in the early 1950s. But during the latter half of the 1950s and early 1960s, Pakistan received superior weapons systems for its armed forces by signing a mutual defence agreement with the United States and enrolling into SEATO and CENTO. India's numerical superiority lay only in the numbers of infantry units, artillery pieces, and frontline aircraft squadrons. By that time, the expansion envisaged by India's 1964 rearmament programme had not come into effect. The emerging entente cordiale between Pakistan and China was also a cause for concern for India. Considering these developments, India's political and army leaderships recalibrated their strategy and war plan. In 1965, Pakistan launched an offensive with Operation Gibraltar and Operation Grand Slam to destroy Indian positions, sever land communications, and capture strategic areas in Jammu and Kashmir. This led the Indian government to resolve a full-scale war against Pakistan. The war plan held the objectives of defeating the Pakistani attempts to seize Kashmir, destroying the power of Pakistan's armed forces, and occupying minimum Pakistani territory. The strategy of exhaustion was adopted to attain strategic success. The doctrine of attrition was adopted, and it involved set-piece battles, phased programmes to secure positions, and undertaking a methodical advance from one position to another only after regrouping and reinforcement. Owing to the absence of a joint plan between the Indian Army and the Indian Air force, the Indian Air Force was not informed about the launch of the offensive across the Punjab border by the Indian Army. Further, the role of the navy was absent in this strategic framework. The lack of strategic clarity at the top military level led to inadequate understanding among military commanders about the type of war they were engaged in (full-scale or limited). In the final outcome of the war, two inter-related factors played a fundamental role, first, the Indian Army's marginal superiority over the Pakistan Army, and second, the limited time available for the doctrine of attrition to produce the desired result. At the end of the war, India can be said to have attained a strategic advantage, instead of the strategic success that it had aimed for. It had prevented Pakistan from militarily wresting Jammu and Kashmir. India's territorial gains were larger than Pakistan's. The prospect of China initiating hostilities and international diplomatic pressure led the Indian government to agree to a ceasefire. In the aftermath of the war, there was no noticeable change in India's overall strategic framework to deal with Pakistan. However, each armed service did effect some changes either in its war plans or doctrines.

Notes

1 This history has not been officially published but is available online. Each chapter of this volume is available separately in pdf format at: http://www.bharat-rakshak.com/LAND-FORCES/Army/History/1965War/PDF/index.html (accessed on 16 April 2009).
2 'Pakistan's Designs in Kutch,' 28 April 1965.
3 Calculated from K. Subrahmanyam, 'Military Aid to Pakistan and Its Repercussions on Bangla Desh.' Also see Nawaz, *Crossed Swords* citing Despatch No. 679, US Embassy Karachi to the Department of State, 29 January 1959.
4 A 1973 study, however, points out that Pakistan actually had 1,100 tanks in 1965 by citing the hearings held before the sub-committee on Near East and South Asia of the US Senate Foreign Relations Committee. But since it does not discuss the number of tanks India possessed at this time, it is difficult to accurately judge the differential between the armoured forces of the two countries (Rao 1973).
5 'India and Military Aid,' Statement by Prime Minister Nehru in Lok Sabha, 1 March 1954 (see Kumar and Sharada Prasad 1999). Nehru's 'Conversations with J.F. Dulles' (see Sharada Prasad and Damodaran 2003).
6 Chaudhuri expressly stated this after a mid-June 1965 conference held at 15th Division's Headquarters in Amritsar.

7 On how the Kennedy and Johnson administrations sought to craft a balanced approach towards India and Pakistan before and after the India–China War (see McMahon 1994, Chapters 8 and 9).

8 On the US effort in this regard and the six rounds of talks held between the foreign ministers of India and Pakistan on the Kashmir issue (Crawford 2002, 1–38).

9 The quoted phrases can be found on pp. 14, 17, and 20.

10 The quoted phrases can respectively be found on pp. 282 and 287.

11 Srivastava also elaborates upon India's own consideration of the China factor, see Srivastava (1996, 225, 253–254).

12 Although Indian newspapers had given the impression that the capture of Lahore was a major objective, Defence Minister Y.B. Chavan and other officials soon declared that it was not so. The city of 1.3 million 'would have been both a military and a political liability', and Indian officials believed that its occupation 'would only intensify Pakistani resistance', see Brines (1968, 329).

13 This lacuna was addressed after the end of the war, see Singh (1991, 173).

14 This figure has been arrived at by considering 'Other' sorties undertaken by fighter-bombers as bombing missions.

15 The first figure in each category is what was recorded by the army and the second by the air force.

16 Nirad C. Chaudhuri, 'The Higher Direction of the Indo-Pakistan War.' The author obtained a copy of this essay from Colonel P.K. Gautam (retd), Research Fellow at IDSA, who, in turn, had received it from the late Lt. Col. Gautam Sharma in December 1997. The copy does not indicate the date of the publication or even where it was published.

17 Singh, 147, citing Air Chief Marshal Arjan Singh's statement that before the 1965 War, 'the IAF was planning operations on fighting a war lasting several months …'

18 Brines citing Selig S. Harrison's report in *The Washington Post*, 14 and 15 September 1965.

19 Sixty-seven Pakistani tanks were destroyed or damaged during the battle for Phillora as against only six Indian tanks.

20 'Statement of the Government of the People's Republic of China, 7 September 1965,' reprinted as Appendix I in *White Paper No. XII, January 1965–February 1966*.

21 'Note given by the Ministry of Foreign Affairs, Peking, to the Embassy of India in China, 8 September, 1965,' reprinted in *White Paper No. XII*.

22 'Note given by the Ministry of Foreign Affairs, Peking, to the Embassy of India in China, 16 September, 1965,' reprinted in *White Paper No. XII.*

23 Defence Minister's diary entry of 21 September 1965.

24 'Note given by the Ministry of External Affairs, New Delhi, to the Embassy of China in India, 12 September, 1965,' reprinted in *White Paper No. XII.*

25 The narrow Siliguri Corridor provides the land link between the northeastern states and the rest of India.

26 Thomas citing D.K. Palit, 'Outmoded Imperial Concepts,' *The Hindustan Times*, 27 and 29 December 1969.

References

Brines, Russell. 1968. *The Indo-Pakistani Conflict.* London: Pall Mall Press.

Chakravorty, B.C. 1992. *History of the Indo-Pak War, 1965.* New Delhi: Ministry of Defence.

Chopra, Pran. 1973. *India's Second Liberation.* New Delhi: Vikas Publishing House.

Crawford, Timothy. 2002. 'Kennedy and Kashmir, 1962–63: The Perils of Pivotal Peacemaking in South Asia'. *India Review*, 1(3): 1–38.

Gupta, Ranjit and Radhakrishna. 1971. *World Meet on Bangla Desh: Report of the International Conference on Bangla Desh, Held in New Delhi from September 18 to 20, 1971.* New Delhi: IMPEX India.

Howard, Michael. 1979. 'The Forgotten Dimensions of Strategy'. *Foreign Affairs*, 57(5): 975–986.

Khan, M. Asghar. 1979. *The First Round: Indo-Pakistan War 1965.* Ghaziabad, UP: Vikas Publishing House.

Khan Chaudhry, A.A. 1977. *September 65: Before and After.* Lahore: Ferozsons.

Kumar, Ravinder and H.Y. Sharada Prasad. eds. 1999. *Selected Works of Jawaharlal Nehru,* Second Series, Vol. 25. New Delhi: Jawaharlal Nehru Memorial Fund.

Lal, P.C. 2008. *My Years with the IAF,* edited by Ela Lal. New Delhi: Lancer.

Lehl, Lachhman Singh. 2005. *Missed Opportunities: Indo-Pak War 1965,* 2nd edn. Dehradun: Natraj Publishers.

Mankekar, D.R. 1967. *Twenty Two Fateful Days: Pakistan Cut to Size.* Bombay: Manaktalas.

McMahon, Robert J. 1994. *The Cold War on the Periphery: The United States, India, and Pakistan.* New York: Columbia University Press.

Mearsheimer, John J. 1989. 'Assessing the Conventional Balance: The 3:1 Rule and Its Critics'. *International Security*, 13(4): 54–89.

Ministry of External Affairs. 1966. *White Paper No. XII: Notes, Memoranda and Letters Exchanged Between the Government of India and China, January 1965–February 1966*. New Delhi: Ministry of External Affairs.

Musa, Mohammad H.J. 1983. *My Version: India–Pakistan War 1965*. Lahore: Wajidalis.

Narayan, B.K. 1978. *General J.N. Chaudhuri: An Autobiography*. New Delhi: Vikas Publishing House.

Nawaz, Shuja. 2008. *Crossed Swords: Pakistan, Its Army, and the Wars Within*. Karachi: Oxford University Press.

Palit, D.K. 1972. *The Lightning Campaign: The Indo-Pakistan War 1971*. New Delhi: Thomson Press.

Palit, D.K. 1991. *War in the High Himalaya: The Indian Army in Crisis, 1962*. New Delhi: Lancer International.

Paul, T.V. 1994. *Asymmetric Conflicts: War Initiation by Weaker Powers*. Cambridge: Cambridge University Press.

Pradhan, R.D. 2013. *Debacle to Resurgence: Y.B. Chavan: Defence Minister (1962–66)*. New Delhi: Atlantic Publishers.

Raghavan, Srinath. 2010. 'Soldiers, Statesmen and Strategy'. *Seminar*, 611. Available at: http://www.india-seminar.com/2010/611/611_srinath_raghavan.htm (accessed on 25 July 2013).

Rao, K.V. Krishna. 1991. *Prepare or Perish: A Study of National Security*. New Delhi: Lancer International.

Rao, R. Rama. 1973. 'Peace in the Sub-Continent'. *Journal of the United Service Institution of India*, 103(430): 173–178.

Sharada Prasad, H.Y. and A.K. Damodaran. eds. 2003. *Selected Works of Jawaharlal Nehru*, Second Series, Vol. 32. New Delhi: Jawaharlal Nehru Memorial Fund.

Shastri, Lal Bahadur. 1974. *Selected Speeches of Lal Bahadur Shastri: June 11, 1964 to January 10, 1965*. New Delhi: Ministry of Information and Broadcasting, 2007 reprint.

Singh, Harbakhsh. 1991. *War Despatches: Indo-Pak Conflict 1965*. New Delhi: Lancer International.

Singh, Jasjit. 2013. *Defence from the Skies: 80 Years of the Indian Air Force*, 2nd edn. New Delhi: Knowledge World and Centre for Air Power Studies.

Singh, Pushpinder. 1997. *Himalayan Eagles: History of the Indian Air Force*, 3 vols. New Delhi: The Society for Aerospace Studies.

Singh, Pushpinder. 2007. *Himalayan Eagles: History of the Indian Air Force*, Vol. II. New Delhi: The Society for Aerospace Studies.

Srivastava, C.P. 1996. *Lal Bahadur Shastri: A Life of Truth in Politics*. Delhi: Oxford University Press.

Subrahmanyam, K. 1971. 'Military Aid to Pakistan and Its Repercussions on Bangla Desh'. In *World Meet on Bangla Desh: Report of the International Conference on Bangla Desh, Held in New Delhi from September 18 to 20, 1971*, edited by Ranjit Gupta and Radhakrishna, 110–118. New Delhi: IMPEX India.

Subrahmanyam, K. 1972. *Bangla Desh and India's Security*. Compiled by D.K. Palit. Dehradun: Palit and Dutt.

The International Institute for Strategic Studies. 1963. *The Military Balance 1963–1964*. London: The International Institute for Strategic Studies.

Thomas, Raju G.C. 1978. *The Defence of India: A Budgetary Perspective of Strategy and Politics*. Delhi: Macmillan.

6

The 1971 War and the Sundarji Doctrine

Even as the post-1965 changes in roles, plans, and doctrines were being introduced and absorbed in the armed services, India's embroilment in the unexpected outbreak of the civil war between the western and eastern wings of Pakistan necessitated a marked change in strategy and the army's doctrine in particular. The underlying cause of Pakistan's civil war lay in the eastern wing's quest for autonomy and the western wing's determination to perpetuate its hegemony. But the immediate trigger was the electoral majority that the East Pakistan-based Awami League won in the December 1970 general elections and the unwillingness of the West Pakistan-based forces (political and military) to concede the League's right to form a national government. The Pakistani military regime's brutal action to crush the resultant protests in East Pakistan ensued in the civil war.[1]

India, which surrounds East Pakistan on three sides, inevitably became embroiled in this crisis for two reasons. First, Indian territory formed a base both for the rebel forces, which later became organised as the Mukti Bahini, as well as the government-in-exile. And second, 10 million refugees poured into Indian territory over the course of the next few months. Not only was the provision of succour to the fleeing millions a huge economic burden, but the refugees also posed a political problem by dint of their concentration in politically sensitive states, which were either jealous about guarding their tribal way of life (Tripura and Meghalaya) or troubled by insurgency (Nagaland and Mizoram) and left-wing rebellion (West Bengal) (Sisson and Rose 1990, 179–181). Given this enormous number of refugees, the Indian prime minister was determined not to simply absorb them, as 4 million fleeing Hindus had already been absorbed until then (Dhar 2000, 158; Ayoob and Subramanyam 1972, 193). This meant that either Pakistan found a political solution that ensured the return of the refugees or

India militarily intervened to bring about a solution that facilitated their return. Given the Pakistan government's determination to find a military solution at the expense of a political accommodation, which was only stiffened by the unstinted support extended by the United States, an Indian intervention became inevitable.[2]

When the extent of the crisis in East Pakistan dawned upon the Indian government during the summer of 1971 with the arrival of millions of refugees, several voices within the government began to call for an immediate military intervention (Chopra 1973, 77–78).[3] But neither the prime minister nor the army leadership was enthusiastic about an intervention at that point in time.[4] The army chief highlighted three reasons for desisting from military action at that juncture. First, the mountain passes along the India–China border would be open, thereby enabling China to initiate hostilities against India for diversionary purposes. Second, the Indian Army had at its disposal only a division plus strength on the East Pakistan front, whereas Pakistan had, during the course of the previous couple of months, built up its forces to more than four divisions. And third, even if the army were to rush reinforcements to this front in the course of the following few weeks, the monsoon, likely to arrive by that time, would pose a serious challenge to the conduct of both land and air operations (Chopra 1973, 78–79). Given all this, the ideal time to intervene, in the Army Chief General Manekshaw's judgement, would be sometime in December 1971 or January 1972 after the winter had well set in. By that time, not only would the Himalayan passes be blocked by snow, preventing China from initiating hostilities, but also the ground in post-monsoon East Pakistan would have dried up to enable military operations.

If an intervention was indeed to be undertaken later, what doctrine would the armed forces employ? Pakistan made it amply clear that a limited Indian military offensive aimed at capturing a portion of territory and establishing a Bangladeshi government there would mean all-out war, including on the western front. Further, to ensure that such an Indian attempt did not succeed, the bulk of Pakistani forces in East Pakistan—three full divisions and two ad hoc divisions—were moved towards the border and established in strong defensive positions centred on key towns (Ministry of Defence 1992, 498; Chopra 1973, 96).[5]

This Pakistani move nullified the contingency plan (discussed above) that the Indian Army had recently evolved for the East Pakistan front. But, at the same time, the forward defence posture adopted by Pakistan also opened up the possibility for the development of a new doctrine based on manoeuvre.[6]

Army Doctrine[7]

The Indian Army adopted the doctrine of manoeuvre for the East Pakistan front for several reasons. First, attrition would make the war a prolonged affair because of the entrenched defensive positions that the Pakistan Army had built up. Further, in the event of these defences being overwhelmed by superior Indian strength, which in itself would take time, Pakistani forces could fall back to an inner defence line made up of 'the great river obstacles', cracking which would consume even more time (Palit 1972, 99–100). In light of these realities, only a plan based on manoeuvre that bypassed strong Pakistani fortifications and prevented them from falling back on the river obstacles would enable the army to gain a swift victory.

A swift conclusion to the war was imperative given the challenges inherent in allocating adequate forces for three fronts simultaneously—West Pakistan, East Pakistan, and China. In the event of an Indian offensive on the East Pakistan front, the Pakistan government was expected to automatically initiate hostilities on the western front. Since India would not be able to afford the risk of lowering its guard on the West Pakistan front, the obvious source of additional forces for the East Pakistan front, which had only a division plus strength at that juncture, was the mountain divisions deployed on the northern front against China (Palit 1972, 100). If the war were to be a prolonged affair involving the Indian Army in a war of attrition against entrenched Pakistani defence positions, the northern frontier would remain denuded for an extended period and, thus, provide China the opportunity of initiating hostilities. In such an eventuality, India would have no choice but to abandon halfway the attempt to establish an independent Bangladesh and, thereby, create the conditions for the refugees to return.

Furthermore, a prolonged war of attrition would also afford the international community an opportunity to intervene diplomatically and impose a ceasefire. Such a denouement would transform Pakistan's civil war into an India–Pakistan dispute, perpetuate the status quo by freezing the birth of an independent Bangladesh, and leave India with the enormous challenge of dealing with millions of refugees concentrated in some of its most politically sensitive states. The United States, in particular, was expected to take the lead in this effort, given its unstinting support to the Pakistani military regime even in the face of the brutal repression in East Pakistan (Bass 2013, 282–286).

India had signed a security treaty with the Soviet Union in August 1971 in the immediate aftermath of the US opening to China, for this was a development that India could not 'look upon … with equanimity' (Dhar 2000, 171).[8] The aim of the security treaty was to neutralise a possible Chinese military challenge, especially in the context of America's expressed reluctance to militarily assist India in such an eventuality (Kennedy 2011, 136; Kapur 1972, 463–474). But subsequent discussions with Soviet leaders in October 1971 indicated their reluctance to contemplate a break-up of Pakistan and their scepticism about India's military capability. Indeed, they advised against military action in East Pakistan (Chopra 1973, 90–92). The resulting uncertainty about complete Soviet support also made it necessary to conduct a swift campaign, lest Moscow wavered in its diplomatic support for India during the course of a long war of attrition.

Consequently, the Indian Army devised a plan based on manoeuvre with the aim of bringing the war to a swift and successful conclusion. The forces that the army's Eastern Command, which spearheaded this effort, had at its disposal were three corps comprising six divisions and one infantry brigade. Five of these were mountain divisions, originally deployed on the China front (Chopra 1973, 149). These were specially equipped, including with bridging equipment and armour and artillery components that were more suitable for operations on the plains (Jacob 2001, 78–83). To assist the army in its offensive, 10 squadrons of fighters and fighter-bombers as well as a Canberra squadron were assigned to this front. At the same time, helicopters and transport aircraft were placed at the army's disposal. In the case of the navy, the sole aircraft carrier was assigned to the Eastern Fleet for operations in the Bay of Bengal.[9] The larger Indian strategy was for these forces on the eastern front to employ a manoeuvre-based offensive even as a defensive, albeit containing a provision for limited offensives to thwart Pakistan's plans, was adopted on the other (western) front with Pakistan.[10]

Eastern Command's plan had two elements. The first was to contain the entrenched Pakistani forces located near the border. At the same time, three powerful, mobile, and flexible thrusts and one minor thrust were to be set in motion. These thrusts would bypass fortified positions, cut lines of communication, and rush along the path of least resistance towards the 'Dacca bowl'—East Pakistan's triangular heartland bordered by the rivers Jamuna and Meghna. The plan envisaged whole brigade groups avoiding roads and moving over paddy fields or being transported by helicopter across rivers, even as their logistics travelled by bicycles and rickshaws (Palit 1972, 102–103). The gamble was that these thrusts would isolate Dacca from the rest of the Pakistani forces deployed closer to the Indian border. The Eastern Command did not formulate a rigid plan that needed to be strictly followed. Instead, the plan was only to be 'used as a basis for general guidance', with formation commanders constantly reviewing 'thrust lines and intermediate objectives' according to the situation. As a result, the plan only envisaged the securing of the general line running along the Jamuna and Meghna rivers. The ultimate aim and prize of Dacca would depend upon the progress made by the various thrusts (Ministry of Defence 1992, 503–504).

Military professionals have critiqued this lack of a plan for the capture of Dacca and suggested that it was captured only because of later improvisations (Jacob 2001, 56, 66–67, 125–127). What they overlook, however, is the fact that the principal objective while adopting a manoeuvre doctrine is the disruption of lines of communication and nodal points with the aim of bringing about a systemic collapse of adversary forces and structures. The capture of this or that area is important only in so far as it causes disruption of the war effort. During the Second World War, the objective given to the German panzer forces effecting the blitzkrieg was not France's capital Paris but the Channel coast. The rationale for assigning them this objective was to cut off 'Belgian, British and French troops in western Belgium and northeastern France ... between the German columns and the Channel' (Armstrong 1940, 75, 90). It was only after attaining this objective that Germany launched a second major offensive with Paris as the aim.

Thus, for instance, the offensive launched by the II Corps from the west involved a part of the force containing the Pakistani strongholds near the border even as other fast-moving columns bypassed these and raced for the Madhumati River. While the former kept Pakistani forces engaged, the latter moved to cut off their path of retreat towards Dacca. In the process, the mobile columns moved across 'paddy fields and waste lands, carrying all the impediments of battle' with them, for which they received considerable help from the local people. And when the columns moved far ahead of their supply lines, they did not pause to allow logistics to catch up. Instead, they depended on air drops or what locals offered to supplement the rations they carried (Palit 1972, 107–108). Similarly, in the offensive launched from the north by the XXXIII Corps, one part of the force invested the Pakistani positions at Hilli, while another sidestepped it and occupied Bogra in the rear, which disrupted the former's line of communication (Ministry of Defence 1992, 528–530).

In the eastern sector, the offensive launched by the IV Corps was aimed at isolating Pakistani defences and advancing towards the line of the Meghna River. Upon completing this task, commanders on the ground, who found the bridge over the river destroyed, improvised with locally available resources (steamers, vehicle tugs, and country boats) to effect the crossing. They were also helped in this task by a fleet of helicopters, which engaged in what has been termed as an 'air bridging' operation.[11] Over the next few days, a substantial force comprising nine infantry battalions supported by armour, artillery, and engineers crossed the river and stood ready to march on Dacca (Ministry of Defence 1992, 552, 556, 567, 571–572).

These multiple prongs of swift advance that sidestepped fortified positions and severed lines of communication and lines of retreat isolated Pakistani forces from each other. The result was that General Niazi's 'theatre headquarters lost contact with his divisional commands ... [and] the divisional commands with the brigade headquarters', while his troops became 'an aimless crowd' (Chopra 1973, 194). At the end of the war, a substantial part of Pakistani forces surrendered en masse because of the paralysis and confusion caused by the deep Indian penetration.

Roles of the Air Force and Navy

In tune with its determination to support the army's operation in a future war (discussed earlier), the Indian Air Force began its efforts by transporting a significant portion of the army's build-up along the East Pakistan front and providing aerial photographs of areas through which the ground offensive would occur. The specific tasks assigned to the service as part of the overall strategy to be employed were four-fold: eliminate the Pakistan Air Force at the earliest; assist the army through close air support, interdiction, and transport operations; help the navy in its task of isolating East Pakistan; and ensure air defence (Ministry of Defence 1992, 592–594). Accordingly, within the first two days of the war, the Pakistan Air Force was neutralised both through bombing missions as well as in dogfights. The resulting decrease in the need for air defence and counter-air missions automatically meant a stepping up of close air support missions (Ministry of Defence 1972, 598, 602). Control of the air also enabled the ground offensive to proceed swiftly without being dogged by concerns about the need for dispersal or camouflage or avoiding a high density of vehicular traffic (Palit 1972, 115). The air force also played an important role in air bridging operations, wherein helicopters were employed to help the advancing army columns cross the many rivers in East Pakistan (Ministry of Defence 1992, 606–608). Overall, during the course of the war on the eastern front, the air force flew 2,033 sorties. Out of these, 68.1 per cent were for close air support and interdiction, 19.2 per cent for counter-air strikes, 9.1 per cent for air defence, 2.5 per cent for special missions such as paradrops, and 1.1 per cent for reconnaissance (Ministry of Defence 1992, 613–614).

The Indian Navy also had its share of air operations for which it employed its carrier-based aircraft. In fact, the air force and navy had agreed upon a division of the airspace over East Pakistan on an east-west axis, with the former focusing its efforts on Dacca and the area north of it while the latter operated south of that line (Chopra 1973, 127; Palit 1972, 116). Naval aircraft specially targeted Chittagong, Cox Bazar, and other ports, and so did surface ships. In addition, the navy effected a blockade of East Pakistan during which a number of Pakistani merchantmen carrying contraband were seized (Ministry of Defence 1992, 645–649). One other task that the navy carried out was an amphibious landing to cut off the escape routes of Pakistani personnel to Burma. Although 1,200 troops along with their complement of arms, ammunition, stores, and equipment were successfully landed, the operation was marked by mishaps due to 'insufficient data on the landing sites and difficult sea condition' (Ministry of Defence 1992, 649–652). Overall, the naval effort did make useful contributions to the ground offensive, where the war was won.

The Sundarji Doctrine

Inspired by the spectacular victory attained in the 1971 War through the doctrine of manoeuvre, military thinking in India began to shift towards offensive armour operations that would reach deep into (the now reduced) Pakistan. Writing in the immediate aftermath of the 1971 War, K. Subrahmanyam, for instance, argued that India would be able to deter Pakistan from embarking upon aggression or 'invoking external political or military support' only by maintaining 'a clear margin of superiority both in numbers and fire-power' as well as by convincing it that, in a future war, India's armoured formations are unlikely to be employed 'restrictively' in the Punjab theatre and that they cannot be 'slowed down and stopped by well-prepared defences and water obstacles' (Subrahmanyam 1972, 53, 58). He, therefore, advocated the build-up of India's offensive armour capabilities that can operate in the desert as well as 'self-contained armoured forces' equipped with medium tanks that have 'water-crossing capability', self-propelled guns, mechanised infantry, and bridging and mine-clearing equipment (Subrahmanyam 1972, 58; Rikhye 1972, 163–168; Rikhye 1973, 137–145).

In pursuit of this line of thinking, the political leadership appointed a three-member expert committee in 1975 to develop a 20-year perspective plan for the Indian Army. Viewing Pakistan and China as the principal threats, the committee, comprising Generals K.V. Krishna Rao, M.L. Chibber, and K. Sundarji, recommended the establishment of a force structure that would make it impossible for these countries to achieve their objectives by war and thus deter them. What this meant in operational terms vis-à-vis Pakistan was the maintenance of 'a force advantage of two corps', increasing the army's tank regiments from 27 to 58, and creating two mechanised infantry divisions (Gupta 1997, 49).[12] This recommendation also coincided with the obsolescence of older tanks in the inventory. Although the British Chieftain and the German Leopard 2 were at first considered, the T-72 was eventually chosen because of the favourable price and production terms offered by the Soviet Union. Over the next five years, 300 T-72s were acquired and orders were placed for another 1,600 (Thomas 1989, 165–166). In addition, the most significant acquisitions of the Indian Army during the 1980s were the Bofors 155 mm Howitzers and infantry combat vehicles. All these acquisitions were made to enhance the army's ability to conduct a deep armoured thrust into Pakistani territory and, thus, attain a swift victory in a war of manoeuvre.

The post-1971 impulse towards undertaking offensive armour operations against Pakistan and the introduction of new weapons in the 1980s resulted in the reformulation of the Indian Army's doctrine. An effort spearheaded by General Sundarji, hence the appellation Sundarji Doctrine, the new doctrine called for deep armoured thrusts into Pakistani territory with the primary objective of capturing or destroying 'nerve centres' like corps' headquarters, operational reserves, military airfields, and even towns that have 'politico-economic importance', while at the same time neutralising 'intermediate objectives' like divisional headquarters, logistics support areas, tactical reserves, and long-range rocket artillery positions (Kanwal 1988, 82).

The idea of carrying out deep armoured thrusts was first tested in 1983 through Exercise Dig Vijay. It was further refined through Exercise Brasstacks, which was held in four stages. Brasstacks started with a map exercise in May 1986 and continued as 'a computerised war game-cum-sand model exercise' in November 1986. The third stage, held in November–December 1986, involved 'segmented exercises by different arms and services' for the purpose of supporting 'divisional-corps-level offensive operations in a mobile battle ground environment'. And the fourth stage, in February–March 1987, saw its culmination as 'a massive field exercise' spread over an area of 100 by 150 kilometres and involving three army commands, two air force commands, and a navy component stimulating an amphibious landing (Bajpai et al. 1997, 28). This last stage was conducted in the general area east of the Indira Gandhi Canal in Rajasthan—the likely theatre of a future conflict with Pakistan, given that Punjab's natural ground features and extant obstacle systems, as seen during the 1965 War, did not provide 'much scope' for manoeuvring 'major mechanised forces' (Thomas 1990, 62).

The political scenario visualised by the exercise was a Pakistani military intervention not only in Kashmir but also in Punjab to aid Sikh militants, who were then engaged in a terrorist campaign to attain independence. Under these circumstances, the only theatre where India would be able to bring to bear effective counter-pressure was across the Rajasthan border. Moreover, such a war in the Rajasthan–Sind sector would also enable India to leverage its superiority in armoured forces as well as in combat aircraft.

In order to fully exploit the potential of deep armoured thrusts, General Sundarji proposed the creation of Reorganised Army Plains Infantry Divisions (RAPIDs).[13] For, it was evident that existing infantry divisions lacked 'mobility, flexibility, firepower and shock-action'. They were, therefore, 'incapable of functioning in support of mechanised forces in fast-moving fluid operations' by clearing axes of advance for the provision of logistics, dealing with pockets of enemy resistance that had been bypassed by the mechanised forces, capturing key nodes, and destroying strong points (Thomas 1989, 92). Consequently, RAPIDs were to be equipped with 'a greater complement of armour, mechanised infantry, reconnaissance, support and surveillance elements, anti-tank guided missile elements, air-defence artillery, attack and heavy-lift helicopter and close air support and wheeled/halftrack troop-carrying vehicles' (Thomas 1989, 92). These modernised infantry divisions were to be employed in both offensive and defensive roles, although they would be designed along the same lines. While those envisaged as offensive RAPIDs would be part of the strike corps, their defensive counterparts would operate with the 'holding corps'. And the mechanised brigade of defensive RAPIDs would perform 'counter-penetration and counter-attack tasks in conjunction with the independent armoured brigade'. This would also have the additional advantage of releasing infantry for other tasks (*India Defence Review* 1988, 38).

Sundarji also proposed the creation of air assault divisions equipped with helicopters to enable deep strikes in enemy territory—a proposal that was considered by at least one critic as unaffordable and logistically nightmarish to sustain, given that such a force would be moving at 200 kilometres an hour and operating over 400,000 square kilometres (Rikhye 1990, 73–77). A subsequent perspective plan that Sundarji developed on what the army should evolve into by the year 2000 advocated a force level of 45 divisions, including four armoured divisions, eight mechanised infantry divisions, seven RAPIDs, and two air assault divisions (Gupta 1997, 59).

Doctrines of the Air Force and Navy

During the 1980s, like in the case of the army, the air force and navy also saw significant accretions to their force levels and capabilities. This concerted build-up of the capabilities of all the three services was premised on the goal of deterring Pakistan in particular, which, during the 1970s, had expanded its army by 70 per cent and emerged in the 1980s as a frontline state receiving significant US military assistance (Subrahmanyam 1982, 150).[14]

The Indian Air Force's experience in the 1971 War made it realise the imperative of attaining control of the air in the initial stages of a conflict. Consequently, it began to emphasise on this priority, with close air support for ground forces coming immediately thereafter in its list of priorities. In order to enable it to attain control of the air, the air force acquired a range of Western (Jaguars and Mirage 2000s) and Soviet aircraft (MiG-23s, 27s, 29s) during the late 1970s and the decade of the 1980s. One other crucial addition to the air force inventory during this period was the Il-76, designed to provide strategic airlift capability for the service. For its part, the Indian Navy, with the addition of a second aircraft carrier, Sea Harriers, Tu-142 maritime patrol aircraft, and Kilo and HDW submarines, planned for maintaining sea control in order to be able to project power onto Pakistani territory (Gupta 1997, 53–54, 60–63).

Summary

In the wake of India's embroilment in the civil war between the western and eastern wings of Pakistan, a marked change in strategy and doctrine was necessary, although the post-1965 changes in roles, plans, and doctrines were being introduced and absorbed in the armed services. The Pakistani military regime's brutal action in the 1970 general elections to crush the resultant protests in East Pakistan resulted in the civil war. With the arrival of millions of refugees in 1971, the extent of the crisis in East Pakistan dawned upon the Indian government, which called for an immediate military intervention. The Indian Army adopted the doctrine of manoeuvre with the aim of bringing the war to a swift and successful conclusion. Inspired by the spectacular victory in 1971, military thinking in India began to shift towards offensive armour operations that would reach deep into (the now reduced) Pakistan. In 1975, the three-member expert committee recommended the establishment of a force structure that would make it impossible for Pakistan and China to achieve their objectives by war and, thus, deter them. The introduction of new weapons in the 1980s resulted in the reformulation of the Indian Army's doctrine. The new doctrine called for deep armoured thrusts into Pakistani territory with the primary objective of capturing or destroying 'nerve centres' while at the same time neutralising 'intermediate objectives'. Since the existing infantry divisions lacked 'mobility, flexibility, firepower and shock-action', in order to fully exploit the potential of deep armoured thrusts, General Sundarji proposed the creation of Reorganised Army Plains Divisions (RAPIDs). Sundarji also proposed the creation of air assault divisions equipped with helicopters to enable deep strikes in enemy territory. During the 1980s, like in the case of the army, the air force and navy also saw significant accretions to their force levels and capabilities.

Notes

1 On the factors that led to the break between the two wings of Pakistan and its denouement into civil war, see Raghavan (2013).
2 On US support for the Pakistan government during the civil war, see Bass (2013).
3 The most prominent advocates of intervention were the finance and defence ministers. But the foreign minister opposed such a venture.
4 The prime minister invited the army chief to a Cabinet meeting where he could voice his reservations and, thus, help to silence the advocates. It is not clear when exactly this meeting took place. In a 1996 interview, the then army chief mentioned that it may have been towards the end of April 1971. For a reproduction of this interview, see Jacob (2001, Appendix 6, pp. 181–183).
5 Except for the Introduction and Chapter 1, the rest of this official history is available at: http://www.bharat-rakshak.com/LAND-FORCES/Army/History/1971War/PDF/ (accessed on 10 November 2013).
6 On what a forward defence posture involves and Pakistan adopting this approach, see Mearsheimer (1983, 48–49, 206).
7 The 1971 War occurred along both the western and eastern fronts. India adopted the defensive on the western front and a manoeuvre-based offensive on the eastern front. The discussion here is limited to events on the eastern front.
8 Phrase used by the then Foreign Minister Swaran Singh during a statement.
9 On the allocation of forces for the Bangladesh operation, see the *Official History of the 1971 War*, pp. 284–285.
10 On India's strategy on the western front, see *Official History of the 1971 War*, Chapters 8, 9, 10, and 11.
11 Several such air bridging operations were carried out during the course of the campaign.
12 The committee considered that existing forces were sufficient to deter China. Its other major recommendation was to enhance the capabilities of domestic research and development in order to reduce the dependence on imports.
13 At the same time, he also mooted the idea of RAMIDs—Reorganised Army Mountain Infantry Divisions—for the Chinese front.
14 During the 1980s, IDSA, in particular, brought to bear intense focus on Pakistan's defence build-up since the 1970s, the financing of this build-up

by West Asian countries, and the provision of US military aid. See, for instance, Singh (1988); Sawhney (1984); and Gupta (1982)

References

Armstrong, Hamilton Fish. 1940. 'The Downfall of France'. *Foreign Affairs*, 19(1): 55–144.

Ayoob, Mohammed and K. Subramanyam. 1972. *The Liberation War*. New Delhi: S. Chand and Co.

Bajpai, Kanti, P.R. Chari, Pervaiz Iqbal Cheema, Stephen P. Cohen, and Sumit Ganguly. 1997. *Brasstacks and Beyond: Perception and Management of Crisis in South Asia*. New Delhi: Manohar.

Bass, Gary J. 2013. *The Blood Telegram: India's Secret War in East Pakistan*. Noida: Random House India.

Chopra, Pran. 1973. *India's Second Liberation*. Delhi: Vikas.

Dhar, P.N. 2000. *Indira Gandhi, the 'Emergency', and Indian Democracy*. New Delhi: Oxford University Press.

Gupta, Amit. 1982. 'Pakistan's Acquisition of Arms: Rationale, Quest and Implications'. *IDSA Journal*, 14(3): 422–443.

Gupta, Amit. 1997. 'Building an Arsenal: The Indian Experience'. In *Building an Arsenal: The Evolution of Regional Power Force Structures*, edited by Amit Gupta, 27–82. Westport, CT: Praeger.

Indian Defence Review. 1988. 'Interview with General K. Sundarji, PVSM, ADC, Chief of the Army Staff'. *Indian Defence Review*, January: 35–41.

Jacob, J.F.R. 2001. *Surrender at Dacca: Birth of a Nation*. New Delhi: Manohar.

Kanwal, Gurmeet. 1988. 'Strike Corps Offensive Operations: Imperatives for Success'. *Indian Defence Review*, January: 81–89.

Kapur, Ashok. 1972. 'Indo-Soviet Treaty and the Emerging Asian Balance'. *Asian Survey*, 12(6): 463–74.

Kennedy, Andrew. 2011. 'India's Nuclear Odyssey: Implicit Umbrellas, Diplomatic Disappointments, and the Bomb'. *International Security*, 36(2): 120–153

Mearsheimer, John J. 1983. *Conventional Deterrence*. New York: Cornell University Press.

Ministry of Defence. 1992. *Official History of the 1971 War*. New Delhi: History Division, Ministry of Defence.

Palit, D.K. 1972. *The Lightning Campaign: The Indo-Pakistan War, 1971*. New Delhi: Lancer International.

Raghavan, Srinath. 2013. *1971: A Global History of the Creation of Bangladesh*. Ranikhet: Permanent Black.

Rikhye, Ravi. 1972. 'Rethinking Mechanised Infantry Concepts'. *Journal of the United Service Institution of India*, 102(427): 163–168.

Rikhye, Ravi. 1973. 'A New Armoured Force for India'. *Journal of the United Service Institution of India*, 103(432): 137–145.

Rikhye, Ravi. 1990. *The Militarization of Mother India*. Delhi: Chanakya Publications.

Sawhney, R.G. 1984. 'Pakistan's Military Capability'. *IDSA Journal*, 16(3): 195–214.

Singh, Jasjit. 1988. 'Pakistan Army: The Growing Offensive Capability'. *Strategic Analysis*, 11(11): 1225–1238.

Sisson, Richard and Leo E. Rose. 1990. *War and Secession: Pakistan, India, and the Creation of Bangladesh*. Berkeley: University of California Press.

Subrahmanyam, K. 1972. *Our National Security*. New Delhi: Economic and Scientific Research Foundation.

Subrahmanyam, K. 1982. *Indian Security Perspectives*. New Delhi: ABC Publishing House.

Thomas, Mathew. 1989. 'The RAPID: An Appraisal of India's New-Look Infantry Division for Warfare in the Plains'. *Indian Defence Review*, January: 92–101.

Thomas, Mathew. 1990. 'An Analysis of the Threat Perception and Strategy for India'. *Indian Defence Review*, January: 61–64.

Thomas, Raju G.C. 1986. *Indian Security Policy*. Princeton, NJ: Princeton University Press.

7

Strategy in the Shadow of Nuclear Weapons

Some of Sundarji's proposals for reorganising the army remained unimplemented because of cuts in defence expenditure in the wake of a national financial crisis in the early 1990s (Singh 2001, xvi–xvii). At the same time, the idea of effecting a deep penetration into Pakistani territory became impossible because of Pakistan's acquisition of nuclear weapons capability. The introduction of nuclear weapons into the India–Pakistan equation also tended to hasten international and, in particular, US diplomatic intervention during crises.[1] This further reduced the time window available for the Indian military to take effective action.

The shadow of the bomb began to induce a degree of caution in exercising the option of an armoured thrust in the desert sector, as is evident from the writings of retired military professionals. In one such view, an armoured offensive was still necessary not only for compelling Pakistan to vacate Indian territory but also to force its reserves into battle and destroy them. But, at the same time, the 'chemical/nuclear threshold' must not be crossed in the process of capturing or threatening Pakistan's 'sensitive territory, or objectives'. Consequently, the distances penetrated in North and Central Rajasthan 'need not be more than 60 to 80 kilometres', although it would be prudent to conduct 'a sector-wise study of the NBC [nuclear-biological-chemical] threshold' in order to validate the distances up to which armoured forces can penetrate in these desert and semi-desert sectors. Even in the South Rajasthan and Gujarat sector, which provided scope for large-scale manoeuvre and where the distances penetrated would depend on the availability of logistical support, armoured penetrations need to be limited to the major river line (Thomas 1990, 62).

It is not clear what influence this caution expressed from the outside had on the army's internal thought process and whether the scale and purpose of the armour penetration envisaged were accordingly changed. But what is clear is the fact that the army seems to have assumed in the early 1990s that its offensive to capture key objectives may well trigger a Pakistani nuclear response. Consequently, it set out to strengthen its ability to fight in such an environment by boosting mobility, shifting to round-the-clock operations, rapidly deploying forces through paradrops, dispersing formations, and developing procedures for decontamination and the ability to maintain forces in contaminated areas (Patel 2004).

Strategy in the Kargil War

That such a risk is unlikely to be contemplated by the political leadership became clear during the summer of 1999 when Pakistani forces occupied mountain heights overlooking a key Indian line of communication in the Kargil region of Jammu and Kashmir. The ensuing border conflict remained restricted to this particular sub-sector because the political leadership adopted a calibrated response, wherein both the army and the air force were instructed not to cross the Line of Control (LoC) during the course of operations (Chari et al. 2008, 122).

During the winter of 1998–1999, the Pakistan Army occupied 'an area of about 130 square kilometres over a front of over 100 kilometres, and a depth ranging between seven to fifteen kilometres' in the Kargil district of Kashmir (Qadir 2002, 26). Its initial, minimal aim of providing a fillip to the waning insurgency in Kashmir subsequently expanded to one of posing a combined Pakistani military–Kashmiri insurgency threat at the front and rear of Indian forces. Pakistani military planners calculated that India's likely decision to augment force levels in Kashmir would erode its overall force advantage for carrying out an all-out offensive, that even such an augmentation would not be able to deal with the combined challenge in Kashmir, and that such a circumstance would force India to the negotiating table where its weak hand would be exploited to seek 'a just and permanent solution to the Kashmir issue in accordance with the wishes of the people of Kashmir' (Quadir 2002, 26–27).

Contrary to this calculation, India was indeed able to orchestrate a strategy to deal with the Pakistani challenge. The broad contours of this strategy were as follows: the exercise of restraint in terms of neither declaring a war nor escalating the conflict by permitting the armed forces to cross the LoC and the adoption of an assertive posture by all three armed services to prevent Pakistan from focusing only on the Kargil sector (Malik 2010, 139). While the exercise of restraint earned India the support of the international community and the United States, in particular, the adoption of an assertive posture enabled it to deter Pakistan.[2] In tune with the strategy approved by the political leadership, the army not only reassigned and built up its force levels, including artillery, in Kashmir but also forward deployed in other theatres some elements of the strike corps along with their logistics (Gill 2009, 113, 128–129).[3] In addition, formations along the International Border and LoC were instructed 'to exert pressure on the Pakistani military through forward deployment, active patrolling and surveillance' (Malik 2010, 128–129). The air force activated its defences in the area covered by its Western Command (Kashmir to parts of Rajasthan), with the proviso that there should be 'no sudden or mass movement of aircraft' (Tipnis 2006, 13). And to strengthen the air effort in the Kargil sector, it built up its aircraft strength in Srinagar airbase as well in Awantipur (Lambeth 2012, 17). For its part, the navy augmented its Western Fleet with some ships from the Eastern Fleet, transferred its amphibious brigade to the west coast, and, in a further effort to signal its 'readiness and resolve', shifted the venue of its 'SUMMEREX' exercise from the Bay of Bengal to the Arabian Sea (Gill 2009, 110).

Within this overall strategic posture, aimed at deterring Pakistan, the doctrinal orientations of the army and the air force were the attrition and pushing back of the intruding forces through a combination of ground battles and the application of firepower from both land and aerial platforms. Thus, before the army commenced each of its tactical battles to physically capture the occupied hill features, such as Tiger Hill and Tololing, artillery firepower was applied to soften these targets and psychologically exhaust the intruders positioned there (Bammi 2002, 199–388; Malik 2010, 161–211). The air force, too, played a critical role in delivering firepower upon the camps, material dumps, and supply routes of the intruders, with its most significant successes being the destruction of the supply depot at Muntho Dalo and of the intruders' command and control bunkers on Tiger Hill. Overall, during the course of the war, the air force undertook a total of 7,631 sorties (Lambeth 2012, 14, 20, 22).

The Practice of Coercive Diplomacy

In the wake of the Kargil conflict, political leaders, military professionals, and independent analysts began to articulate the existence of space below the nuclear threshold for waging conventional wars that are limited in terms of space and force levels employed.[4] This idea of limited war was reinforced by the India–Pakistan crisis that occurred in the wake of the terrorist attack on the Indian Parliament in December 2001. The attack represented a new degree of escalation in the campaign that Pakistan-based and -supported terrorist groups began to unleash from the mid-1990s. India interpreted the attack, in the words of the then Home Minister L.K. Advani, as 'undoubtedly the most audacious' and 'the most alarming act of terrorism in the nearly two-decade-long history of Pakistan-sponsored terrorism in India (*The Hindu* 19 December 2001). Its threshold of tolerance breached, India ordered general mobilisation of its armed forces in an attempt to compel Pakistan into ceasing support for the anti-India terrorist groups based in its territory.

Known as Operation Parakram, the mobilisation lasted 10 months until October 2002. Given the fact that it had been mobilised and could well be asked to initiate hostilities, the army had to necessarily evolve a plan of action. Its first plan was an offensive into Pakistan-occupied Kashmir with the aim of occupying those patches of territory that would stem the infiltration of terrorists. But the plan was subsequently abandoned because the element of surprise was lost in the absence of an immediate political decision to initiate hostilities. Soon, Pakistan mobilised its own armed forces. With the other side prepared, the Indian Army calculated that an offensive in mountainous terrain was bound to lead to high levels of attrition without, at the same time, gaining anything substantial. It, thereafter, devised a new plan to conduct an armoured thrust across the Rajasthan border during the summer of 2002, especially because of the superiority enjoyed in terms of the number of strike corps possessed—three versus Pakistan's two. The army's calculation was that Pakistan would be forced to move both its strike corps to meet the Indian offensive in the desert sector, thereby presenting India an opportunity to attrite them. That would not only cause the destruction of Pakistan's centre of military gravity—its two strike corps—but also result in the capture of territory for use as a bargaining chip in peace negotiations (Sood and Sawhney 2003, 73–76, 80–81).

It seems to have escaped the attention of military planners that such destruction of Pakistan's centre of military gravity would tantamount to total victory and that such an objective is best pursued in a full-scale war and not in a limited war, that too under a nuclear overhang. In any event, the political leadership was far more focused on leveraging the military mobilisation, which had been recommended by the military leadership as a preliminary to carrying out any operation for diplomatic coercion.[5]

What Is Coercive Diplomacy?

Diplomacy is about bargaining. Its objective is to seek mutually acceptable outcomes. Concepts like deterrence, compellence, and nuclear blackmail reflect the bargaining power that comes from the physical harm that one country can do to another. While the armed forces can be used to achieve an objective forcibly, their capacity to inflict harm can also be used as leverage to influence other countries. Used as bargaining power, the military capacity to cause harm is part of diplomacy. The purpose of causing harm or threatening to cause harm is to influence the other side's policy choice. 'The power to hurt is bargaining power. To exploit it is diplomacy …' (Schelling 1966, 2). Thomas Schelling used the term 'compellence' to describe diplomacy of this kind (Schelling 1966, 69–78). But compellence is itself part of the larger concept of strategic coercion, which later has been defined as 'the deliberate and purposive use of overt threats to influence another's strategic behaviour' (Jakobsen 1998, 11).[6]

Deterrence and compellence are the two major subsets of strategic coercion. Both rely on threats to persuade the adversary to behave in a way that it would prefer not to. They are, however, used in different phases of a conflict and have different objectives (Jakobsen 1998, 11–12). Deterrence is passive in nature and is aimed at discouraging an adversary from undertaking certain actions through fear induced by the threat to use force. It involves the communication of a threat that pain will be inflicted *if* the adversary initiates certain actions. The initiative is, thus, left to the adversary (Schelling 1966, 71–72). Compellence, in contrast, is active in nature. Its aim is to force an adversary to do something or stop doing something that it would prefer not to. It involves the initiation of an action 'or an irrevocable commitment to action' to convince the adversary that the costs of non-compliance with the stated demand will be high and that punishment will be administered until compliance occurs (Schelling 1966, 70, 72).

Schelling identified a few necessary conditions for the success of compellence. First, the threat conveyed must be potent enough to convince an adversary that non-compliance will be too costly. At the same time, it must also be credible, i.e., the adversary must be convinced that the coercing power has the will and the capability to execute the threat in case of non-compliance. Second, the coercing power must give its adversary adequate time to comply with the demand and also reassure the latter that compliance will not lead to more demands in future. Finally, neither party must perceive the conflict as a zero-sum game and must share a degree of common interest in avoiding a full-scale war. In other words, both sides must believe that they have more to gain from striking a bargain than through recourse to unilateral action (Schelling 1966, passim).

Blackmail and coercive diplomacy are the two subsets of compellence (Jakobsen 1998, 12). Their respective aims are to persuade the adversary to do something or stop doing something. There is, however, one difference between the two. Blackmail is used to persuade the adversary *to do something* that it would prefer not to. For example, it would be blackmail were Pakistan to threaten the use of nuclear weapons against India if the latter did not vacate Jammu and Kashmir.

In contrast, coercive diplomacy is used to force an adversary *to stop doing, or undo, something* that it has already initiated. The coercive threat is issued after the adversary has already initiated its move. The aim is to persuade it to stop doing something and *not physically preventing it from doing so*. Coercive diplomacy does not rely upon the application of overwhelming or quick use of force. Even when force is eventually used when threats have not sufficed, it is employed in a limited, selective, and demonstrative manner as well as in controlled increments. The aim underlying any use of force is to induce the adversary to revise its calculations and agree to a mutually acceptable termination of the conflict. Force is also used to demonstrate resolve to protect national interests as well as to convey the determination to use more force if necessary. The threat or use of force is thus subordinated to a larger politico-diplomatic strategy and is coupled with appropriate communications to the adversary. Coercive diplomacy, thus, has 'a signalling, bargaining, negotiating character that is built into the conceptualisation and conduct of military operations …' (George et al. 1971, 18).

Alexander George identified two essential variables that determine the success of coercive diplomacy: the demand placed on the adversary by the coercing power and the strength of the adversary's disinclination to comply with this demand (George et al. 1971, 22–26). Each influences the other. The strength of the adversary's motivation not to comply depends to a great extent on what is demanded of it and how it perceives this demand. Here, one can distinguish between two types of demands. Either the adversary is asked to *stop* what it is doing, or it is asked to *undo* what it has been doing or has already accomplished. The first type of demand is easier to comply with as well as simpler to enforce since it asks appreciably less of the opponent than the second. Stronger threats and greater pressure will, thus, be necessary to enforce the second type of demand. But against a determined opponent or a country which feels that it is on the verge of an important success, even a stronger coercive threat may not be effective.

An additional factor that comes into play here is the coercing power's own motivation level. This, too, is affected by the nature and magnitude of the demand that it places on its opponent. Relative motivation levels of the two sides play a critical role in the eventual outcome. The chances of success will be appreciably greater if the coercing power chooses only the most important of its national objectives since this is more likely to create an asymmetry of motivation in its favour.

The successful exercise of coercive diplomacy also depends upon positive inducements offered to the adversary to reduce its disinclination to comply with the demand placed upon it. Threats alone, i.e., sheer coercion, may not suffice to induce compliance. The threat to use force must be accompanied by genuine concessions as part of a quid pro quo that secures the coercing power's essential demands. At the same time, the adversary must view the inducement offered as credible and something that will be honoured after the crisis is over.

In a subsequent revised edition of their work, Alexander George and William Simons identified four variants of the coercive diplomacy strategy: ultimatum, tacit ultimatum, gradual turning of the screw, and the try-and-see methods.

The 'ultimatum' variant has three elements: a demand on the adversary, a time limit for compliance with the demand, and a specific threat of punishment in case of non-compliance. The threat of punishment may or may not be accompanied by the promise of rewards for compliance.

The 'tacit ultimatum' variant differs in two respects from the above. It does not contain a specific time limit for compliance with the demand, and the nature of the punishment to be meted out for non-compliance is not specified. Instead, a sense of urgency or an indication of the nature of the punishment contemplated is conveyed by other means such as military preparations.

In the 'gradual turning of the screw' method, the coercing power neither creates a sense of urgency for compliance with its demand nor does it signal the nature of the punishment that it is contemplating in case of non-compliance. Instead, its demands are accompanied by a threat that punishment will be gradually increased if compliance is not forthcoming. As a first step, economic sanctions may be imposed, followed by their tightening, later the use of limited military force, and so on.

The 'try-and-see' method is the weakest of the four variants. When it conveys its demand and the threat of punishment to the adversary, the coercing power neither places a time limit for compliance nor threatens escalation in case of non-compliance. In case of non-compliance, the coercing power simply executes its threat and then waits to see whether this produces the desired effect (George 1994, 16–19).

The India–Pakistan Context

The concepts of compellence and coercive diplomacy were, however, articulated with superpower rivalry or situations involving a superpower and a minor power in mind. Hence, they cannot be applied wholesale to the India–Pakistan context.

While drawing upon these articulations on coercive diplomacy, we need to keep the following caveats in mind. The circumstances are quite different in the India–Pakistan context. The United States and the former Soviet Union did not share a common border and, more importantly, did not dispute territories that the other possessed. Their rivalry was geopolitical in nature, and the world at large was the stage on which it played itself out. As a result, they had greater freedom for manoeuvre and a more elaborate menu of options. Compromise was also easier, given that the contest was invariably over third countries.

Where a superpower confronted a weaker adversary, the menu of options available to the former was even larger. Relative strength was in favour of the superpower across the military–diplomatic spectrum. This, of course, did not always result in the successful exercise of coercive diplomacy, especially where motivation levels were skewed in favour of the weaker party. A good example is the US failure to coerce North Vietnam into ceasing support for the Viet Cong. But the point being emphasised here is the unequal nature of the contest and the weaker power's lack of military capability to threaten or cause major harm to its more powerful adversary.

In contrast, India and Pakistan are not all that mismatched at the conventional level.[7] They not only share a common border but are also parties to a territorial dispute over 'Kashmir', which is tied to their contending conceptions of national identity. This enmeshing of national identity with national interest makes their conflict that much more intense and limits the scope for compromise. The motivation levels of both parties are, thus, quite high, and each perceives the conflict as a zero-sum game. Moreover, unlike in the superpower context, the geopolitical context influencing the India–Pakistan conflict is rather limited. In the absence of a periphery in which their mutual antagonism can play itself out, or alternatively, given their limitations in projecting power beyond their borders, outlets for their rivalry are mainly focussed on each other's territory.

One complicating factor in this regard is the possession of nuclear weapons by both countries. For India especially, Pakistan's nuclear weapons capability has imposed restrictions on its scope for the use of force. A corollary to the nuclear issue is international concern about the fears of a nuclear war and the diplomatic intervention that it induces. In January and May/June 2002, for example, Western leaders streamed into New Delhi advising military restraint. That these visits and the advice rendered by them and their governments did have an impact on India's decisions can be discerned from the statement made by Prime Minister Vajpayee on 26 May 2002: the time for military action was in the immediate aftermath of the terrorist attack on the Indian Parliament, but his government had decided against it at that time because of the advice rendered to that effect by the United States and other major powers (Kanwar 2002). Whether intended or not, New Delhi even perceived the travel advisories issued by the United States and its allies in late May 2002 as a signal not to initiate hostilities (*The Hindu* 2 June 2002).[8]

The Post-September 11 Strategic Environment

In the wake of September 11, Pakistan, the epicentre of modern-day jihad and its mujahideen cohorts since the early 1980s, had to make a choice between supporting the fundamentalist zealots that it had helped spawn and the US-led campaign against terrorism. Confronted by President George Bush's offer of a stark choice—'either you are with us, or you are with the terrorists'—as well as the private threats conveyed by Secretary of State Colin Powell, President

Pervez Musharraf opted for a 'frontline state' status for Pakistan. This was made doubly necessary by India's prompt offer to be a part of the anti-terrorism coalition. India's participation, even in a passive capacity, would have further consolidated the relationship that it had been forging with the United States through the 1990s. These apprehensions were reflected in Musharraf's televised address to the Pakistani people on 19 September 2001:

> Pakistan is facing an extremely delicate situation; and in my opinion, it is the most delicate phase since 1971. At this moment, our decisions may have far-reaching and wide repercussions.... The worst results, God forbid, may endanger our territorial integrity and our survival. Our critical concerns may be harmed. And, when I talk about critical concerns, I mean that our nuclear strength and our Kashmir cause may be harmed. This is the worst case scenario.... Now let us see what are the designs of our neighbouring country. They have readily offered all their bases, facilities, and logistic support to the United States. They want the United States to side with them and to declare Pakistan a terrorist state. They also want our strategic assets and our Kashmir cause to be harmed.... India does not have any border with Afghanistan. It has no connections with Afghanistan.... In my view, they want a change in Afghanistan and the establishment of an anti-Pakistan government there. What is regrettable that while the whole world is talking about this terrorist incident, our neighbouring country, with which we were talking about peace and cooperation, wants to harm and malign Islam and Pakistan. (BBC News 19 September 2001)

India's offer to be a partner in the US-led campaign against terrorism was a function of its national interests. September 11 represented a watershed in international perceptions about terrorism. Terrorists could no longer masquerade as 'freedom fighters', and their actions could no longer be glorified in terms of martyrdom. Western acknowledgement of Pakistan's symbiotic relationship with the Taliban and other jihadi groups bent on wreaking havoc on India, Israel, and the United States meant that September 11 constituted a window of opportunity for New Delhi to compel Islamabad to roll back its use of cross-border terrorism as an instrument of policy.

In the wake of Musharraf's decision to co-operate with the United States, New Delhi's options were limited to bringing into focus the umbilical links between the Pakistani establishment and the hydra-headed jihadi monster. But the situation changed when terrorists from the Lashkar-e-Taiba (LeT) and Jaish-e-Mohammed (JeM) attacked the Indian Parliament on 13 December 2001, which, according to the then Home Minister L.K. Advani, was an attempt to 'wipe out the entire political leadership of India' (*The Hindu* 20 December 2001). For his part, Prime Minister Atal Bihari Vajpayee described it as an attack on the 'very existence and honour' of the nation (*The Hindu* 2001). Such an affront to the national honour had to be responded to.

Military Mobilisation and the Threat of War

The menu of options available for New Delhi was, however, limited. Non-military measures like economic sanctions had only a symbolic value, given the low levels of trade between the two countries. Severance of transport links would affect only a small section of the population with links on the other side, and Islamabad could no longer even be isolated diplomatically, given its central role in the campaign against terrorism. To begin with, such non-military options were indeed exercised: the severance of rail and road links, the recall of the Indian high commissioner and halving the strength of diplomatic missions, and the denial of Indian air space to Pakistan International Airlines. At the same time, however, military mobilisation was authorised, including the movement of the army's strike elements towards the international border. The air force was placed on full alert (Dikshit 2001). And landmines were laid all along the LoC and the international border in preparation for hostilities (Tisdall and MacAskill 2002).

It appears that the first reaction of the government was to attack terrorist camps located across the LoC in Pakistan-occupied Kashmir. Hot pursuit and surgical strikes were options that were favoured and advocated by both senior members of Vajpayee's Cabinet and leaders of the Bharatiya Janata Party (*The Telegraph* 12 August 2000; *The Times of India* 19 October 2001). In the immediate aftermath of the terrorist attack, the then Home Minister L.K. Advani indicated that there would be some 'action' against terrorist groups based in Pakistan-occupied Kashmir. The then Foreign Minister Jaswant Singh added, 'These are extraordinary days and because these are extraordinary days, the response has to be extraordinary' (Khare 2001).

This mood, however, changed after the debate in Parliament on 18 December 2001, during which even Advani 'refrained from adding to the hype' (*The Hindu* 19 December 2001). For its part, the opposition counselled restraint: while Manmohan Singh, the then leader of opposition in the Rajya Sabha, urged the government to desist from 'loose talk', Shivraj Patil, the then deputy leader of the Congress party in the Lok Sabha, suggested that the government exhaust diplomatic and other options before embarking upon 'hot pursuit' of terrorists across the border or a war (*The Hindu* 19 December 2001).

In any event, strikes against terrorist camps would not have served any useful purpose, given that they could be easily relocated or reassembled. As early as 17 December 2001, the top Indian military brass reportedly conveyed to the Cabinet Committee on Security that strikes against terrorist camps would have little impact since these were 'no more than drill squares and firing ranges' (Kalyanaraman 2002, 484). In addition, they highlighted the importance of weighing the psychological impact of the strikes against the military escalation it might cause 'including the possibility of a full-fledged conflagration'. Although they were '[n]ot averse to carrying out "surgical strikes" or "hot pursuit" across the Line of Control', they favoured 'a carefully calibrated reply' that took into account 'all possible scenarios' (*The Hindu* 19 December 2001).

Some retired military officers contended at the time that the Indian Armed Forces simply did not have the capacity to carry out hot pursuit or surgical strikes across the border. According to Raja Menon, for instance, the navy had 'a competent force of marine commandos' but only three helicopters, that is, a capacity to transport only 40 men. The army also had its commando units, but it did not have a helicopter that could carry more than four people. Whereas the army needed helicopters that could operate in the dark, the helicopters in the inventory of the air force could fly only during the day. Helicopters possessed by the navy were capable of flying over the sea but not over land. None of the services actually possessed a helicopter 'that can fly low over rough terrain on a dark night'. Finally, the most important platform that India lacked was an airborne warning and control system (AWACS) aircraft, which 'would have given us the edge in both the strike and in smothering the riposte that would inevitably follow' (Menon 2001).

If calibrated strikes were difficult, if not impossible, to carry out, and moreover would not have served a useful purpose, a general war was simply inconceivable under the nuclear shadow. Even a limited war under the then prevalent diplomatic and military circumstances was difficult to envisage. Yet, Chief of the Army Staff General Padmanabhan advocated general mobilisation as a prelude to a war for either degrading Pakistani forces or capturing portions of the territory of Jammu and Kashmir under Pakistan's control. Calibrated strikes, in his assessment, would be 'totally futile', and the only way to 'punish someone for something very terrible he has done' was to 'smash him ... destroy his weapons and capture his territory' (Swami 2004).

Prime Minister Vajpayee was dismayed by the military options suggested by General Padmanabhan: liberating Pakistan-occupied Kashmir, annihilating the Pakistani armed forces, or destroying Pakistan altogether. He did not wish to initiate a war in anger and understood the impossibility of controlling its progress (Gupta 2014). Yet, it was also imperative to convey to both Pakistan and the international community that Pakistan's continued sponsorship of terrorism against India and the escalating terrorist campaign of Pakistani jihadi groups in Indian territory is unacceptable and needed to stop. Faced with these twin imperatives, Vajpayee and the other members of the Cabinet Committee on Security grasped at the military leadership's recommendation of general mobilisation as a prelude to military operations that would be authorised subsequently (Panag 2019). Vajpayee was, however, not in favour of undertaking precipitate military action. When Admiral Sushil Kumar, the chief of the naval staff, asked him to spell out the political aim of the war for which the mobilisation was being undertaken so that the armed forces could derive their military objectives therefrom, Vajpayee responded with a cryptic 'mobilize for the present, rest will follow' (*The Times of India* 6 November 2011; *Rediff.com* 4 November 2011).

Any major military operation launched by India would have been impeded by the presence of US forces operating from, around, and through Pakistani territory. The massive American naval presence in the northern part of the Arabian Sea reportedly restricted the strategic sea space available for Indian warships and made it difficult for the Indian Navy to carry out even routine or surveillance missions. And the Americans ignored a discreet Indian request that US naval forces stay away west of a certain longitude (Kalyanaraman 2002, 484). The situation was even more constraining on land. General Padmanabhan publicly acknowledged to journalists that the presence of American troops in Pakistani air bases would indeed inhibit military operations (Dugger 2002). Although the then Foreign Minister Jaswant Singh would subsequently, in May 2002, dismiss the presence of US forces as 'not an inhibiting factor in policy determinations' (Singh 2002), the fact was that India was under considerable American and Western pressure to exercise military restraint.

As early as 16 December 2001, the then Secretary of State Colin Powell had publicly advised the Indian government to exercise restraint (*The Hindu* 17 December 2001). Simultaneously, President George W. Bush urged both India and Pakistan to consider the 'very difficult situation in the region … [which] could spiral out of control' and, therefore, 'take no action that would in any way hinder the war against terrorism, to which both India and Pakistan have committed themselves' (*The Hindu* 19 December 2001). And as the crisis intensified, first in January 2002, and flared up again in May/June 2002, a string of Western leaders streamed through New Delhi advising restraint, including Prime Minister Tony Blair of the United Kingdom, US Secretary of State Colin Powell, US Secretary of Defense Donald Rumsfeld, US Deputy Secretary of State Richard Armitage, Deputy Prime Minister John Manley of Canada, the British Foreign Secretary Jack Straw, and the Japanese Vice-Foreign Minister Seiken Sugiura.

Given that the overt application of military force was not a viable course of action under the circumstances, one option India had was *to generate and manage* a crisis in order to bring to bear on Islamabad direct military pressure as well as diplomatic pressure from the international community. In other words, military mobilisation could be used as an integral part of a politico-diplomatic strategy to pressurise Islamabad into ceasing official support for anti-India terrorists within its territory.

The Indian government appears to have had two sets of audiences in mind. One was the Pakistani leadership, which was sought to be convinced that New Delhi was not averse to escalating the crisis and even waging war if Islamabad did not roll back official patronage to anti-India jihadi groups. The other was the international community, with the United States at the forefront. Mobilisation and the impending threat of war were the means by which New Delhi sought to leverage the international community into exerting pressure on Islamabad and force it to dissociate itself from the jihadi apparatus.

The initial set of demands, communicated through the 14 December 2001 démarche to the Pakistani High Commissioner in New Delhi, was general in character and called for the termination of the activities of the LeT and JeM, including the detention of their leaders, sealing off their offices, and blocking their access to funds (Aneja 2001).[9] But these were later modified into four specific demands. Describing them as 'legitimate' demands, Home Minister Advani reiterated them during a visit to the United States in early January 2002. These were as follows:

1. The hand-over of 20 criminals and terrorists residing in Pakistan, six of whom were Pakistani citizens and the rest being holders of Indian passports. This demand was first articulated on 31 December 2001.
2. The stoppage of cross-border infiltration of terrorists into Indian territory.
3. The closure of facilities, training camps, arms supply routes, funding channels, and all direct and indirect assistance to terrorists operating from Pakistani soil.
4. A 'categorical and unambiguous renunciation' of terrorism in all its manifestations (Krishnaswami 2002).

Drawing upon the four approaches to coercive diplomacy detailed earlier, New Delhi can be said to have adopted the 'tacit ultimatum' variant. Specific demands were placed on Islamabad, but no time limit for compliance was indicated. Though the entire military apparatus was mobilised to communicate a sense of urgency, New Delhi did not specify how exactly it intended to apply force to mete out punishment. While there was no actual (as opposed to apparent) intent to initiate combat, the threat to do so was essential to bring pressure to bear on Islamabad. Drawing upon Schelling's articulations, New Delhi's threat to initiate hostilities had to be perceived by Islamabad as both potent and credible. Hence the necessity for total mobilisation, which included the movement of strike corps towards the Pakistan border, naval assets from the eastern seaboard to the Arabian Sea, aircraft and Prithvi missiles to contingency positions. Later, in May 2002, a unified command structure was created by bringing the Coast Guard and the Border Security Force under the control of the navy and army, respectively—a move that was considered a prelude to the commencement of hostilities (Aneja 2002). That Islamabad recognised the reality of the threats being conveyed by New Delhi was evident from the comment made in December 2001 by Pakistani spokesperson Rashid Qureshi that New Delhi 'is putting itself into a corner where it would be difficult for them [*sic*] to now back off' (Jones 2001).

At the same time, India also understood the necessity of practising crisis management. Brinkmanship is the art of manipulating the shared risk of a war that neither wants in order to force the other side to back down. Thus, any dangerous or unforeseen development had to be promptly dealt with to prevent the situation from slipping out of hand. The removal of Lieutenant General Kapil Vij as commander of the army's II Corps needs to be seen in this light. American satellite imagery had revealed that some armour formations of this Corps had moved from their concentration areas to strike areas, some within two kilometres of the border in the Rajasthan sector. It appears that Vij took this decision on his own initiative so as to have an advantageous position for prosecuting an attack as soon as the political leadership gave the go-ahead for war. When Washington brought this movement to its notice during the visit of Colin Powell, the Indian government promptly recalled Vij from his command (Gupta 2002; *The Times of India* 21 January 2002).

One aspect missing in the Indian exercise was the offer of rewards to induce Pakistani compliance. But what could have India really offered, especially on 'Kashmir'? The only concession that India could have made was negotiations for the formalisation of the territorial status quo, that is, the transformation of the LoC into an international border. As detailed in chapter 2, this has been evident since the late 1940s, although a standing resolution of Parliament passed on 22 February 1994 demands that Pakistan 'vacate the areas of the Indian State of Jammu and Kashmir' which it has 'occupied through aggression', a stand that is desultorily repeated by political leaders and government officials.[10] Even the international community is largely inclined in favour of such a settlement. During the Kargil conflict, the United States and most other countries had emphasised on respecting the sanctity of the LoC, with President Bill Clinton referring to it thus in his direct address to the Pakistani people: 'this era does not reward people who struggle in vain to redraw borders with blood' (CNN 25 March 2000). And, at the height of the May/June 2002 crisis, Joseph Biden, the then chairman of the Senate Foreign Relations Committee, commented that if India 'is willing to make substantive changes in its policy towards Kashmir, Pakistan must be willing to accept the LoC as a border and end its support for insurgency' (Mattoo 2002).

As discussed in chapter 2, this solution remains unacceptable to Pakistan. It was partly to delegitimise the LoC as a possible future boundary that Islamabad initiated the Kargil intrusions (Dixit 1999). During the crisis, Musharraf repeatedly reiterated the Pakistani position on the 'Kashmir' issue and support for Kashmir's liberation. Thus, in his 12 January 2002 speech, Musharraf not only asserted that 'Kashmir runs in our blood. No Pakistani can afford to sever links with Kashmir.... We will continue to extend our moral, political and diplomatic support to Kashmiris', but he also insisted that India–Pakistan relations cannot become normal until the Kashmir issue is resolved (BBC News 12 January 2002). Again, when the crisis hit its second peak in May 2002, Musharraf insisted that 'Kashmir resides in the heart of every Pakistani. Pakistan would always fulfil its duty of providing moral, political and diplomatic support to the cause of Kashmir. Pakistan will always support the Kashmiris' struggle for liberation' (BBC News 27 May 2002).

Clearly, there was nothing that New Delhi could have credibly offered as a starting point for a negotiated compromise. As we saw in chapter 2, even concerted back-channel talks spread over several years to arrive at a status quo plus solution in the aftermath of this crisis were abandoned by Musharraf's political successors, while those who succeeded him at the helm of the Pakistan military fell back to the default option of using terrorism as an instrument of policy as demonstrated by LeT's terrorist attacks in Mumbai in November 2008.

Evaluating the Results

The pressure that New Delhi brought to bear on Pakistan did have an impact. But it worked more effectively through the efforts made by the international community to cajole Musharraf into addressing India's grievances about cross-border terrorism. This, of course, would not have happened if India had not mobilised its military and threatened punitive action. Islamabad, though, remained defiant throughout the stand-off. It sought to counter India through its own military build-up, the movement of ballistic missiles closer to the border, and, in late May 2002, test-firing three ballistic missiles in four days (Kalyanaraman 2003, 737–738; Aneja and Dikshit 2001). Musharraf also flatly refused to oblige on the list of twenty persons demanded by India (BBC News 12 January 2002).

It was, in fact, Washington that took the lead in first freezing the assets of the LeT and later designating it along with the JeM as 'foreign terrorist organisations' (*The Hindu* 22 December 2001; Krishnaswami 2001). Subsequently, President George W. Bush called upon Musharraf 'to take action against the LeT and the JeM, and other terrorist organisations, their leaders and their finances' (*The Hindu* 23 December 2001).[11] It was in response to this exhortation that Musharraf first froze the assets of the LeT on 24 December 2001 and then arrested the chief of the JeM a day later (*The Hindu* 26 December 2001; Reddy 2001).[12] Even Musharraf's speech of 12 January 2002 appears to have been prompted by Washington. For instance, on 7 January 2002, Bush said that 'it is very important for President Musharraf to make a clear statement to the world that he intends to crack down on terror' (Krishnaswami 2002). Again, during the second peak of the crisis in May/June 2002, Bush repeatedly reiterated that Musharraf must deliver on his promises to stop the cross-border infiltration of terrorists. For instance, on 30 May 2002, Bush stated that Musharraf 'must stop the incursions across the Line of Control; he must do so. He said he would do so. We and others are making it clear to him that he must live up to his word' (Krishnaswami 2002).

Russia, Britain, Japan, Australia, Israel, and multilateral organisations, like the European Union and the Group of Eight, also urged Pakistan to stop the cross-border infiltration of terrorists into Indian territory. The only concession that the international community was willing to make in response to the constant Pakistani refrain about the 'Kashmir dispute' was that a dialogue can resume only after the cross-border infiltration of terrorists stopped. Thus, in January 2002, Russian Foreign Minister Igor Ivanov told Asfandyar Wali Khan, a special envoy of President Musharraf, that 'through its concrete actions Islamabad should create a favourable base for resumption of dialogue with New Delhi' (*The Hindu* 22 January 2002). Subsequently, in June 2002, Prime Minister Tony Blair of the United Kingdom noted that the only way in which India and Pakistan can come together and resolve the issue is 'on the basis of Pakistan ceasing completely and absolutely its support for terrorism in Kashmir, or indeed exported from Kashmir. And the Indian Government recognising that if that is the case it is sensible to offer dialogue on all the issues' (Suroor 2002).

On 12 January 2002, Musharraf made a historic speech in which, while reaffirming Pakistan's support for the Kashmiri right to self-determination, he proclaimed:

> No organisation will be allowed to indulge in terrorism in the name of Kashmir. We condemn the terrorist acts of September 11, October 1 and December 13. Anyone found involved in any terrorist act would be dealt with sternly. Strict action will be taken against any Pakistani individual, group or organisation found involved in terrorism within or outside the country. (Musharraf 12 January 2002)

He reaffirmed this commitment in May 2002 after India turned the heat up in the wake of the massacre at Kaluchak:

> I had said in my January 12 address that Pakistani soil would not be allowed to be used for terrorism against anybody. I repeat we will not allow this. I also want to tell the world and give the assurance that no infiltration is taking place across the Line of Control.... Pakistan is doing nothing across the Line of Control and Pakistan will never allow the export of terrorism anywhere in the world from within Pakistan. (Musharraf 27 May 2002)

In early June, Government of India sources were reported to have said that Musharraf may have issued orders to the commander of the Pakistan Army's X Corps deployed along the LoC to curb terrorist infiltration into India (Aneja 2002). On 11 June, Colin Powell confirmed that Musharraf had given assurances to the United States two weeks earlier that 'infiltration activity across the Line of Control' would cease. Powell also stated that his deputy, Richard Armitage, had more recently received further assurances from Pakistan that infiltration would visibly and permanently cease across the LoC and that it 'would be followed by other activities that had to do with the dismantling of the camps that led to the capacity to conduct these kinds of operations' (Krishnaswami 2002). A week later, Defence Minister George Fernandes, Army Chief General S. Padmanabhan, and Ministry of External Affairs Spokesperson Nirupama Rao all confirmed that there had been a 'considerable decline' in cross-border infiltration of terrorists into Jammu and Kashmir during the first two weeks of June (Dikshit 2002).

New Delhi responded to this development by recalling its warships from the Arabian Sea, opening its air space to Pakistani civil airlines, and identifying a new envoy to Islamabad. Following the successful completion of the electoral process in Jammu and Kashmir in early October 2002 and partly as a result of the diminishing returns flowing from the forward military deployment, the Government of India decided on 16 October to de-escalate partially by withdrawing troops from the international border (*The Hindu* 18 October 2002).

So, what did India achieve from this exercise in coercive diplomacy? It was indeed successful in compelling Pakistan to comply with its initial set of demands, i.e., action against the LeT and the JeM. But out of the four subsequent demands, Pakistan formally complied with only one: the public undertaking not to permit terrorism in the name of 'Kashmir' from within its territory. This did not, however, result in the total cessation of cross-border terrorist infiltration. Neither did Islamabad dismantle the infrastructure it had established to facilitate terrorist operations against India. Pakistan also dismissed the demand for the handing over of 20 criminals and terrorists wanted in India. Thus, in the overall analysis, New Delhi cannot be said to have been successful in its exercise of coercive diplomacy.

What determined this outcome? Pakistan's stake in the 'Kashmir' issue is extremely high, given the perception that Muslim-majority Jammu and Kashmir should be a part of Pakistan. Consequently, its motivation to persist with the policy of providing moral, political, and diplomatic support for 'Kashmiri' self-determination is also very high. Conceding the Indian demand to completely stop support for the 'freedom fighters' would tantamount to the abnegation of a fundamental national duty. The Indian demand was, thus, unrealistic and unrealisable, however great the pressure exerted on Islamabad. Even a comprehensive victory in war, just as Germany found out in the aftermath of its victory over France in 1871, would not force Pakistan to permanently concede its claims on Jammu and Kashmir. Linked to this was Pakistan's understanding that neither India nor the international community could generate sufficient pressure to force it to compromise on the 'Kashmir' issue. India did not have the option of going to war, and the international community needed Pakistan's cooperation in the campaign against terrorism in general and the stabilisation of post-Taliban Afghanistan in particular.

Some analysts like Rear Admiral Raja Menon (retd) had argued that the government should have taken incremental steps instead of initiating a full-scale mobilisation and threatening an all-out war (Kalyanaraman 2002, 488). India could indeed have limited itself to exerting military pressure only across the LoC, as it did after the decision to de-escalate in October 2002. But such a step was not possible, according to Lieutenant General Satish Nambiar (retd), because of the government's initial inclination to carry out limited strikes across the LoC. That necessitated mobilisation in order to foreclose for Pakistan the option of opening a front of its own in response (Author's discussion with Gen. Nambiar 29 October 2001).

Other analysts insist that what India practised was not coercive diplomacy at all. Instead, it simply attempted to cow down Pakistan. It had no intention of arriving at a compromise solution and 'deliberately clogged' diplomatic channels and rejected dialogue, all of which are antithetical to the practice of coercive diplomacy (Noorani 2002). Indeed, New Delhi's decision to recall its ambassador from Islamabad and halve the strength of its diplomatic mission as soon as the crisis began to unfold demonstrated a lack of appreciation of the essentials of coercive diplomacy. More than at any other time, a crisis demands regular diplomatic contact. Cutting off all contact is not a recipe for success. If coercive diplomacy is a way of bargaining, a bargain can be struck only through talks.

Part of the trouble with coercing Pakistan lay in the inexplicable expansion of Indian objectives. It is not clear why this expansion—however legitimate and in accordance with the United Nations Security Council Resolution 1373—took place. Expanding Indian demands went against a tenet of coercive diplomacy, viz., compliance should not lead to further demands. This introduced a competitive element into the coercive diplomatic process, which strengthened Islamabad's non-cooperation. For example, in response to India's demand for the extradition of 20 criminals and terrorists, Pakistan announced that it was preparing its own list of wanted persons from India. Although it eventually chose not to present a list of wanted persons, it did invite India 'for talks to discuss the subject' (Reddy 2002).

The deployment of the military along the border was also needlessly prolonged. India's persistence with the mobilisation seems to have been influenced by domestic and electoral calculations. The flip side of the coin, however, was that New Delhi had to react to subsequent terrorist provocations, as happened in the wake of the attack on the Kaluchak army camp in May 2002. Moreover, when this crisis arose, international attention shifted from Pakistan-sponsored terrorism towards efforts to prevent the outbreak of war between the two nuclear adversaries. As *The Hindu* editorialised on that occasion:

> Coercive diplomacy as practised by New Delhi had blurred its own case as to which was the aggrieved party and which the belligerent. Instead of fully utilising the potential to focus global attention on the terrorist threat that it faces, New Delhi had caused international diplomatic energies to be frittered away in efforts to block armed conflict between two nuclear-armed adversaries. International consternation was further compounded when New Delhi did not heed the opportunities that it had to de-escalate and did not seem to appreciate that there were limits both to the quantum of third party pressure that could be applied and the results it could achieve. (*The Hindu* 18 October 2002)

There was, however, one limited gain that accrued from the attempt at coercive diplomacy: the international acknowledgement that one basic cause of the troubles in Jammu and Kashmir was Pakistan's support for, and sponsorship of, terrorist activities. It was this that impelled the United States and other major powers to exert pressure on Musharraf to crack down on Pakistani terrorist groups targeting India. Musharraf would not have conceded even the little that he did without such pressure. In a sense, Indian policy can be said to have been directed more towards the United States and other major powers in order to coax them into exerting pressure on Islamabad. A corollary was the further consolidation of international support for the Indian position that the territorial status quo is the most practical solution to the 'Kashmir' issue.

The Cold Start Doctrine

After Operation Parakram, military planners realised that the war plans they had drawn up during the crisis were unviable and a limited war had to be more precisely planned for. Two critical factors and three failings identified with this operation determined the army's response to the imperative of devising plans for waging a limited war (Ladwig 2007/08, 162–163). The two critical factors were the lack of political will to exercise the military option, which was further reinforced by international diplomatic intervention to prevent the outbreak of a conflict. It was, therefore, necessary to devise plans that would circumvent these two factors. At the same time, the need for fresh plans was reinforced by the three failings identified with Operation Parakram. First, the great size of the strike corps and their location in the interior meant that it took time for them to move to their forward concentration areas. It is the resultant time lag that led to the Indian political leadership losing its nerve and provided an opportunity for major external actors to intervene diplomatically. A second feature of the strike corps is their inability to cause surprise and unsettle the adversary. Given their size and composition, the movement and destination of the strike corps could be easily monitored and countered by the adversary through suitable redeployment. Third, the obverse side of the complete dependence on the strike corps to pose an offensive threat was the lack of offensive punch held by the holding corps. This too prevented India from responding rapidly.

To overcome these limitations and constraints, the Indian Army proposed a new doctrine in 2004 termed the Cold Start, which seeks to creatively employ both attrition and manoeuvre. In order to implement a war plan based on this doctrine, it has begun to reorganise the structure and capabilities of its defensive corps. Redesignated as the pivot corps, these are now being assigned offensive capabilities in the form of division-sized integrated battle groups (IBGs). These battle groups possess integral armour, artillery, and aviation assets, which would give them the ability to launch a quick offensive along multiple axes and, thus, exploit Pakistan's unpreparedness in the early stages of a conflict (Kanwal 2010; Gokhale 2011). In other words, the idea is to take Pakistan by surprise. Further, this early offensive would subsequently be used as a pivot by the strike corps to effect a deeper armoured penetration, but without crossing Pakistan's nuclear red lines.

During the course of these successive offensives, the army and air force would apply massive firepower to attrite Pakistani forces. And, the thin slice of territory that would be captured all along the border would be used as a bargaining chip for compelling Pakistan to cease support for anti-India terrorist groups on its soil (Kanwal 2010). In sum, the Cold Start seeks to catch Pakistan by surprise through an early offensive, capture territory by effecting a shallow armoured penetration, and attrite Pakistani forces with massive firepower delivered from the ground and the air.

Since its promulgation in April 2004, various elements of the doctrine are being tested in frequent exercises, in which the air force has also been participating (Ladwig 2007/08, 178–181). But because of international diplomatic pressure, particularly from the United States, the Indian political leadership did not formally endorse the doctrine in the last 10 years (Roemer 2010).[13] This, in turn, compelled an army chief to declare that the Cold Start is only one among many 'contingencies and options' (Pubby 2010). Nevertheless, the political leadership seems to have tacitly endorsed the doctrine, which is evident from the regular exercises that the army, with the participation of the air force, has been carrying out to validate the concepts involved (*The Times of India* 10 May 2011; *The Hindu* 6 December 2011; *Nation* 23 December 2013). In effect, the Cold Start is not a 'doctrine stillborn' but a work in progress (Joshi 2013, 512–540).

What that means is that in a future limited war, the army is likely to implement the strategy of exhaustion through a creative doctrinal combination of attrition and manoeuvre. The air force would play a critical role in such a limited war through its doctrine of attaining in-theatre command of the air even as it carries out aerial and ground interdiction. For its part, the navy is likely to aim at exercising control over designated sea areas. Its tasks would include preventing the Pakistan Navy from carrying out a surprise attack on the Indian coast, raising the cost of Pakistan's seaborne commerce, and distract the attention of its decision makers from events on the land.

Contours of a Strategy for Limited War

In crafting a strategy for limited war, three factors need to be kept in mind. First, the political objective for which it is to be waged must be precise and limited. Compelling Pakistan to stop cross-border terrorism is not a precise and limited objective, especially given the growing radicalisation within Pakistani society and even within its armed forces as well as the Pakistani state's loss of control over radical terrorist groups. However, compelling Pakistan to vacate any Indian territory it may capture through military aggression is a limited objective, as was demonstrated during the Kargil conflict.

Second, a limited war must ideally remain confined within a particular geographical area and preferably in an area that is part of the periphery rather than the heartland. Citing examples from the Cold War era is not appropriate. Neither superpower waged a limited war in the central theatre of Europe. Limited wars occurred only in peripheral theatres. Similarly, China and the Soviet Union engaged in a limited border conflict along the Ussuri River, far from their heartlands.

Finally, the means employed in war must also remain limited. While one obvious limitation is the employment of nuclear weapons, it is also essential that even conventional means are employed in a calibrated manner to avoid the risk of escalation. After all, the purpose of limited war or calibrated military strikes is to raise the cost for the adversary, not to militarily defeat it.

Summary

In the early 1990s, because of Pakistan's acquisition of nuclear weapons capability, the idea of effecting a deep penetration into Pakistani territory became impossible. Seemingly assuming that its offensive to capture key objectives may well trigger a Pakistani nuclear response, the Indian Army set out to strengthen its ability to fight in such an environment by boosting mobility, shifting to round-the-clock operations, and rapidly deploying forces. In the wake of the Kargil conflict, political leaders, military professionals, and independent analysts began to articulate the existence of space below the nuclear threshold for waging limited wars in terms of space and force levels employed. This idea was reinforced by the India–Pakistan crisis that occurred in the wake of the terrorist attack on the Indian Parliament in December 2001. New Delhi can be said to have adopted the 'tacit ultimatum' variant of coercive diplomacy. Specific demands were placed on Islamabad, but no time limit for compliance was indicated. Though the entire military apparatus was mobilised to communicate a sense of urgency, New Delhi did not specify how exactly it intended to apply force to mete out punishment. While there was no actual (as opposed to apparent) intent to initiate combat, the threat to do so was essential to bring pressure to bear on

Islamabad. At the same time, India also understood the necessity of practising crisis management. After Operation Parakram, military planners realised that the war plans they had drawn up during the crisis were unviable and a limited war had to be more precisely planned for. It was, therefore, necessary to devise plans that would circumvent the two critical factors, viz., the lack of political will to exercise the military option and the international diplomatic intervention to prevent the outbreak of a conflict. At the same time, the need for fresh plans was reinforced by the three failings identified with Operation Parakram, namely, time taken by the strike corps to move forward resulting in the opportunity provided to external actors to intervene diplomatically, the inability of the strike corps to cause surprise and unsettle the adversary, and the lack of offensive punch by the holding corps.

These failings had prevented India from responding rapidly. To overcome these limitations and constraints, the Indian Army proposed a new doctrine in 2004 termed the Cold Start. This doctrine seeks to creatively employ both attrition and manoeuvre. The defensive corps, redesignated as the pivot corps, was assigned offensive capabilities in the form of division-sized IBGs.

In crafting a strategy for limited war, three factors need to be kept in mind. First, the political objective must be precise and limited. Second, a limited war must ideally remain confined within a particular geographical area and preferably in an area that is part of the periphery rather than the heartland. Finally, the means employed in war must also remain limited. Within the limitation of nuclear weapons, employment of conventional means of a limited war in a calibrated manner, to avoid the risk of escalation, serves the purpose of raising the cost for the adversary. The idea is to take Pakistan by surprise.

Notes

1 On this aspect, see Chari et al. (2008).

2 India's restraint was the principal factor in the United States not equating India and Pakistan during the conflict, with President Clinton even asserting that 'borders cannot be redrawn in blood'. Clinton's statement is

cited in Ganguly (2006, 53). For the US role during the conflict, see Riedel (2009, 130–143); Bommakanti (2011, 304–315).

3 In the Kargil sector alone, the army built up its force level nearly to a corps' worth, with one division serving as reserve.

4 For statements on limited war made by the then defence minister and army chief, see Raghavan (2001, 5). Others who have articulated this view include Malik (2010, 342); Singh (2000, 1205–1220); Sethi (2009, 415–425).

5 The discussion of coercive diplomacy that follows is an updated version of the author's article published in 2002.

6 The term was first articulated and defined by Lawrence Freedman.

7 For comparative figures, see, for example, International Institute for Strategic Studies, *The Military Balance 2000–2001*, 2000, 168–170, 173–174.

8 About 50 'non-emergency' staff members and dependents of the US Embassy officials left India within hours of the issue of the travel advisory. Nearly two-thirds of the US Embassy staff reportedly came under the 'non-emergency' category. Similarly, about 60 of the 110 members who make up the British High Commission and its allied offices lined up to leave India.

9 The démarche was issued on 14 December 2001 by Indian Foreign Secretary Chokila Iyer to Pakistan's ambassador in India, Ashraf Jehangir Qazi.

10 The text of the resolution is available at: http://www.satp.org/satporgtp/countries/india/document/papers/parliament_resolution_on_Jammu_and_Kashmir.htm (accessed on 2 May 2016).

11 This was stated by Ari Fleischer, White House press secretary, in the course of a media briefing on 22 December 2001.

12 Azhar was, however, arrested for making provocative speeches disturbing internal peace.

13 US ambassador to India Timothy Roemer queried 'very high level' officials of the Indian government, including the national security advisor, about their support for the doctrine and was assured that 'they have never endorsed, supported, or advocated for this doctrine'.

References

Aneja, Atul and Sandeep Dikshit. 2001. 'Pakistan Moves Missiles Closer to Border'. *The Hindu*, 26 December.

Aneja, Atul. 2001. 'Lashkar Responsible for Attack, Says Jaswant'. *The Hindu*, New Delhi, 15 December.

Aneja, Atul. 2002. 'Army Takes Command of First Tier of Defence'. *The Hindu*, 20 May.

Aneja, Atul. 2002. 'We Will Respond if Pak. Shows Results on Ground: PM'. *The Hindu*, 3 June.

Bammi, Y.M. 2002. *Kargil 1999: The Impregnable Conquered*. Noida: Gorkha Publishers.

BBC News. 2001. 'Text: Musharraf Rallies Pakistan'. BBC News, 19 September 2001.

BBC News. 2002. 'Excerpts of Musharraf's Speech'. BBC News, 27 May.

BBC News. 2002. 'Musharraf Speech Highlights'. BBC News, 12 January.

Bommakanti, Kartik. 2011. 'Coercion and Control: Explaining India's Victory at Kargil'. *India Review*, 10(3): 304–315.

Chari, P.R., Pervaiz Iqbal Cheema, and Stephen P. Cohen. 2008. *Four Crises and a Peace Process: American Engagement in South Asia*. New Delhi: HarperCollins Publishers India.

CNN. 2000. 'Clinton Addresses Pakistani People'. CNN, 25 March.

Dikshit, Sandeep. 2001. 'Strike Forces Moved Closer to the Border'. *The Hindu*, New Delhi, 21 December.

Dikshit, Sandeep. 2001. 'Troop Movement a Precautionary Measure'. *The Hindu*, 22 December.

Dikshit, Sandeep. 2002. 'Decline in Infiltration, Admits Fernandes'. *The Hindu*, 20 June.

Dixit, J.N. 1999. 'Beyond Kargil'. *The Journal of the United Service Institution of India*, 129: 537.

Dugger, Celia W. 2002. 'A Blunt-Speaking General Says India Is Ready for War'. *New York Times*, 11 January.

Ganguly, Sumit. 2006. 'Will Kashmir Stop India's Rise?'. *Foreign Affairs*, 85(4): 45–56.

George, Alexander L., David K. Hall, and William E. Simons. 1971. *The Limits of Coercive Diplomacy: Laos, Cuba, Vietnam*. Boston: Little, Brown and Company.

George, Alexander. 1994. 'Theory and Practice'. In *The Limits of Coercive Diplomacy*, edited by Alexander George and William E. Simons. Boulder, Colorado: Westview Press.

Gill, John H. 2009. 'Military Operations in the Kargil Conflict'. In *Asymmetric Warfare in South Asia: The Causes and Consequences of the Kargil Conflict*, edited by Peter R. Lavoy, 92–129. New Delhi: Cambridge University Press.

Gokhale, Nitin. 2011. 'India's Doctrinal Shift?'. *Diplomat*, 25 January. Available at: http://thediplomat.com/2011/01/25/india%E2%80%99s-doctrinal-shift/?all=true (accessed on 29 November 2012).

Gupta, Shekhar. 2014. 'Narendra Modi: Getting His Foreign Policy Right'. *India Today*, 4 September.

Gupta, Shishir. 2002. 'Controversial Transfer of Key Corps Commander Fuels Speculation about India-Pakistan War'. *India Today*, 4 February.

Hindu. 2001. 'War Should be the Last Option: Opposition'. *The Hindu*, New Delhi, 19 December.

Hindu. 2001. 'All Options Are Open: PM'. *The Hindu*, New Delhi, 20 December.

Hindu. 2001. 'Armed Forces for Weighing All Possibilities'. *The Hindu*, New Delhi, 19 December.

Hindu. 2001. 'Attack Aimed at Wiping Out Top Leadership: Advani'. *The Hindu*, New Delhi, 19 December.

Hindu. 2001. 'Bush Blocks Lashkar Finances'. *The Hindu*, 22 December.

Hindu. 2001. 'India Must Exercise Restraint: Powell'. *The Hindu*, 17 December.

Hindu. 2001. 'U.S. Asks Pak. to Act Against Jaish, Lashkar'. *The Hindu*, 23 December.

Hindu. 2001. 'U.S. Asks Pak. to Control Terrorist Activities'. *The Hindu*, 19 December.

Hindu. 2002. 'More Foreigners Leaving India'. *The Hindu*, New Delhi, 2 June.

Hindu. 2002. 'Russia Puts the Onus on Pak'. *The Hindu*, 22 January.

Hindu. 2002. 'Towards De-escalation'. *The Hindu*, 18 October

International Institute for Strategic Studies. 2000. *The Military Balance 2000–2001*. London: Oxford University Press/IISS.

Jakobsen, Peter Viggo. 1998. *Western Use of Coercive Diplomacy after the Cold War: A Challenge for Theory and Practice*. New York: St. Martin's Press.

Jones, Keith. 2001. 'India and Pakistan on Threshold of War'. *World Socialist Web Site*, 29 December.

Joshi, Shashank. 2013. 'India's Military Instrument: A Doctrine Stillborn'. *Journal of Strategic Studies*, 36(4): 512–540.

Kalyanaraman, S. 2002. 'Operation Parakram: An Indian Exercise in Coercive Diplomacy'. *Strategic Analysis*, 26(4): 478–492.

Kalyanaraman, S. 2003. 'The India–Pakistan–United States Break-Dance: A Chronology—September 11, 2001 to October 16, 2002'. *Strategic Digest*, 33(8): 730–743.

Kanwal, Gurmeet. 2010. 'India's Cold Start Doctrine and Strategic Stability'. *IDSA Comment*, 1 June. Available at: http://www.idsa.in/idsacomments/IndiasColdStartDoctrineandStrategicStability_gkanwal_010610 (accessed on 2 June 2010).

Kanwar, Yogendra. 2002. 'We Should Have Responded After December 13: PM'. *The Hindu*, New Delhi, 27 May.

Kattakayam, Jiby. 2011. '"Sudarshan Shakti" Aims to Transform Armed Forces'. *The Hindu*, Chennai, 6 December.

Khare, Harish. 2001. 'Govt. Under Pressure to "Act"'. *The Hindu*, New Delhi, 15 December.

Krishnaswami, Sridhar. 2001. 'U.S. Brands Lashkar, Jaish Terrorist Outfits'. *The Hindu*, 27 December.

Krishnaswami, Sridhar. 2002. 'Act Tough on Terrorism, Bush Tells Musharraf'. *The Hindu*, 9 January.

Krishnaswami, Sridhar. 2002. 'Bush Expects Musharraf to Take All Steps Against Terrorism'. *The Hindu*, 11 January.

Krishnaswami, Sridhar. 2002. 'Musharraf Has Promised to Dismantle Terrorist Camps'. *The Hindu*, 12 June.

Krishnaswami, Sridhar. 2002. 'Rumsfeld Coming to Defuse Tension'. *The Hindu*, 31 May.

Ladwig, Walter C. 2007/08. 'A Cold Start for Hot Wars? The Indian Army's New Limited War Doctrine'. *International Security*, 32(3): 158–190.

Lambeth, Benjamin S. 2012. *'Air Power at 18000': The Indian Air Force in the Kargil War*. Washington D.C.: Carnegie Endowment of International Peace.

Malik, V.P. 2010. *Kargil: From Surprise to Victory*. New Delhi: HarperCollins.

Mattoo, Amitabh. 2002. 'The Endgame Over Kashmir', *The Hindu*, 24 June.

Menon, Raja. 2001. 'Hot Pursuit, Cold Turkey'. *Outlook*, 31 December.

Musharraf, Pervez. 2002. 'President General Pervez Musharraf's Address to the Nation'. 27 May. Available at: https://presidentmusharraf.wordpress.com/2006/07/20/musharraf-address-27-may-2002/ (accessed on 20 December 2018).

Musharraf, Pervez. 2002. 'President of Pakistan General Pervez Musharraf's Address to the Nation'. 12 January. Available at: https://presidentmusharraf.wordpress.com/2007/04/01/address-12-january-2002/ (accessed on 20 December 2018).

Nation. 2013. 'India Conducts Wargames Near Pak Border'. *Nation*, Lahore, 23 December.

Noorani, A.G. 2002. 'Of War-Mongering and Accountability'. *Frontline*, 19(3). Available at: https://frontline.thehindu.com/static/html/fl1903/19030220.htm (accessed on 20 December 2018).

Panag, H.S. 2019. 'Operation Parakram: The War That Wasn't But Could Have Reined in Pakistan'. The Print, 3 January.

Patel, Y.I. 2004. 'Dig Vijay to Divya Astra: A Paradigm Shift in the Indian Army's Doctrine'. *Bharat Rakshak Monitor*, 6(6). Available at: http://www.bharat-rakshak.com/MONITOR/ISSUE6-6/patel.html (accessed on 7 May 2011).

Pubby, Manu. 2010. 'No "Cold Start" Doctrine: India Tells US'. *Indian Express*, New Delhi, 9 September.

Qadir, Shaukat. 2002. 'An Analysis of the Kargil Conflict 1999'. *RUSI Journal*, 147(2): 24–30.

Raghavan, V.R. 2001. 'Limited War and Nuclear Escalation'. *The Nonproliferation Review*, 8(3): 1–18.

Reddy, B. Muralidhar. 2001. 'Lashkar Chief Quits as Pak. Freezes Assets'. *The Hindu*, 25 December.

Reddy, B. Muralidhar. 2001. 'Pakistan Detains Masood Azhar'. *The Hindu*, 26 December.

Reddy, B. Muralidhar. 2002. 'We Are for Talks on Extradition of Fugitives: Pak'. *The Hindu*, 22 February.

Rediff.com. 2011. 'Sir, Can You Give Us Your Political Aim?'. Rediff.com, 4 November.

Riedel, Bruce. 2009. 'American Diplomacy and the 1999 Kargil Summit at Blair House'. In *Asymmetric Warfare in South Asia: The Causes and Consequences of the Kargil Conflict*, edited by Peter R. Lavoy, 130–143. New Delhi: Cambridge University Press.

Roemer, Timothy. 2010. 'Cold Start—A Mixture of Myth and Reality'. 16 February. Available at: http://www.wikileaks.nl/cable/2010/02/10NEWDELHI295.html (accessed on 7 May 2011).

Schelling, Thomas C. 1966. *Arms and Influence*. New Haven/London: Yale University Press.

Sethi, Manpreet. 2009. 'Conventional War in the Presence of Nuclear Weapons'. *Strategic Analysis*, 33(3): 415–425.

Singh, Jasjit. 2000. 'Dynamics of Limited War'. *Strategic Analysis*, 24(7): 1205–1220.

Singh, Jasjit. 2001. *India's Defence Spending: Assessing Future Needs*. New Delhi: Knowledge World and IDSA.

Singh, Jaswant. 2002. 'Transcript of Press Conference by Shri Jaswant Singh, External Affairs Minister at 15:30 hours on May 28, 2002'. Available at: http://pmg-assets.s3-website-eu-west-1.amazonaws.com/docs/2002/020612pcforeignpressconference.doc (accessed on 20 December 2018).

Sood, V.K. and Pravin Sawhney. 2003. *Operation Parakram: The War Unfinished.* New Delhi: Sage.

Suroor, Hasan. 2002. 'Pak. Must Stop Support to Terrorism in Kashmir: Blair'. *The Hindu*, 22 June.

Swami, Praveen. 2004. 'Gen. Padmanabhan Mulls Over Lessons of Operation Parakram'. *The Hindu*, 6 February.

Telegraph. 2000. 'Hot Pursuit Back on BJP Agenda'. *The Telegraph*, New Delhi, 12 August.

Thomas, Mathew. 1990 'An Analysis of the Threat Perception and Strategy for India'. *Indian Defence Review*, January: 61–64.

Times of India. 2001. 'Hot Pursuit Legitimate: Advani'. *The Times of India*, New Delhi, 19 October.

Times of India. 2002. 'Lt-Gen Vij Moved Forces "Too Close" to Border'. *The Times of India*, 21 January.

Times of India. 2011. 'Getting Leaner and Meaner? Army Practises Blitzkrieg to Strike Hard at Enemy'. *The Times of India*, New Delhi, 10 May.

Times of India. 2011. 'Operation Parakram After Parliament Attack Lacked Cleared Objectives: Ex-Navy Chief Sushil Kumar'. *The Times of India*, New Delhi, 6 November.

Tipnis, A.Y. 2006. 'Operation Safed Sagar'. *Force*, October: 6–16.

Tisdall, Simon and Ewen MacAskill. 2002. 'India's Deadly Defence: The 1,800 Mile Long Minefield'. *The Guardian*, 10 January.

Conclusion

Strategy and Civil–Military Relations

It is on the basis of the distinctions between the types of war, strategies, and doctrines that the overall politico-military framework governing India's military posture towards Pakistan can be characterised as defensive in nature, given that India has invariably not initiated a war (Pant 1989, 212–213). However, in tune with Clausewitz's definition of defence, and given India's conscious policy of maintaining a measure of military superiority over Pakistan, its strategy has invariably contained an integral counter-offensive element.

Three distinct phases can be discerned in the evolution of India's strategy towards Pakistan during the last seven decades. In the first phase between 1950 and 1970, India adopted the first pole of Delbrück's strategy of exhaustion, whereby it sought to attain strategic success and forge a favourable peace with Pakistan. This strategy of exhaustion gave way to the strategy of annihilation during the 1971 War but only on the East Pakistan front. In the wake of the splendid victory attained in that war, which led to the emergence of East Pakistan as independent Bangladesh, India retuned and refocused its strategy of annihilation towards the western and now only front with Pakistan. The third phase in the evolution of India's strategy towards Pakistan began with the latter's acquisition of nuclear weapon capability in the late 1980s. Because Pakistan's possession of nuclear weapons has rendered full-scale war impossible to contemplate, India has had to perforce adopt the second pole of Delbrück's strategy of exhaustion in the context of limited war. Now, the objective is no longer the military defeat of Pakistan but only the vacation of that country's aggression or the imposition of costs for pursuing a particular course of action.

While India's strategy towards Pakistan has thus evolved in tune with the changing military balance and nuclear equation between the two countries, the doctrines of its armed services have had to adapt to these changes in the overall strategic framework. Until the 1971 War, the Indian Army's preferred doctrine, which it had imbibed by 'training and tradition', was attrition: 'the set-piece battle, phased programmes to capture strong points—and venturing on further advance only after due regrouping and re-inforcement' (Palit 1972, 100). For its part, the Indian Air Force, impelled by a fighter-pilot ethos exemplified in its motto of 'Touching the Sky with Glory' (Lambeth 2011) as well as by the political leadership's fear of Indian cities being subject to retaliatory attacks, largely favoured a combination of the direct doctrines of aerial combat and air interdiction to attain a 'local favourable air situation'.[1] And, the rather weak navy was forced to continue its British-era mission of coastal defence and the custody of maritime assets during this period (Hiranandani 2000, 1; Tellis 1991, 137). Although, in the latter half of the 1960s, it began to adopt a more expansive approach that was inspired, in the words of one critic, by the 'Imperial tradition' and the 'grandiose, world-power outlook' of its mentor, the British Navy (Thomas 1978, 205; Palit 1969).

These doctrinal orientations of the services changed during the course of the 1971 War when India adopted the strategy of annihilation on the East Pakistan front. To attain a swift victory, the army chose the indirect doctrine of manoeuvre; the navy practised the indirect doctrine of blockade to attain a working control of the sea off East Pakistan; the air force adopted a combination of aerial combat (direct doctrine) and air interdiction (indirect) to gain command of the air and adversely affect Pakistan's logistical ability to continue the war. India's splendid victory in this war led to these doctrines getting further consolidated during the course of the next two decades.

But with Pakistan's acquisition of nuclear weapons capability in the late 1980s and the consequent shift in India's strategy to one of exhaustion in the context of a limited war, the armed services, and particularly the army, have been forced to revisit their doctrines. Through its Cold Start doctrine, the army is attempting to creatively combine attrition and manoeuvre within a single doctrinal framework. For their part, the air force and navy appear to be adapting their extant doctrines for respectively attaining in-theatre air superiority and a working control of designated sea areas.

Applying this typology to India–Pakistan wars and crises, we can see that India has invariably pursued limited political aims that did not threaten Pakistan's survival or form of government or regime in power. Thus, in the Kashmir conflict of 1947–1948, the Indian aim was to consolidate national territory and safeguard the population from Pakistani tribal invaders. During the 1951 crisis, India sought to deter Pakistan from initiating war to annex Jammu and Kashmir. When Pakistan initiated such a war in 1965, India endeavoured to safeguard national territory in Jammu and Kashmir, in particular, and also in the rest of the states sharing a border with West Pakistan. Indian political aims in the 1971 War were liberating Bangladesh on the eastern front and safeguarding territory, including Jammu and Kashmir, on the western front. In 1999, India limited itself to seeking the eviction of Pakistani troops occupying the Kargil heights. Two years later, during the 2001–2002 crisis, India ordered general mobilisation to intimidate Pakistan into cracking down on anti-India terrorist groups on Pakistani territory. Finally, during the last few years, India has sought to deter Pakistan and its terrorist proxies through the surgical strikes of 2016 and 2019.

Turning to strategy, with the exception of the East Pakistan front in the 1971 War, India has relied upon the strategy of exhaustion and the pursuit of limited objectives in its wars with Pakistan. This has been a function of India's lack of sufficient military superiority (see chapter 3) and the operation of nuclear deterrence since the 1990s. Thus, in the 1947–1948 operations in Kashmir, the Indian military objective was to push the tribal raiders out of the territory of Jammu and Kashmir. When Pakistan made a renewed effort to annex the rest of Jammu and Kashmir in 1965, India expanded its military objective to the capture of territory in the Pakistani heartland, thereby imposing a greater cost and pain on Pakistan. During the 1971 War, India adopted the defensive on the western front but pursued the strategy of annihilation to defeat Pakistani forces in East Pakistan. In 1999, the Indian military objective was limited to evicting the Pakistani forces occupying the Kargil heights because of both the constraint imposed by nuclear deterrence and the imperative of gaining international diplomatic support. These two factors were also responsible for India's decision to not initiate hostilities during the 2001–2002 crisis caused by the attack on Parliament by Pakistani terrorists. Likewise, the Cold Start doctrine devised in the early 2000s envisages only shallow offensives to capture slices of Pakistani territory and cause military setbacks to Pakistani armed forces.

With respect to the doctrines employed, the Indian Army's campaigns in the 1947–1948 conflict, 1965 War, and Kargil conflict were all marked by the employment of attrition. In 1947–1948, the army employed attrition to roll back Pakistani tribal raiders. During the 1965 War, its twin offensives towards Lahore and Sialkot were classic campaigns of attrition that compelled Pakistan to concentrate on defending its own territory instead of stepping up the offensive to wrest Jammu and Kashmir. In the 1999 Kargil conflict, the Indian Army took back the mountain heights through the concerted application of firepower and infantry assaults on the positions occupied by Pakistani forces. The only occasion India employed blitzkrieg, or rather a variant of blitzkrieg, was in the East Pakistan front during the 1971 War. In its bid to penetrate as deeply as possible into East Pakistan, Indian infantry units bypassed strongholds and went cross-country, which ultimately enabled some of them to reach Dhaka itself and cause the collapse of the Pakistani military effort.

For its part, the Indian Navy played no role in the 1947–1948 conflict and was directed by the political leadership to assume the defensive during the 1965 War because several warships, including the aircraft carrier, were undergoing repair and refit. The navy, however, played a major role in the 1971 War by imposing a blockade of East Pakistan and projecting power ashore through both air strikes and an amphibious landing. Given the rather limited character of the Kargil conflict, the navy's role in 1999 was restricted to manoeuvring in the Arabian Sea in order to exert concerted military pressure on Pakistan.

Finally, the Indian Air Force has neither aspired for nor acquired the capability to practice strategic bombing. Consequently, it has only practised the Counter Air doctrine during the various wars with Pakistan. In the 1947–1948 conflict, its missions were limited to armed reconnaissance, ground attacks on Pakistani irregulars, and provision of close air support for army formations. During the 1965 War, the air force adopted a defensive approach by devoting the bulk of its sorties to aerial combat and combat air patrol missions over India's own airspace. However, six years later, it attained total superiority over East Pakistan airspace and a high degree of air superiority on the western front through a combination of offensive and defensive counter-air operations. Finally, during the Kargil conflict, Pakistan's non-use of air power automatically permitted the Indian Air Force to fully concentrate on the counter surface force missions of bombing the positions occupied by Pakistani irregulars.

This appraisal of the evolution of India's strategic praxis highlights the critical importance of enmeshing the political aim and the military objectives within a well-crafted strategy. A prerequisite for devising an effective strategy is civil–military coordination and the harmonisation of the political aim with what the armed services can actually deliver. That, in turn, depends upon the existence of a well-structured mechanism for civil–military dialogue on a regular basis.

The creation of the post of chief of defence staff (CDS) in August 2019 and the follow-up establishment of the Department of Military Affairs (DMA) in the Ministry of Defence (MoD) in December have addressed the long-standing imperative of reforming the higher defence management structure. These decisions are set to transform the pattern of civil–military relations that has prevailed until now. What would be the characteristics of the new pattern of civil–military relations and how different would it be from its forerunner? What factors influenced the formation of the previous pattern and how relevant are these likely to be for the unfolding one? These are the questions explored in this final chapter.

Democracy and Civil–Military Relations

The central issue in civil–military relations is the structuring of the relationship between those who govern the polity and those who lead the military apparatus that protects it from internal and external threats. How political authorities relate to and interact with the military leadership is determined by the form of government prevalent in a state. In democracies, civil–military relations are structured to ensure that the fundamental principle of accountability of the elected to the electors extends to the military apparatus that the elected oversee. Since the people are ultimately in charge, civil–military relations in democracies involve the people's 'designated political agents controlling designated military agents' (Feaver 1999, 215).

In addition to this democratic dictate, the exercise of civilian authority over the military is essential to establish a sustainable balance in the distribution of national resources for the pursuit of security, on the one hand, and the furtherance of economic objectives, on the other. Given its role as the sword arm of the state, the military leadership's focus is on building up its capabilities for meeting existing and potential threats. As the representatives of the people, democratic leaders are aware of not only the importance of safeguarding the polity from threats but also of meeting the economic aspirations of the people through developmental programmes.

The exercise of civilian authority over the military is essential to establish a balance between these imperatives of security and development. Overemphasis on either is undesirable. Privileging economic goals would result in a relatively weaker military, which would prove incapable of meeting security threats. A narrow focus on developing the military apparatus would deny adequate resources to productive activities that not only address people's aspirations but are ultimately the key to sustaining the military build-up itself in the long term. Further, undue emphasis on the security imperative might result in a powerful military institution that proves 'impossible to contain' within the political order (Huntington 2005, 2). That is, a powerful military apparatus might resort to praetorianism through the seizure of power and the annulment of democracy.

The structure of civil–military relations established in a democracy should, therefore, strive to establish a balance between these two necessities. One, it should minimise the military's role in the political order and subordinate the military leadership to political authority. Two, it should enable the build-up of a powerful military apparatus that is moreover led by an officer corps skilled in the application and 'management of violence' (Huntington 2005, 11–13). To put it differently, the structure of civil–military relations should enable the development of a military that is 'strong enough to prevail in war' and, at the same time, prevent it from employing its 'overwhelming advantage in coercive power' to overthrow the political order, or make excessive demands on national resources, or dictate the course of foreign policy. In short, the ideal to be aspired for is a military that is not only 'strong enough to do anything the civilians ask' but is also 'subordinate enough to do only what civilians authorise' (Feaver 2003, 1, 2, 4, 5).

Political Conception of Civil–Military Relations

Indian political leaders have grappled with these issues of civil–military relations since Independence. Three specific concerns have influenced their approach to civil–military relations. First, they have taken the view that defence and development must go together and that one cannot come at the expense of the other. Thus, in the immediate aftermath of Independence, Prime Minister Jawaharlal Nehru called for building 'an economically strong and well-balanced India with a strong enough defence apparatus' (Nehru 1996, 96). At the same time, however, he warned that the defence apparatus should not simply come to mean the possession of an army, navy, and air force. Instead, these spearheads must necessarily rest on a broad industrial and technological base and a sound economy (Nehru 1996, 283).

Nehru's emphasis on defence and development going together has persisted to date. In a 2013 lecture on national security challenges and priorities, P. Chidambaram, the then finance minister in the United Progressive Alliance government, emphasised that sustained high rate of economic growth is the key for India becoming a 'comprehensive national power' and advocated that the country embrace 'the twin goals of prosperity and security' (Chidambaram 2013). His successor as finance minister, Arun Jaitley, acknowledged that 'the security challenge … involves a lot of national resources being diverted in that direction' (*The Times of India* 2016). Prime Minister Narendra Modi also highlighted the link between development and security in one of his early addresses to the commanders of the armed forces by noting that economic growth is essential for India to secure itself better. Indeed, in his view, India can never call itself 'a secure nation and a strong military power' unless domestic capabilities are developed. Further, domestic defence industrial development would, in turn, serve as a 'catalyst for industry, employment and economic growth'. Finally, he urged the military leadership to reconsider its penchant for expanding the size of the armed forces when major powers were actually 'reducing their forces' and relying 'more on technology'. His conclusion was that 'modernisation and expansion of forces at the same time is a difficult and unnecessary goal' (Press Information Bureau 2015).

The second concern of Indian political leaders has been the subordination of the military to civilian authority. A week after assuming charge of the interim government in early September 1946, Nehru wrote to both the defence secretary and General Claude Auchinleck, the commander-in-chief of the British Raj's Indian Army, highlighting the importance of making the army fully responsible to the elected representatives of the people. Another early indication of this thought process came on the eve of Independence. Resistance within the military to the plan for celebrating Independence Day led Nehru to address another letter to Auchinleck, which he copied to several senior officers. His message was crystal clear:

> In any policy that is to be pursued, in the army or otherwise, the views of the Government of India and the policy they lay down must prevail. If any person is unable to carry out this policy, he has no place in the Indian army or in the Indian structure of government. (Wilkinson 2015, 101–103)

Nehru subsequently reiterated this message in 1959 during a discussion in Parliament on the episode involving General Thimayya's resignation. On this occasion, he firmly stated that 'civil authority is and must remain supreme' (Raghavan 2010, 269). That this concern was not limited to the early years of Independence is evident from the sacking in December 1998 of Admiral Vishnu Bhagwat from the position of chief of naval staff for similar reasons. The National Democratic Alliance government described its decision in this regard as one taken 'consciously and deliberately, in the face of action which threatened the established structures of democracy, the traditional neutrality, and objectivity of our armed forces as well as national security'. For his part, Prime Minister Atal Bihari Vajpayee emphasised that the reason for Bhagwat's sacking lay in the latter's 'deliberate defiance of the established system of cabinet control over the defence forces' (Joshi and Chawla 1999).

A third concern in the minds of political leaders was the accretion of too much power in the hands of a military supremo and its consequences for the democratic political system. This concern manifested in the six-decades-long opposition to the establishment of the post of CDS (discussed later), although it has been long acknowledged that such a post was necessary to foster inter-service coordination and effect financial savings (Jayal 2012, 63).

Pattern of Civil–Military Relations

The interplay of these concerns largely determined the pattern of civil–military relations in India after Independence. Two contrasting assessments exist with respect to the form of civil–military relations in India. One holds that, with the exception of the period during which Krishna Menon was the defence minister, India practised the Huntingtonian idea of objective civilian control in terms of the political leadership not interfering in operational issues and granting considerable autonomy to the military leadership (Chari 1977, 13; Raghavan 2009, 172–174). The other contends that India has actually practised subjective civilian control by interfering excessively in military affairs (Nayar 2008).

Neither is, however, an accurate description. While political leaders have indeed granted a broad degree of internal autonomy to the armed forces, they have not given carte blanche to the military leadership during various wars and crises (discussed later). At the same time, they have also treated military advice as just that—advice to be considered during the decision-making process and not as a course of action to be automatically endorsed. In effect, the pattern of civil–military relations practised by Indian leaders is a modified form of objective civilian control. Until now, this pattern has been distinguished by four main features: conscious subordination of the military to civilian authority, grant of a broad degree of autonomy to the military leadership on issues internal to the armed forces, reluctance to introduce major reforms lest they result in the emergence of a military supremo, and intrusive monitoring of the military by the civilian bureaucracy.

Formal Subordination of the Military

Formal subordination of the military to civilian authority began with the formation of the interim government headed by Nehru in September 1946. The handover of power to Indian hands by the British necessitated a change in the colonial system of civil–military relations. In the colonial system, the commander-in-chief of the Indian Army 'dominated the defence apparatus' because of the authority he enjoyed over all the three services as well as because of his position as the war member of the Viceroy's Executive Council (Chari 1977, 7). In that system, ultimate civilian control lay in the hands of the secretary of state for India, the British Cabinet, and the British Parliament. With the transfer of power, that system had to be necessarily changed, and formal civilian authority over the military had to be vested in Indian hands.

Consequently, as a first step, a political leader—Sardar Baldev Singh—assumed the position of defence member in the interim government. At the same time, the commander-in-chief was stripped of his formal authority over the other two services, which then emerged as independent entities with their own chiefs. This latter measure was recommended by Lord Hastings Ismay, who essentially devised the institutional structure of civil–military relations (Sinha 1980, 6). It was, however, only after the adoption of the Constitution that civilian authority over the military was formalised. The Constitution made the president the supreme commander of the armed forces and vested responsibility for national defence with the Cabinet. The Cabinet, in turn, discharged its responsibility for defence through the MoD headed by the defence minister (Vohra 2013).

The formal subordination of the military to civilian authority did not stop there. In a highly symbolic move, Nehru transformed the commander-in-chief's house, Teen Murti Bhavan, into his official residence (Wilkinson 2015, 25). Subsequent years saw the position of the military leadership being consciously downgraded 'both administratively and socially'. In 1955, the designation of the three service chiefs was changed from commander-in-chief to chief of staff. According to Lloyd and Susanne Rudolph, this 'reflected some nervousness concerning the military's potential role' in political affairs and 'a consequent desire to "trim" their tails' (Rudolph and Rudolph 1964, 9–10). In fact, Nehru told them in an interview that 'the demotion ... certainly was a deliberate decision to reduce the role of the military on the Indian Scene' (Wilkinson 2015, 105).

Other measures adopted to reduce the status of the military leadership included the abolition of the entitlement of lieutenant general rank officers to gun salutes and placing the chief of the army staff at the 25th place in the Warrant of Precedence behind the comptroller and auditor general, chief justices of High Courts and members of the erstwhile planning commission. All these measures were designed with a single intent: to reduce the high pre-war status and position enjoyed by the military leadership in the colonial government hierarchy and, thus, their salience in the democratic political order.

That the political leaders have been acutely conscious about subordinating the military to civilian authority can be observed through the following cases. One of the earliest episodes that shed light on this feature was General Thimayya writing a letter of resignation and subsequently retracting it upon Nehru's persuasion. According to Srinath Raghavan, Thimayya submitted his resignation not simply because of the vitiated atmosphere generated by the then Defence Minister Krishna Menon's 'irascible behaviour' and Thimayya's disagreements with Menon over which senior army officers should be promoted, but more fundamentally due to differences on fundamental issues of defence policy (Raghavan 2009, 152–153).[2]

Those policy differences pertained to three related issues: whether it was China or Pakistan that posed the more immediate and intense threat, how to respond to the threat from China militarily, and the diplomatic practicability of forging a joint defence arrangement with Pakistan to meet the China challenge. Menon was not concerned about the China challenge but was obsessed with the threat posed by

Pakistan. Consequently, he was impervious to the army's demand for raising additional forces for the China front and was dead set against President Ayub Khan's suggestion of forging a joint India–Pakistan defence arrangement for dealing with China. Thimayya, in contrast, was conscious of India's military weakness and resultant inability to tackle on its own the threat posed by China.

As he noted in an article published after retirement, India simply cannot take on China

> in an open conflict on its own. China's present strength in manpower, equipment and aircraft exceeds our resources a hundredfold with the full support of the USSR, and we could never hope to match China in the foreseeable future. It must be left to the politicians and the diplomats to ensure our security. (Guha 2007, 330)

Consequently, he favoured consideration of Ayub Khan's joint defence proposal and urged Nehru to meet the Pakistani president, who was transiting through New Delhi, and discuss the issue. Nehru, according to Srinath Raghavan, interpreted Thimayya's urging on this issue as 'interference in matters of policy' and the army chief's subsequent resignation as 'a step to force his hand on Menon and on questions of policy'. When Thimayya's resignation became known, and the issue was raised in Parliament, Nehru consequently asserted that 'civil authority is and must remain supreme' (Raghavan 2009, 153).

A second, more recent, episode, which demonstrates the political leadership's penchant to consciously subordinate the military leadership, occurred in 1998. On 30 December that year, the Vajpayee government sacked Admiral Vishnu Bhagwat because of 'loss of confidence in his fitness to continue as' chief of naval staff. The government later contended that Bhagwat's actions 'threatened the established structures of democracy, the traditional neutrality and objectivity of our armed forces as well as national security'. Prime Minister Vajpayee himself later asserted that Bhagwat's services were terminated because of his 'deliberate defiance of the established system of cabinet control over the defence forces' (Joshi and Chawla 1999).

Finally, more recently in 2016, the Modi government asserted the prerogative of civil authority over the military when it selected General

Bipin Rawat as Chief of the Army Staff by ignoring the customary seniority principle. In response to not only opposition parties but even sections among retired military officers describing Rawat's appointment as 'political interference', a 'bad precedent', and 'the beginning of the end of an apolitical Army' (Kumar 2016; *The Times of India* 19 December 2016), the government explained its rationale for the deep selection thus:

> The appointment of the Chief of Army Staff is based on selection from a panel of officers in the rank of Army Commanders. All officers in the panel are very competent officers and the most suitable among them is selected. However, it must be emphasised that the prerogative of selecting the most eligible from the panel is that of the government. (Singh 2016)

Internal Autonomy to the Military

The second feature in the Indian pattern of civil–military relations was the importance that the political leadership gave to fostering professionalism in the military. It is because of this imperative that the political leadership did not reinduct into the armed forces any officer who had chosen to join the Indian National Army under Subhas Chandra Bose. The decision 'not only cemented the loyalties of the old officers to the new regime but also strengthened the idea that professional competence, not political initiatives, was the first requirement of the Indian Army' (Rudolph and Rudolph 1964, 8).

That the imperative of military professionalism and autonomy can be ignored only at a high cost was tellingly brought home to political leaders when Krishna Menon's tenure as defence minister ended with the collapse of the military effort in the North-East Frontier Agency in 1962. Since then, the imperative of fostering professionalism and avoiding politicisation has led political leaders to grant a broad degree of autonomy to the military leadership. They rarely, if ever, ask questions about the doctrine that each service chooses to employ or stress upon in performing its role. Given that political leaders have generally refrained from probing the military leadership on these larger aspects that relate to strategy and doctrine, it is only natural that they do not also interfere with issues relating to training, military education, and even appointments up to a certain rank (Mukherjee 2020, 173–221).

That, however, does not mean that the political leadership has given carte blanche to the military. During major crises and wars, they have indeed exercised close supervision of the military effort and even laid down limits within which military operations should be conducted. Thus, in November 1947, during operations to rescue Jammu and Kashmir from the depredations of the tribal *lashkars* (armies) sponsored by Pakistan and led by Pakistani servicemen, the Cabinet set aside the advice given by Lieutenant General Dudley Russell, the then commander of the Delhi and East Punjab Command, that an immediate advance be undertaken towards Muzaffarabad. Instead, the army was instructed to send a relief column to the besieged town of Poonch, where not only the State Forces Garrison but also 40,000 non-Muslim refugees remained trapped. In effect, as Lieutenant General S.K. Sinha has concluded after narrating this incident, 'political considerations outweighed military requirements', and rightly so (Sinha 1977, 31–32).

That was not, however, a one-time practice. During the 1965 War, the Lal Bahadur Shastri government laid down ground rules for the operations of the air force and navy driven by larger political and strategic considerations. The air force was prohibited from undertaking offensive retaliatory action against East Pakistan because of the need to avoid 'wasteful escalation' along a secondary front and the imperative of not provoking China (Pradhan 2013, 255). For its part, the navy was not only advised to play a defensive role but was instructed 'not to operate beyond the latitude of Porbandar' (Chakravorty 1992, 287).

Subsequently, during the Kargil conflict of 1999, the army and air force were expressly prohibited from undertaking operations that involved crossing the Line of Control (Malik 2010, 139). Nor have political leaders always and automatically endorsed the options provided by the military leadership. During the crisis generated by the December 2001 attack on the Parliament by Pakistani terrorists, Vajpayee responded to military inputs thus:

> [W]hen the history of this war is written, what name will be given to it? The war of destruction of Pakistan, the liberation of Kashmir, annihilation of the Pakistani army, what? We must have a clear objective before we go to war. We can't launch what history would merely call a war of anger.... The problem with a war is, how you start it, when and where you start it, is in your hands. But how it will end, and when, is never in your control. That is why the decision to go to war is never taken lightly or in anger. (Gupta 2014)

Reluctant Reformers

The third feature of the Indian pattern of civil–military relations is the reluctance to meaningfully reform the institutional structure of civil–military relations. The structure designed by Lord Ismay at the time of Independence has largely remained the same, although marginal changes have been affected from time to time. Thus, at the apex level, the Defence Committee of the Cabinet was successively renamed the Emergency Committee of the Cabinet, the Cabinet Committee on Political Affairs, and the Cabinet Committee on Security. The Defence Minister's Committee ceased to exist and was replaced by the system of informal morning meetings chaired by the defence minister. At the apex level, only the name of the Chiefs of Staff Committee has remained unchanged. At the same time, new committees were established to foster greater coordination among civilian and military officials, the most prominent of which was the Committee for Defence Planning and its replacement, the Directorate General of Defence Planning Staff (Behera 2010, 127–128).

Even the post-Kargil reforms did not fundamentally alter the organisational structure of civil–military relations. The National Security Council and its associated offices—the National Security Advisor (NSA), the National Security Council Secretariat (NSCS), the Strategic Policy Group (SPG), and the National Security Advisory Board (NSAB)—were constituted as an additional layer for inter-agency coordination. In the same vein, new tri-services agencies were established, such as Headquarters of the Integrated Defence Staff, Defence Intelligence Agency, and Andaman and Nicobar Command, to foster coordination among the armed forces. Neither set of institutions, however, functioned efficiently in the absence of fully empowered officials—NSA for broader national security issues and CDS on military issues (Mukherjee 2011).

The reluctance to establish the post of NSA was much less evident from its creation in November 1998. But the political discomfort with the CDS proposal persisted for six decades since Mountbatten began to advocate it in 1960 (Mukherjee 2020, 51–52). Nehru was against creating such a position and fobbed off Mountbatten with a series of excuses. When the CDS proposal was revived in the early 1980s, the Indira Gandhi government rejected the need for it and expressed concerns about too much power accreting in the hands of one general officer (Elkin and Ritezel 1984, 1069). Even though the Vajpayee government was in favour of creating the CDS and the group of ministers led by Home Minister L.K. Advani had recommended such a step, a decision was not taken because of the inability to forge a political consensus. The Manmohan Singh government not only refused to view the idea of CDS favourably but even rejected an alternate proposal put forward by a task force that it had taken the initiative to appoint, namely, the idea of a permanent chairman of the Chiefs of Staff Committee proposed by the Naresh Chandra Task Force (IDSA 2013; Samanta 2014).

Political reluctance to appoint a CDS was reinforced by opposition from the air force and, to a lesser extent, from the navy due to concerns about being dominated by the much larger army. In addition, top military leaders of all three services were reluctant to support a proposal that would considerably reduce their own power and role. For their part, civilian bureaucrats were even more determined in their opposition to the idea of a CDS because that would empower the military at the bureaucracy's expense (Prakash 2012; Elkin and Ritezel 1984; Sinha 1980, 16–21). This wide range of opposition within the government ensured that the CDS proposal never gained purchase until Prime Minister Modi chose to ignore all opposition and do what for long has been considered necessary.

In his Independence Day speech in 2019, Prime Minister Modi emphasised the need for India's military power to 'work in unison'.

He said, 'It should be in line with the changing war and security environment with the world. After formation of this post (CDS), all the three forces will get effective leadership at the top level' (Press Information Bureau 2019).

Intrusive Bureaucratic Monitoring

The fourth feature of civil–military relations is the intrusive monitoring of the armed forces by the civilian bureaucracy. As early as 1967, two committees established by the Administrative Reforms Commission highlighted the issue by stating that civilian control over the military should not be interpreted to mean bureaucratic control (Sinha 1980, 14). Nothing much changed thereafter. As Admiral Arun Prakash has noted,

> [E]ach case emanating from the SHQ is required to be steered through multiple layers of bureaucracy that exist in [the] four departments of the MoD as well as its Finance Division. Queries are sequential, repetitive, and often raised to prevaricate; and every file movement takes weeks, if not months.

As a result, forced modernisation has been thwarted and combat readiness affected (Prakash 2014). In effect, driven by concerns about the military emerging as too powerful an institution in what is still a young and poor democracy, political leaders have consciously sought to keep the military contained and constrained through an intrusive bureaucratic monitoring process.

This daily process of what is often seen as over-intrusive bureaucratic monitoring has led to two related conclusions. Exasperated commentators have repeatedly asserted since the 1960s that civil–military relations in India are characterised not by civilian control but by bureaucratic control. And since what prevails is bureaucratic control, there is an absence of dialogue between the political and military leaderships (Mukherjee 2009). This vice-like grip of the bureaucracy has now been broken by the Modi government's decision to establish a separate DMA in the MoD headed by the CDS.

A New Pattern of Civil–Military Relations

The Modi government's two decisions in 2019 to create the post of CDS and establish a DMA in the MoD to service and coordinate the affairs of the three services are set to alter the pattern of civil–military relations that had prevailed until now. In the new scheme of things, the DMA's remit extends to the three services, their headquarters, and all their revenue expenditure, as well as to the Territorial Army—all of which were earlier administratively serviced by the Department of Defence headed by the defence secretary and reporting to the minister of defence (Secretariat 2020). The DMA's mandate is to promote jointness in 'procurement, training, and staffing for the Services', facilitate the restructuring of military commands, and encourage the use of indigenous weapons and equipment (Press Information Bureau 2019).

The CDS has been appointed to head the DMA in the rank of a secretary to a government department (Philip 2019). What is not clear is the status of the CDS vis-à-vis the defence secretary in terms of their working relationship—co-equal or superior or subordinate. Although the CDS formally outranks the defence secretary in the Warrant of Precedence (Secretariat 2020), an ideal working relationship would be what the group of ministers recommended in 2001—the two enjoying 'an equivalent status' as they perform their distinct functions of 'Principal Military Advisor' and 'Principal Defence Advisor' (GoI 2001).

In addition to heading the DMA, the CDS will also serve as the permanent chairman of the Chiefs of Staff Committee from now on. In that capacity, he has been authorised to act as the principal military advisor to the defence minister on all tri-services issues, administer all tri-services organisations and commands, serve as a member of both the Defence Acquisition Council and the Defence Planning Committee (DPC), and function as military advisor to the Nuclear Command Authority. His responsibilities include 'the promotion of jointness among the three services including in operations, logistics, training, and communications; ensure the optimal utilisation of infrastructure; implement the two-year and five-year acquisition plans; and assign prioritisation to inter-Services capital acquisition proposals' (Press Information Bureau 2019).

This reordering of responsibilities within the MoD and the empowerment of the CDS in matters relating to the services was preceded by a similar rearrangement of functions in 2018 in favour of the NSA and at the expense of the Cabinet secretary. On that occasion, the NSA was made the chair of both the newly established DPC and of the Strategic Planning Group which was until then chaired by the Cabinet secretary. In addition, the Modi government has reconstituted the NSAB into a smaller focused group comprising retired defence, diplomatic, and intelligence officials and considerably expanded funding for the NSCS (Patil 2019).

Together, these reforms of the defence organisation and national security management system demonstrate that Prime Minister Modi personally, and his government more broadly, have no concerns regarding the emergence of an unelected civil or military supremo. If this thought process were to last and become absorbed by other leading actors and parties in the political arena, then two of the characteristics of Indian civil–military relations—reluctance to reform and highly intrusive bureaucratic monitoring—are bound to fade away. It is, however, too early to gain a sense of what new characteristics might emerge from the new thought process and new institutional structure.

The three sets of actors involved in determining the new characteristics, and thus the new pattern, need to keep in mind the fact that all three have important roles to play in defence policy. Indeed, defence policy involves three distinct functions, each of which is ideally performed by one of the three actors: the professional military function by leaders of the armed forces, the administrative–fiscal function by an entirely civilian or a wholly military or an integrated civilian–military bureaucracy, and the policy–strategy function by the elected leaders (Huntington 2005, 428–429). Understanding this reality and acting in accordance with it is essential for structuring a pattern of civil–military relations that provides security at an affordable price and without compromising on democratic values.

Notes

1 According to Jasjit Singh, both the Staff College and Air War College continued to emphasise upon the attainment of a 'local favourable air situation' for decades, see Singh (2013, 134).

2 The quoted phrase can be found on p. 152.

References

Behera, L.K. 2010. 'Defence Planning in India'. *Defence Studies*, 4(3): 126–135.

Chakravorty, B.C. 1992. *History of the Indo-Pak War, 1965*. New Delhi: Ministry of Defence.

Chari, P.R. 1977. 'Civil–Military Relations in India'. *Armed Forces and Society*, 41: 3–28.

Chidambaram, P. 2013. *India's National Security—Challenges and Priorities*. Available at: http://idsa.in/keyspeeches/IndiasNationalSecurityChallengesandPriorities (accessed on 27 July 2020).

Elkin, J.F. and W.A. Ritezel. 1984. 'The Debate on Restructuring India's Higher Defense Organization'. *Asian Survey*, 24(10): 1069–1085.

Feaver, P.D. 1999. 'Civil–Military Relations'. *Annual Review of Political Science*, 2: 211–241.

Feaver, P.D. 2003. *Armed Servants: Agency, Oversight and Civil–Military Relations*. Cambridge: Harvard University Press.

Government of India (GoI). 2001. *Reforming the National Security System—Recommendations of the Group of Ministers*. New Delhi: Government of India.

Guha, Ramchandra. 2007. *India After Gandhi: The History of the Word's Largest Democracy*. London: Picador.

Gupta, S. 2014. 'Narendra Modi: Getting his Foreign Policy Right'. *India Today*, 4 September.

Hiranandani, G.M. 2000. *Transition to Triumph: History of the Indian Navy 1965–1975*. New Delhi: Naval Headquarters and Lancer.

Huntington, S.P. 2005. *The Soldier and the State: The Theory and Politics of Civil–Military Relations*. Dehradun: Natraj Publication.

IDSA. 2013. *Starred Question No 168 Chief of Defence Staff, 19 August*. Available at: http://idsa.in/resources/parliament/QUESTIONNO168CHIEFOFDEFENCESTAFF (accessed on 27 July 2020).

Jayal, B. 2012. 'Management and Delivery of Joint Military Capabilities'. In *A Call for Change: Higher Defence Management in India*, edited by A. Mukherjee, 52–71. New Delhi: Institute for Defence Studies and Analysis.

Joshi, M. and P. Chawla. 1999. 'Naval Chief Admiral Vishnu Bhagwat Sacked for Defiance of Civilian Authority'. *India Today*, 11 January.

Kumar, Dinesh. 2016. 'Selection of Army Chief a Sensitive Issue'. *The Tribune*, 26 December.

Lambeth, Benjamin. 2011. 'India's Transforming Air Posture: An Emerging 21st Century Heavyweight'. *IDSA Round Table*. Available at: http://idsa.in/event/IndiasTransformingAirPostureBenjamin_SLambeth (accessed on 3 March 2014).

Malik, V.P. 2010. *Kargil: From Surprise to Victory*. New Delhi: HarperCollins.

Mukherjee, Anit. 2009. 'The Absent Dialogue'. *Seminar*, no. 599, July. Available at: http://www.india-seminar.com/2009/599/599_anit_mukherjee.htm (accessed on 28 June 2013).

Mukherjee, Anit. 2011. *Failing to Deliver: Post-Crises Defence Reforms in India, 1998–2010*. New Delhi: Institute for Defence Studies and Analyses.

Mukherjee, Anit. 2020. *The Absent Dialogue: Politicians, Bureaucrats, and the Military in India*. New Delhi: Oxford University Press.

Nayar, V.K. 2008 'Civil–Military Relations'. *Journal of the United Service Institution of India*, CXXXVIII(574): 498–508.

Nehru, Jawaharlal. 1996. 'Production, The First Essential'. In *Jawaharlal Nehru: Selected Speeches: 1946–1949*, 6th edn., Vol. 1. New Delhi: Ministry of Information and Broadcasting.

Nehru, Jawaharlal. 2003. 'True Meaning of Defence'. In *Selected Works of Jawaharlal Nehru*, Vol. 32. edited by H.S. Prasad and A.K. Damodaran. New Delhi: Jawaharlal Nehru Memorial Fund.

Palit, D.K. 1969. 'Outmoded Imperial Concepts', *The Hindustan Times*, 27 and 29 December.

Palit, D.K. 1972. *Lightening Campaign, the Indo-Pakistan War 1971*. New Delhi: Thompson Press.

Pant, K.C. 1989. 'Philosophy of Indian Defence'. In *Non-Provocative Defence, the Search for Equal Security*, edited by Jasjit Singh. New Delhi: Lancer International.

Patil, K. 2019. 'Defence Modernisation and Production'. In *India's Evolving National Security Agenda: Modi and Beyond*, edited by H. Pant. New Delhi: Konark Publishers.

Philip, S.A. 2019. 'CDS to be Secretary of New Department of Military Affairs, No Impact on Defence Secy Post'. *Print*, New Delhi, 24 December.

Pradhan, R.D. 2013. *Debacle to Resurgence: Y.B. Chavan: Defence Minister (1962–1966)*. New Delhi: Atlantic Publishers.

Prakash, A. 2012. 'Defence Reforms: Contemporary Debates and Issues'. In *A Call for Change: Higher Defence Management in India*, edited by B.D. Jayal, V.P. Malik, Anit Mukherjee, and Arun Prakash, 18–36. New Delhi: Institute of Defence Studies and Analysis.

Prakash, A. 2014. 'Civil–Military Dissonance: A Chink in India's Armour'. In *Third K Subrahmanyam Memorial Lecture*. New Delhi: Global India Foundation. Available at: https://www.globalindiafoundation.org/Admiral%20Arun%20Prakash%20Speech[1].pdf (accessed on 27 July 2020).

Press Information Bureau. 2015. 'PM Chairs Combined Commanders Conference on Board INS Vikramaditya at Sea'. Delhi, 15 December.

Press Information Bureau. 2019. 'Cabinet Approves Creation of the Post of Chief of Defence Staff in the Rank of Four-Star General'. Delhi, 24 December.

Raghavan, S. 2009. 'Civil–Military Relations in India: The China Crisis and After'. *Journal of Strategic Studies*, 32(1): 149–179.

Raghavan, S. 2010. *War and Peace in Modern India: A Strategic History of the Nehru Years*. Ranikhet: Permanent Black.

Rudolph, Lloyd I. and Susanne Hoeber Rudolph. 1964. 'Generals and Politicians in India'. *Pacific Affairs*, 371: 5–19.

Samanta, P.D. 2014. 'Govt Rejects Chandra Panel Proposal for a Four-Star General'. *Indian Express*. New Delhi, 3 May.

Secretariat, Cabinet. Government of India (Allocation of Business) Rules, 1961. Available at: https://cabsec.gov.in/writereaddata/allocationbusinessrule/completeaobrules/english/1_Upload_1972.pdf (accessed on 27 July 2020).

Secretariat, P.o. Table of Precedence. Available at: https://mha.gov.in/sites/default/files/Tableofprecedence_28112018_0.pdf (accessed 27 July 2020).

Secretariat, President's. *Table of Precedence*. Available at: https://www.mha.gov.in/sites/default/files/Tableofprecedence_28112018_0.pdf (accessed on 27 July 2020).

Singh, Jasjit. 2013. *Defence from the Skies, 80 Years of the Indian Air Force*. New Delhi: KW Publishers.

Singh, Sushant. 2016. 'Govt Defence on Army Chief Appointment: Selection on Anti-terror Experience, General Dynamism, Merit'. *The Indian Express*, 19 December.

Sinha, S.K. 1977. *Operation Rescue: Military Operations in Jammu and Kashmir 1947–1949*. New Delhi: Vision Books.

Sinha, U.P. 1980. 'Higher Defence Organisation in India'. *USI Papers No. 7*. New Delhi: United Service Institution of India.

Tellis, Asley. 1991. 'Securing the Barrack: The Logic, Structure and Objectives of India's Naval Expansion', *Indian Defence Review*, July: 133–156.

Thomas, Raju. 1978. *Defence of India, a Budgetary Perspective of Strategy and Politics*. Delhi: Macmillan.

Times of India. 2016. 'Amid Pakistan Tension, Arun Jaitley Hints at Upping Defence'. *The Times of India*, Mumbai, 28 September.

Vohra, N.N. 2013. 'Civil–Military Relations: Opportunities and Challenges'. In *USI National Security Lecture*. New Delhi. Available at: http://idsa.in/resources/speech/CivilMilitaryRelations_NNVohra (accessed on 27 July 2020).

Wilkinson, S.I. 2015. *Army and Nation: The Military and Indian Democracy since Independence*. Ranikhet: Permanent Black.

Index

About the Author

S. Kalyanaraman was a research fellow at the Manohar Parrikar Institute for Defence Studies and Analyses, New Delhi. His research focus was India's defence and security policies. He was a visiting faculty member at the National Defence College, Army War College, Sushma Swaraj Institute of Foreign Service, and Bhutan's Royal Institute for Governance and Strategic Studies. His most recent publication is the co-edited volume *India's Great Power Politics: Managing China's Rise* (2021).